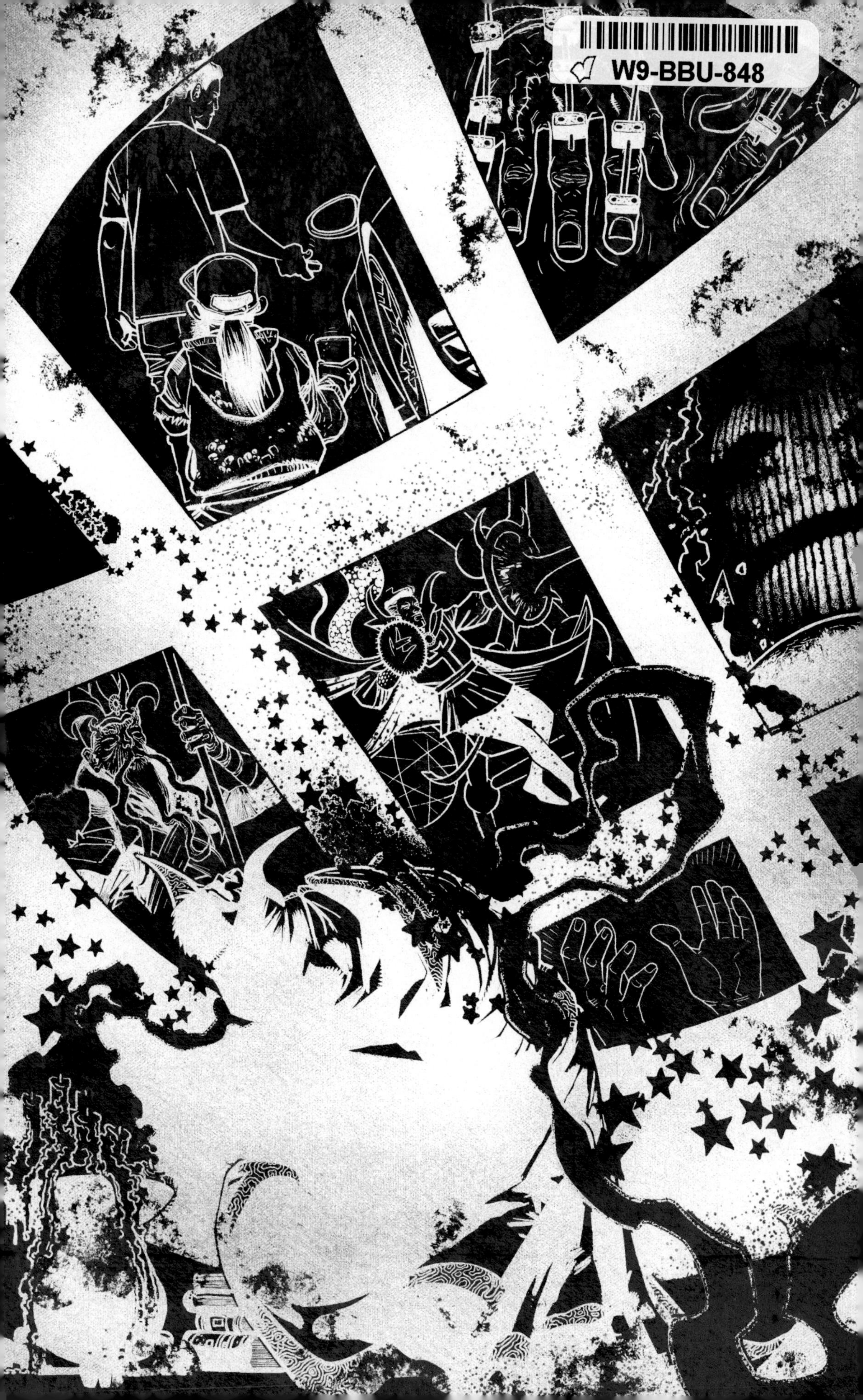

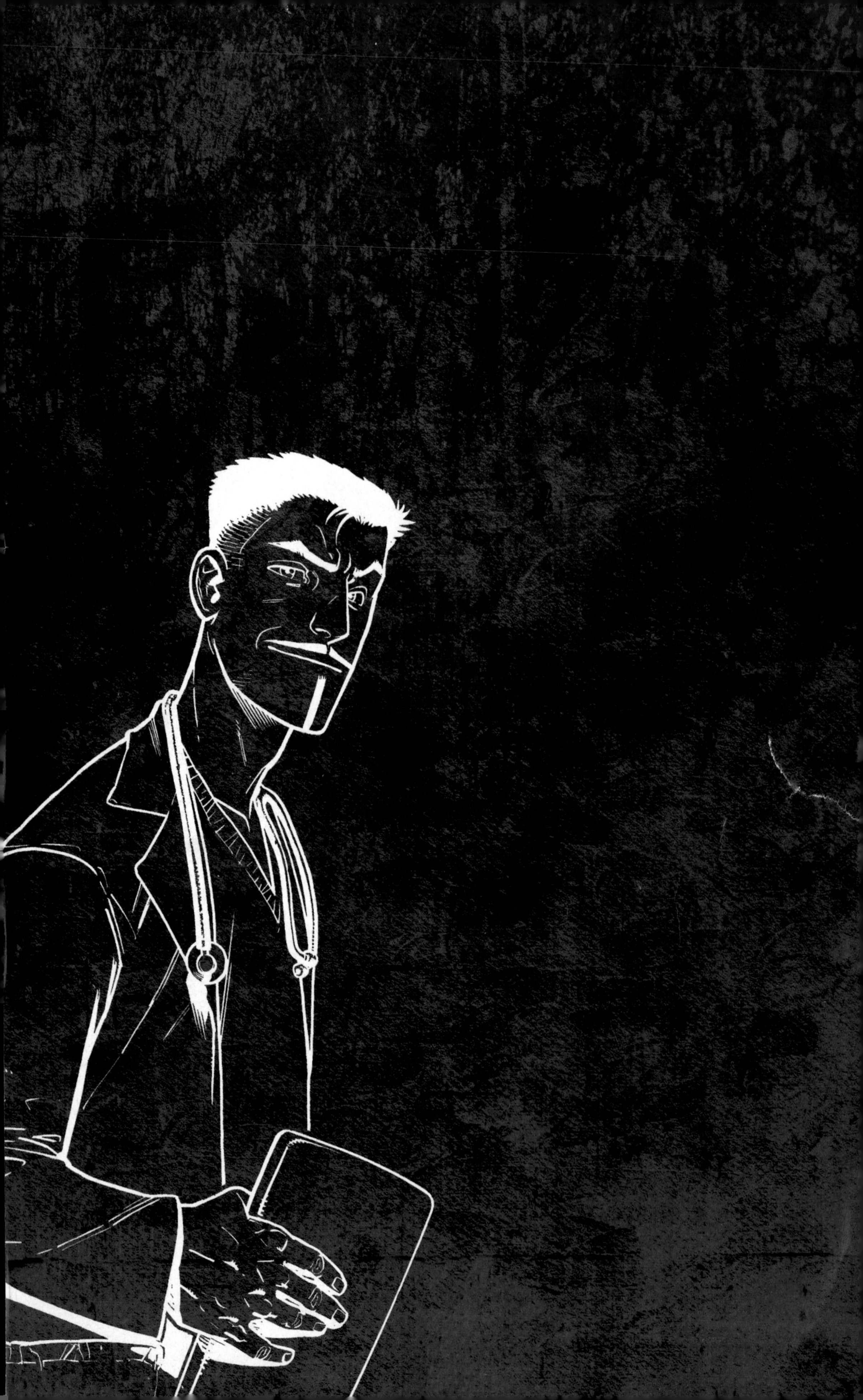

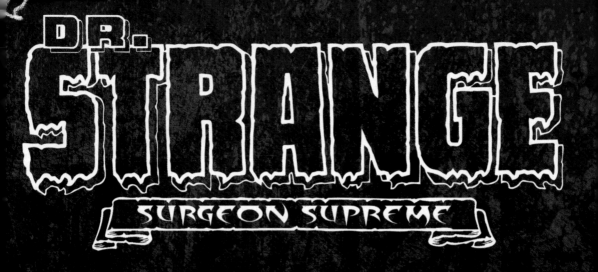

DR. STRANGE
SURGEON SUPREME

MARK WAID & **KEV WALKER**
storytellers

JAVA TARTAGLIA with **Antonio Fabela** (#4)
colorists

VC's CORY PETIT (#1-3, #5-6) & **Clayton Cowles** (#4)
letterers

Phil Noto (#1, #3-6) & **Max Fiumara** (#2)
cover artists

LAUREN AMARO
assistant editor

DARREN SHAN
editor

DOCTOR STRANGE created by **STAN LEE & STEVE DITKO**

JENNIFER GRÜNWALD collection editor
MAIA LOY assistant managing editor
LISA MONTALBANO assistant managing editor
MARK D. BEAZLEY editor, special projects

JEFF YOUNGQUIST vp production & special projects
ADAM DEL RE with **ANTHONY GAMBINO** book designers
DAVID GABRIEL svp print, sales & marketing
C.B. CEBULSKI editor in chief

DR. STRANGE, SURGEON SUPREME VOL. 1: UNDER THE KNIFE. Contains material originally published in magazine form as DR. STRANGE (2019) #1-6. First printing 2020. ISBN 978-1-302-92105-7. Published by MARVEL WORLDWIDE, INC., a subsidiary of MARVEL ENTERTAINMENT, LLC. OFFICE OF PUBLICATION: 1290 Avenue of the Americas, New York, NY 10104. © 2020 MARVEL No similarity between any of the names, ...itution is intended, and any such similarity which may exist is purely coincidental. **Printed in Canada.** ...her; JOE QUESADA, EVP & Creative Director; TOM BREVOORT, SVP of Publishing; DAVID BOGART, ...ital Publishing; JEFF YOUNGQUIST, VP of Production & Special Projects; DAN CARR, Executive ... Managing Editor; RICKEY PURDIN, Director of Talent Relations; SUSAN CRESPI, Production ...arvel.com, please contact Vit DeBellis, Custom Solutions & Integrated Advertising Manager, ... **between 10/16/2020 and 11/17/2020 by SOLISCO PRINTERS, SCOTT, QC, CANADA.**

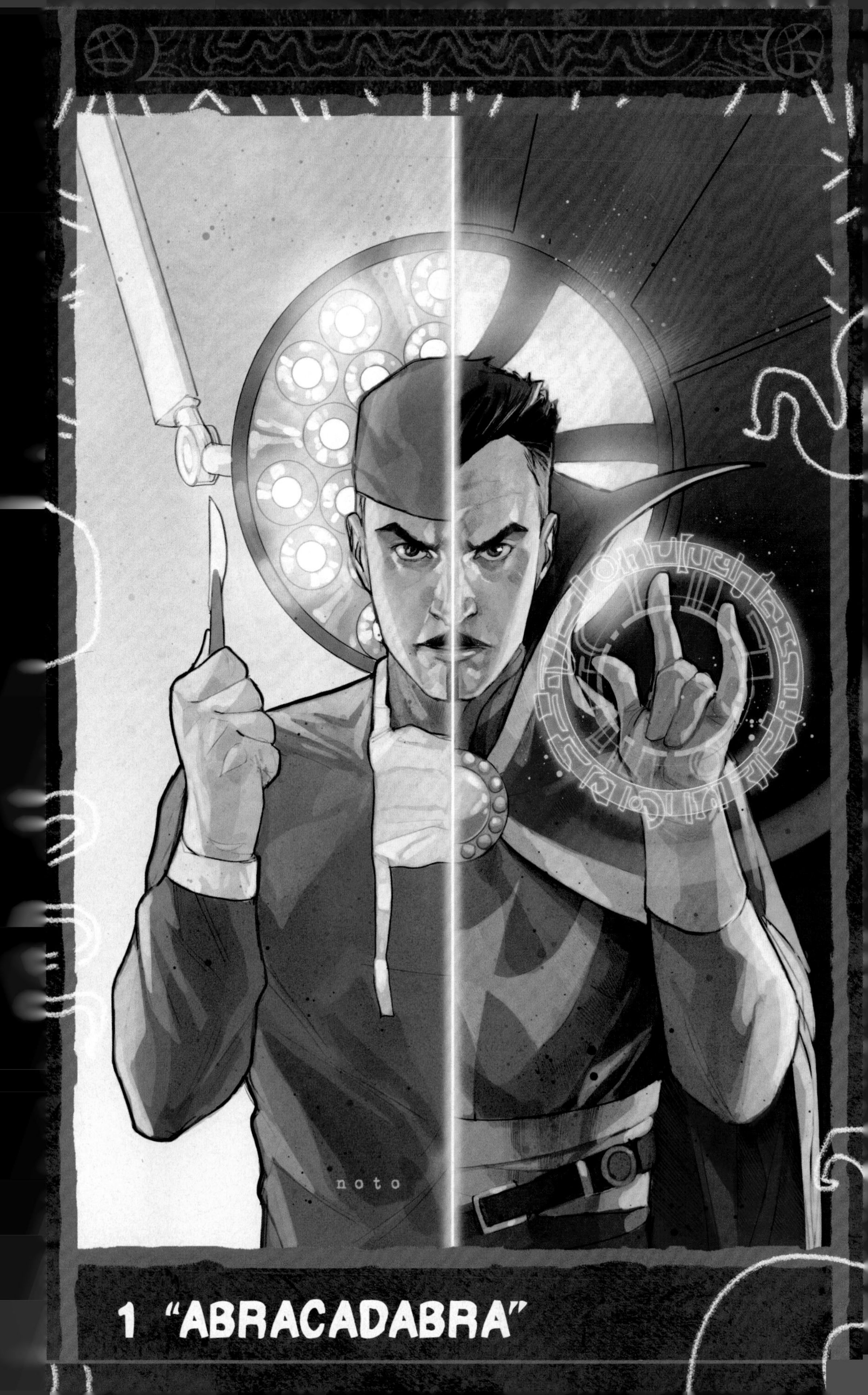
noto

1 "ABRACADABRA"

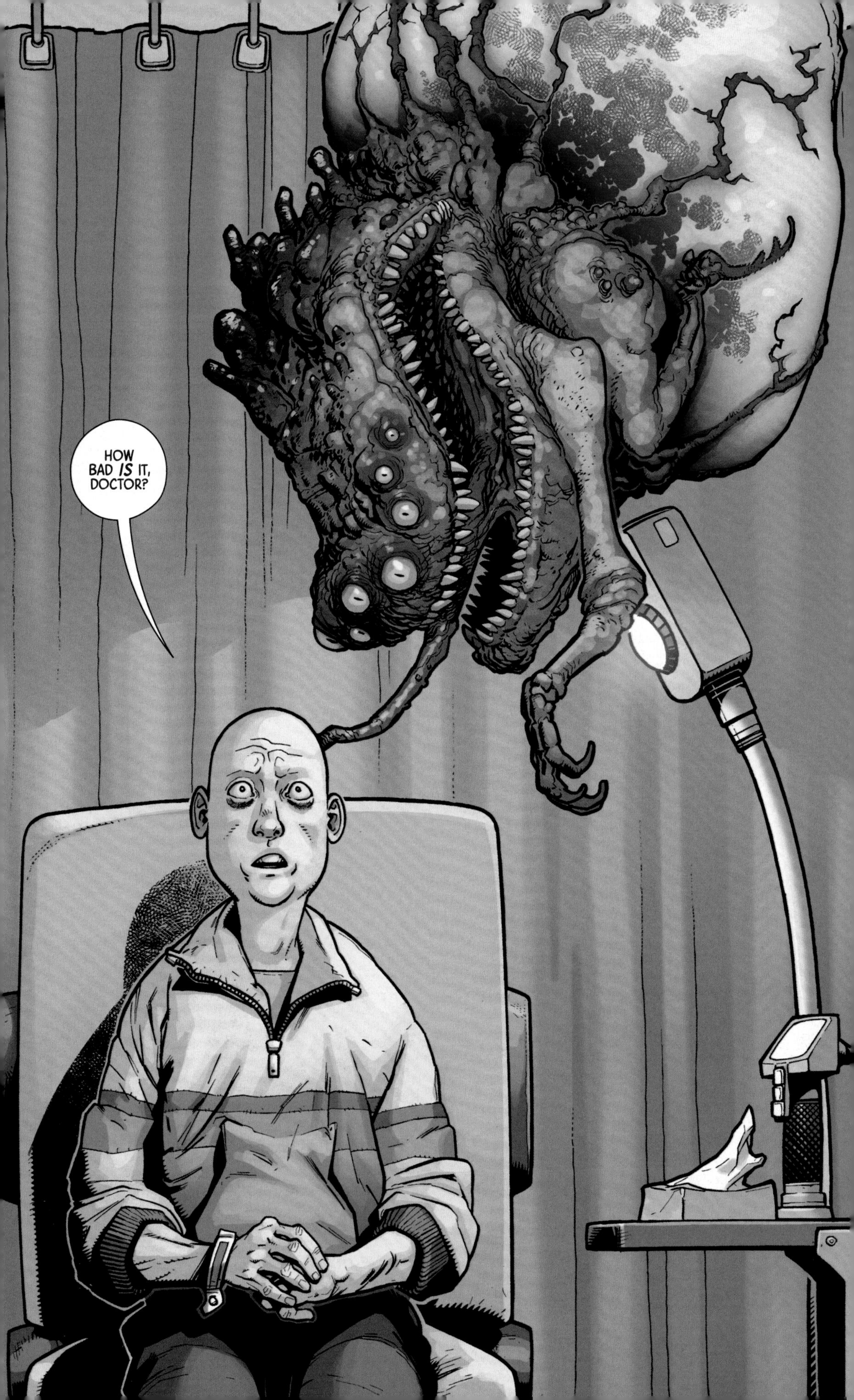
HOW BAD *IS* IT, DOCTOR?

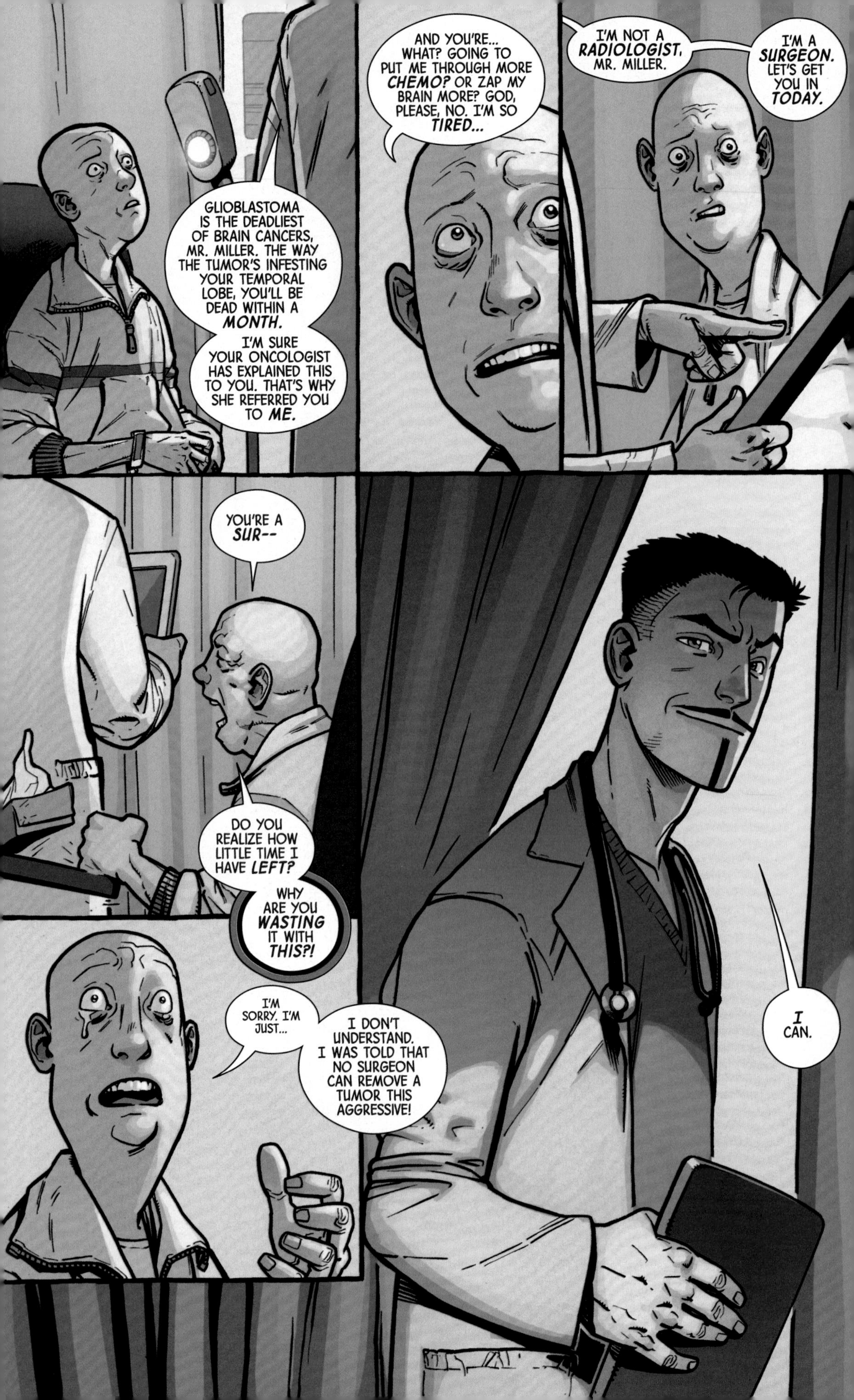
GLIOBLASTOMA IS THE DEADLIEST OF BRAIN CANCERS, MR. MILLER. THE WAY THE TUMOR'S INFESTING YOUR TEMPORAL LOBE, YOU'LL BE DEAD WITHIN A MONTH.
I'M SURE YOUR ONCOLOGIST HAS EXPLAINED THIS TO YOU. THAT'S WHY SHE REFERRED YOU TO ME.
AND YOU'RE... WHAT? GOING TO PUT ME THROUGH MORE CHEMO? OR ZAP MY BRAIN MORE? GOD, PLEASE, NO. I'M SO TIRED...
I'M NOT A RADIOLOGIST, MR. MILLER.
I'M A SURGEON. LET'S GET YOU IN TODAY.
YOU'RE A SUR--
DO YOU REALIZE HOW LITTLE TIME I HAVE LEFT?
WHY ARE YOU WASTING IT WITH THIS?!
I'M SORRY. I'M JUST...
I DON'T UNDERSTAND. I WAS TOLD THAT NO SURGEON CAN REMOVE A TUMOR THIS AGGRESSIVE!
I CAN.

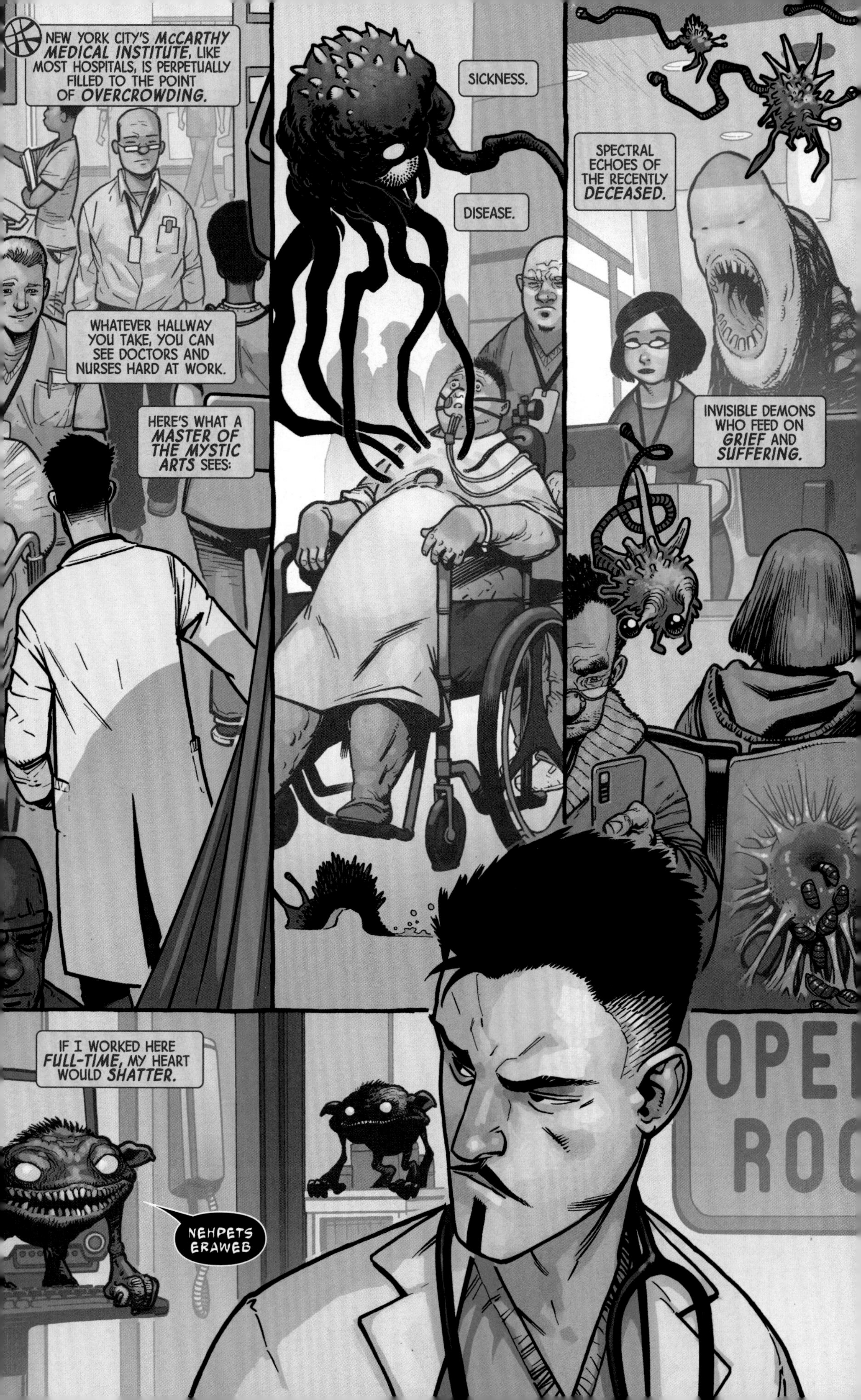
NEW YORK CITY'S McCARTHY MEDICAL INSTITUTE, LIKE MOST HOSPITALS, IS PERPETUALLY FILLED TO THE POINT OF OVERCROWDING.
WHATEVER HALLWAY YOU TAKE, YOU CAN SEE DOCTORS AND NURSES HARD AT WORK.
HERE'S WHAT A MASTER OF THE MYSTIC ARTS SEES:
SICKNESS.
DISEASE.
SPECTRAL ECHOES OF THE RECENTLY DECEASED.
INVISIBLE DEMONS WHO FEED ON GRIEF AND SUFFERING.
IF I WORKED HERE FULL-TIME, MY HEART WOULD SHATTER.
NEHPETS ERAWEB
OPE
ROO

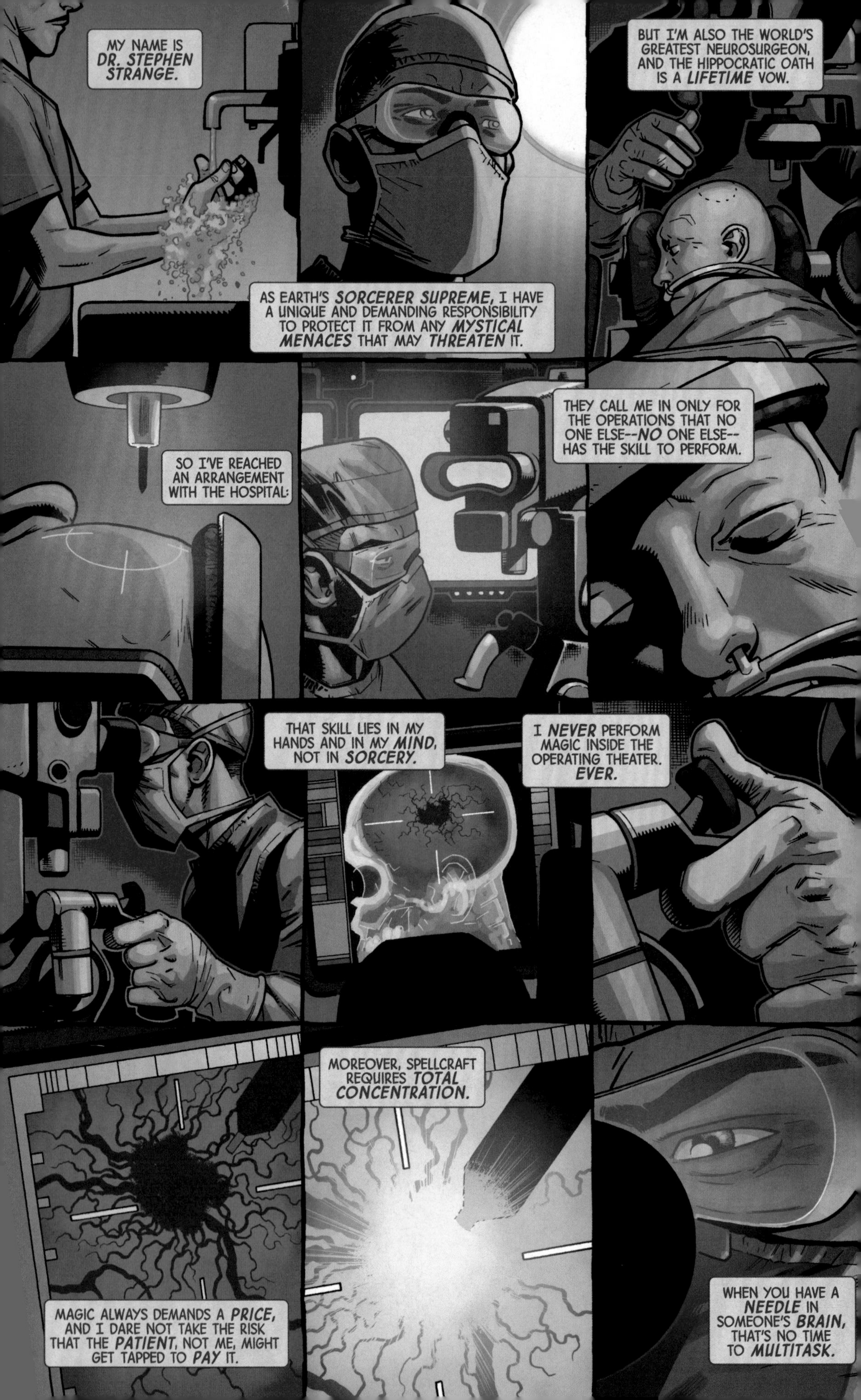
MY NAME IS DR. STEPHEN STRANGE.
AS EARTH'S SORCERER SUPREME, I HAVE A UNIQUE AND DEMANDING RESPONSIBILITY TO PROTECT IT FROM ANY MYSTICAL MENACES THAT MAY THREATEN IT.
BUT I'M ALSO THE WORLD'S GREATEST NEUROSURGEON, AND THE HIPPOCRATIC OATH IS A LIFETIME VOW.
SO I'VE REACHED AN ARRANGEMENT WITH THE HOSPITAL:
THEY CALL ME IN ONLY FOR THE OPERATIONS THAT NO ONE ELSE--NO ONE ELSE--HAS THE SKILL TO PERFORM.
THAT SKILL LIES IN MY HANDS AND IN MY MIND, NOT IN SORCERY.
I NEVER PERFORM MAGIC INSIDE THE OPERATING THEATER. EVER.
MAGIC ALWAYS DEMANDS A PRICE, AND I DARE NOT TAKE THE RISK THAT THE PATIENT, NOT ME, MIGHT GET TAPPED TO PAY IT.
MOREOVER, SPELLCRAFT REQUIRES TOTAL CONCENTRATION.
WHEN YOU HAVE A NEEDLE IN SOMEONE'S BRAIN, THAT'S NO TIME TO MULTITASK.

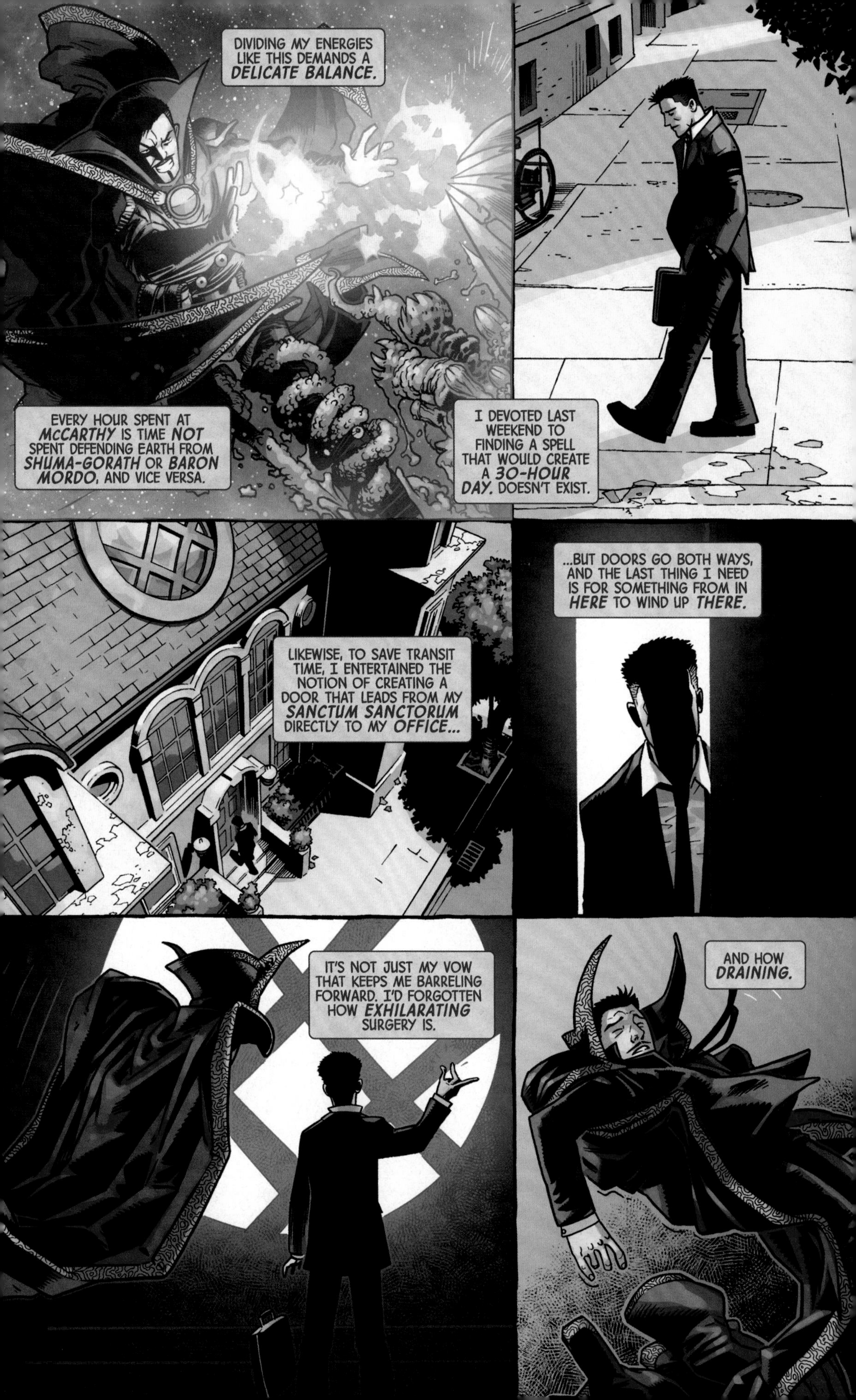
DIVIDING MY ENERGIES LIKE THIS DEMANDS A DELICATE BALANCE.
EVERY HOUR SPENT AT McCARTHY IS TIME NOT SPENT DEFENDING EARTH FROM SHUMA-GORATH OR BARON MORDO, AND VICE VERSA.
I DEVOTED LAST WEEKEND TO FINDING A SPELL THAT WOULD CREATE A 30-HOUR DAY. DOESN'T EXIST.
LIKEWISE, TO SAVE TRANSIT TIME, I ENTERTAINED THE NOTION OF CREATING A DOOR THAT LEADS FROM MY SANCTUM SANCTORUM DIRECTLY TO MY OFFICE...
...BUT DOORS GO BOTH WAYS, AND THE LAST THING I NEED IS FOR SOMETHING FROM IN HERE TO WIND UP THERE.
IT'S NOT JUST MY VOW THAT KEEPS ME BARRELING FORWARD. I'D FORGOTTEN HOW EXHILARATING SURGERY IS.
AND HOW DRAINING.

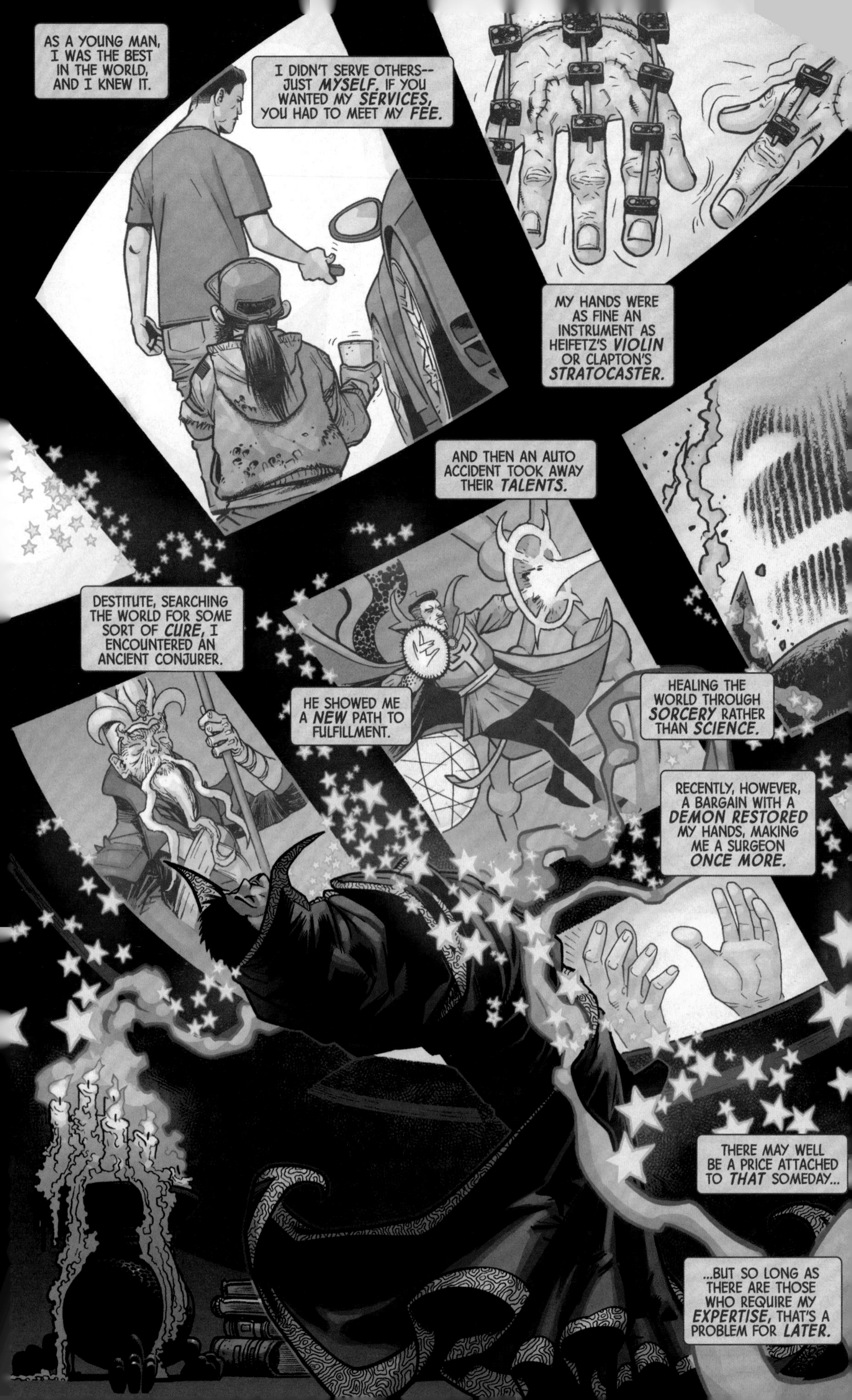
AS A YOUNG MAN, I WAS THE BEST IN THE WORLD, AND I KNEW IT.
I DIDN'T SERVE OTHERS-- JUST MYSELF. IF YOU WANTED MY SERVICES, YOU HAD TO MEET MY FEE.
MY HANDS WERE AS FINE AN INSTRUMENT AS HEIFETZ'S VIOLIN OR CLAPTON'S STRATOCASTER.
AND THEN AN AUTO ACCIDENT TOOK AWAY THEIR TALENTS.
DESTITUTE, SEARCHING THE WORLD FOR SOME SORT OF CURE, I ENCOUNTERED AN ANCIENT CONJURER.
HE SHOWED ME A NEW PATH TO FULFILLMENT.
HEALING THE WORLD THROUGH SORCERY RATHER THAN SCIENCE.
RECENTLY, HOWEVER, A BARGAIN WITH A DEMON RESTORED MY HANDS, MAKING ME A SURGEON ONCE MORE.
THERE MAY WELL BE A PRICE ATTACHED TO THAT SOMEDAY...
...BUT SO LONG AS THERE ARE THOSE WHO REQUIRE MY EXPERTISE, THAT'S A PROBLEM FOR LATER.

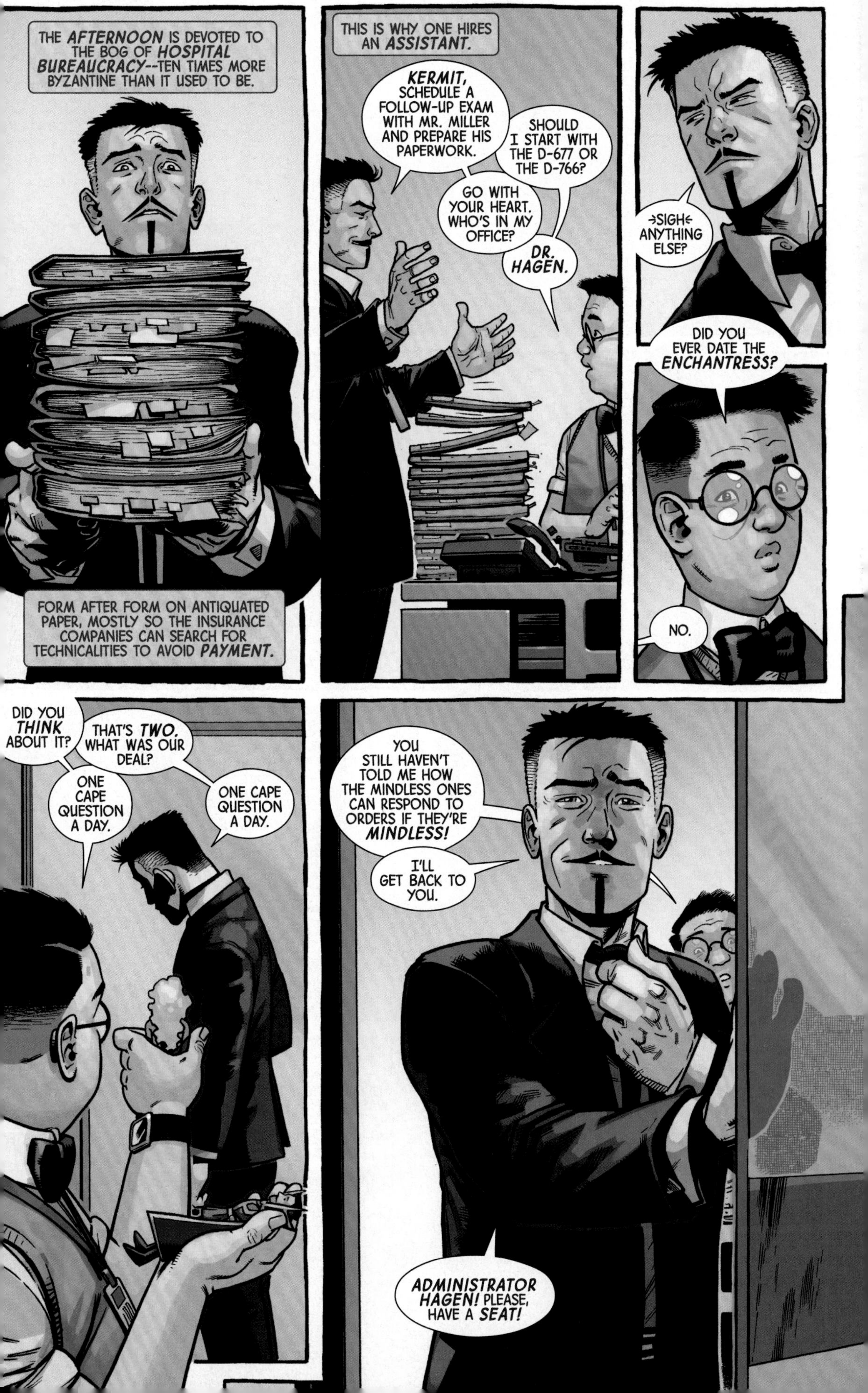
THE AFTERNOON IS DEVOTED TO THE BOG OF HOSPITAL BUREAUCRACY--TEN TIMES MORE BYZANTINE THAN IT USED TO BE.
FORM AFTER FORM ON ANTIQUATED PAPER, MOSTLY SO THE INSURANCE COMPANIES CAN SEARCH FOR TECHNICALITIES TO AVOID PAYMENT.
THIS IS WHY ONE HIRES AN ASSISTANT.
KERMIT, SCHEDULE A FOLLOW-UP EXAM WITH MR. MILLER AND PREPARE HIS PAPERWORK.
SHOULD I START WITH THE D-677 OR THE D-766?
GO WITH YOUR HEART. WHO'S IN MY OFFICE?
DR. HAGEN.
>SIGH< ANYTHING ELSE?
DID YOU EVER DATE THE ENCHANTRESS?
NO.
DID YOU THINK ABOUT IT?
THAT'S TWO. WHAT WAS OUR DEAL?
ONE CAPE QUESTION A DAY.
ONE CAPE QUESTION A DAY.
YOU STILL HAVEN'T TOLD ME HOW THE MINDLESS ONES CAN RESPOND TO ORDERS IF THEY'RE MINDLESS!
I'LL GET BACK TO YOU.
ADMINISTRATOR HAGEN! PLEASE, HAVE A SEAT!

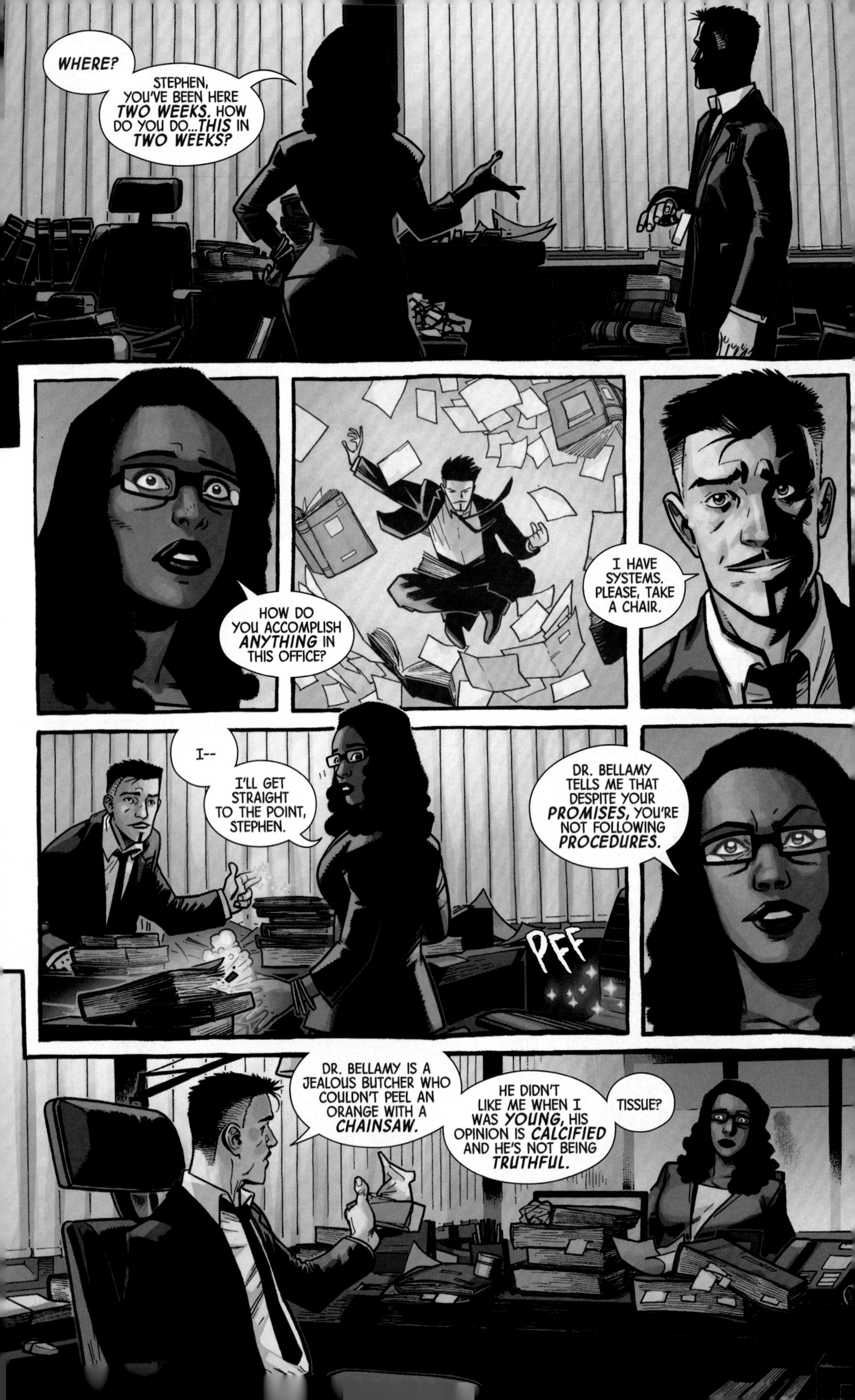
WHERE?
STEPHEN, YOU'VE BEEN HERE TWO WEEKS. HOW DO YOU DO...THIS IN TWO WEEKS?
HOW DO YOU ACCOMPLISH ANYTHING IN THIS OFFICE?
I HAVE SYSTEMS. PLEASE, TAKE A CHAIR.
I--
I'LL GET STRAIGHT TO THE POINT, STEPHEN.
PFF
DR. BELLAMY TELLS ME THAT DESPITE YOUR PROMISES, YOU'RE NOT FOLLOWING PROCEDURES.
DR. BELLAMY IS A JEALOUS BUTCHER WHO COULDN'T PEEL AN ORANGE WITH A CHAINSAW.
HE DIDN'T LIKE ME WHEN I WAS YOUNG, HIS OPINION IS CALCIFIED AND HE'S NOT BEING TRUTHFUL.
TISSUE?

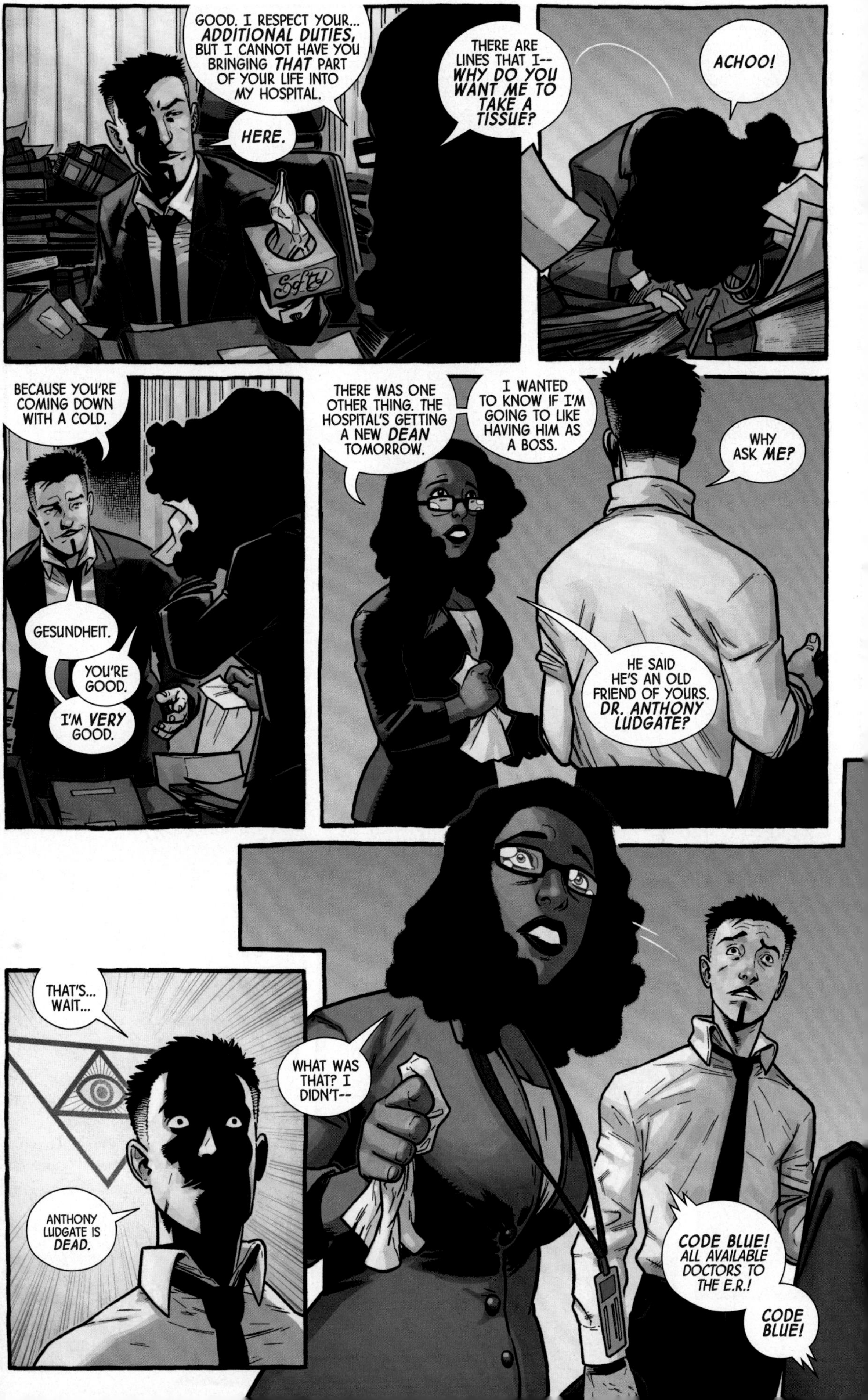
GOOD. I RESPECT YOUR... ADDITIONAL DUTIES, BUT I CANNOT HAVE YOU BRINGING THAT PART OF YOUR LIFE INTO MY HOSPITAL.
HERE.
THERE ARE LINES THAT I-- WHY DO YOU WANT ME TO TAKE A TISSUE?
ACHOO!
BECAUSE YOU'RE COMING DOWN WITH A COLD.
GESUNDHEIT.
YOU'RE GOOD.
I'M VERY GOOD.
THERE WAS ONE OTHER THING. THE HOSPITAL'S GETTING A NEW DEAN TOMORROW.
I WANTED TO KNOW IF I'M GOING TO LIKE HAVING HIM AS A BOSS.
WHY ASK ME?
HE SAID HE'S AN OLD FRIEND OF YOURS. DR. ANTHONY LUDGATE?
THAT'S... WAIT...
ANTHONY LUDGATE IS DEAD.
WHAT WAS THAT? I DIDN'T--
CODE BLUE! ALL AVAILABLE DOCTORS TO THE E.R.!
CODE BLUE!

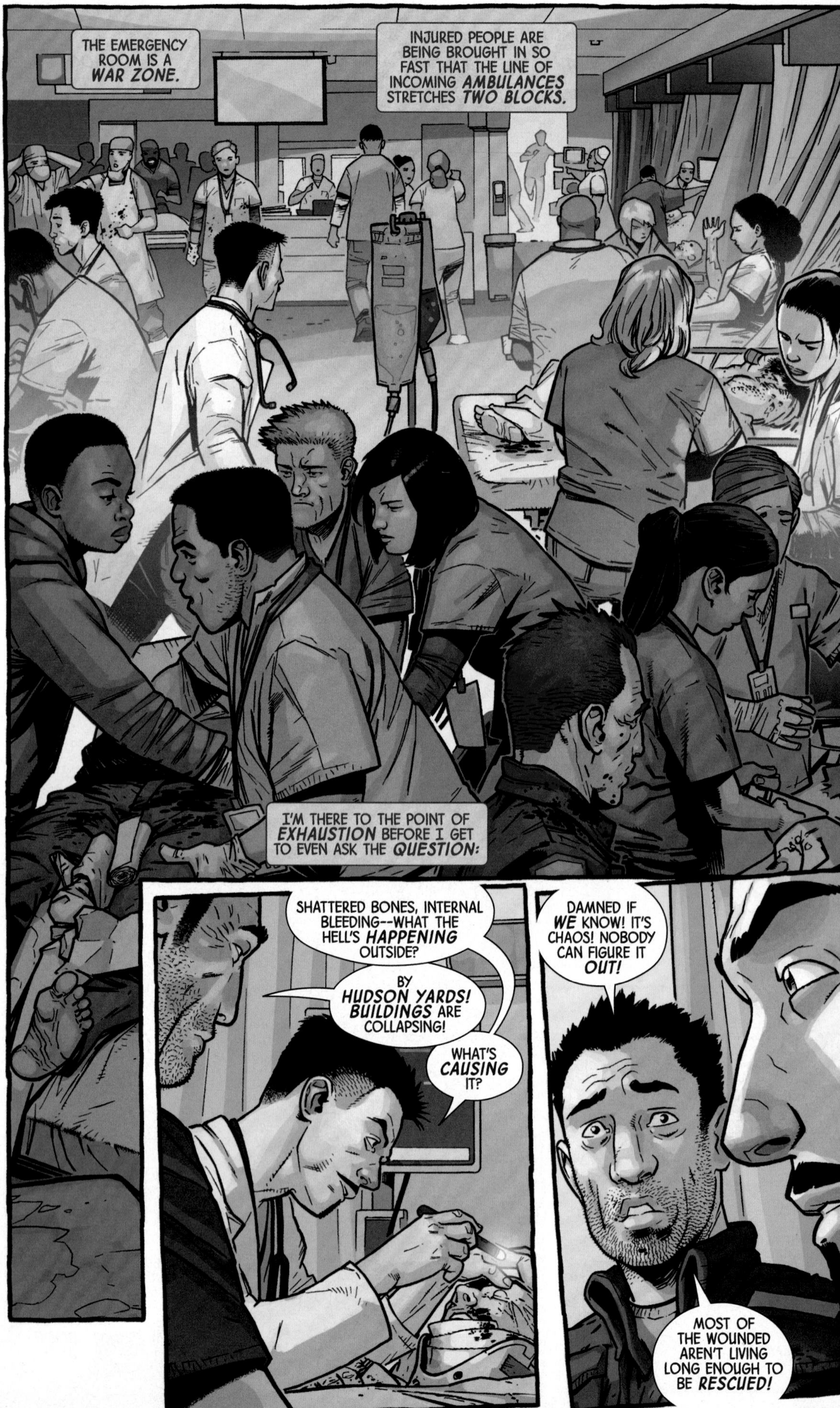
THE EMERGENCY ROOM IS A WAR ZONE.
INJURED PEOPLE ARE BEING BROUGHT IN SO FAST THAT THE LINE OF INCOMING AMBULANCES STRETCHES TWO BLOCKS.
I'M THERE TO THE POINT OF EXHAUSTION BEFORE I GET TO EVEN ASK THE QUESTION:
SHATTERED BONES, INTERNAL BLEEDING--WHAT THE HELL'S HAPPENING OUTSIDE?
BY HUDSON YARDS! BUILDINGS ARE COLLAPSING!
WHAT'S CAUSING IT?
DAMNED IF WE KNOW! IT'S CHAOS! NOBODY CAN FIGURE IT OUT!
MOST OF THE WOUNDED AREN'T LIVING LONG ENOUGH TO BE RESCUED!

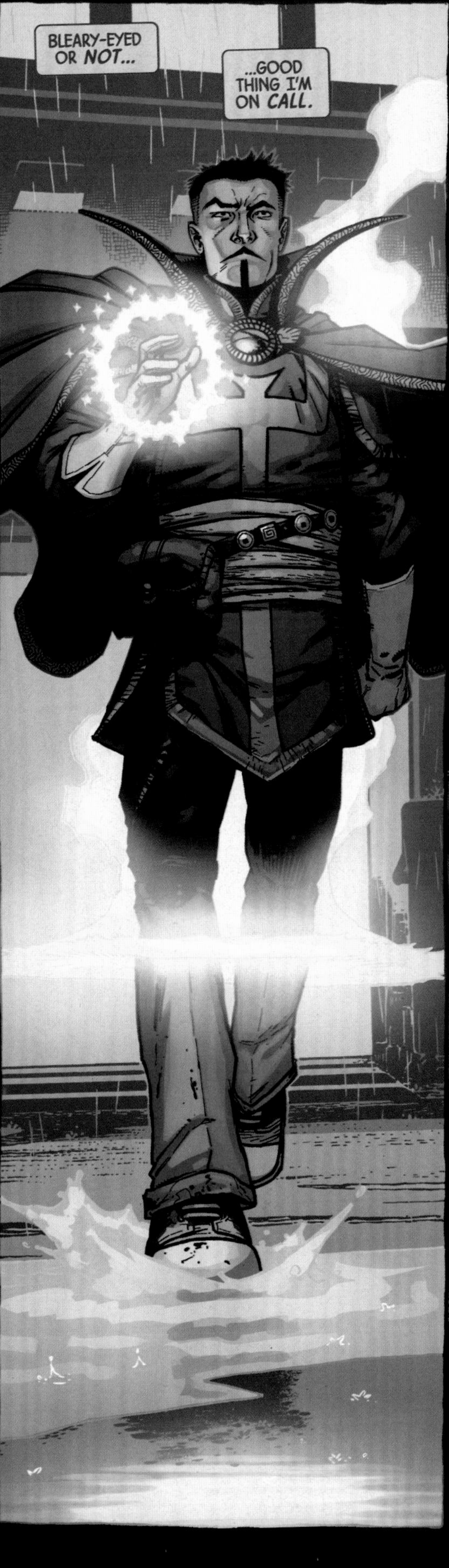
BLEARY-EYED OR NOT...
...GOOD THING I'M ON CALL.
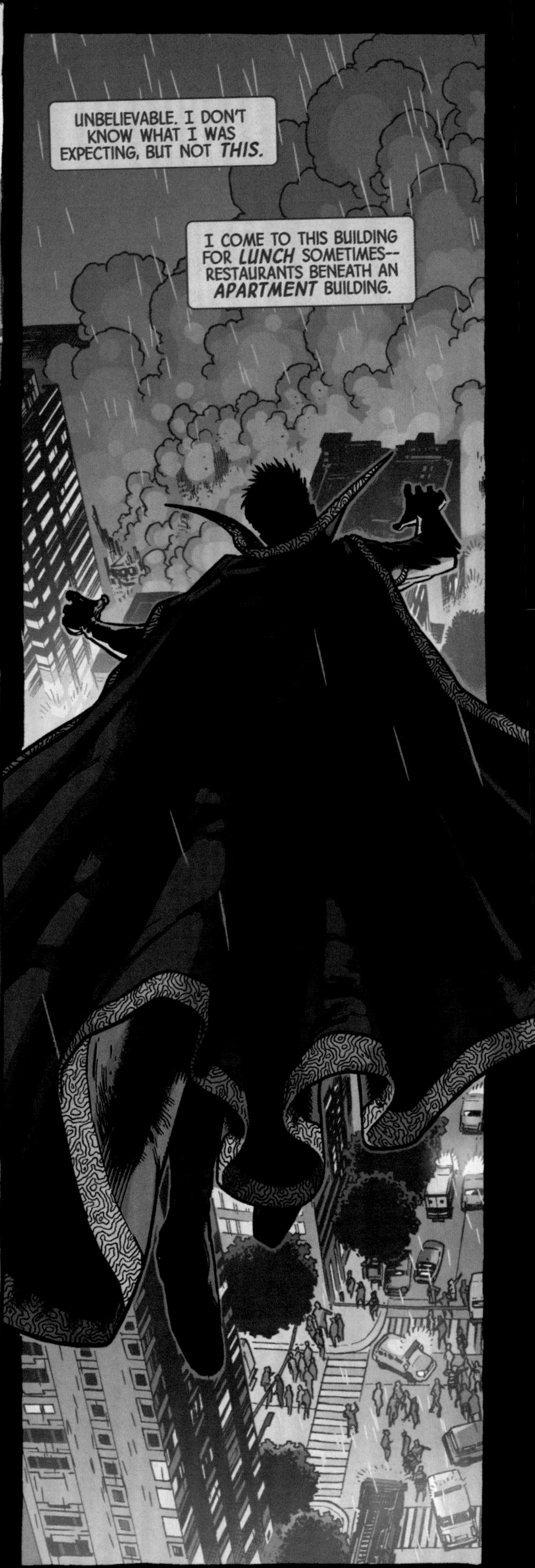
UNBELIEVABLE. I DON'T KNOW WHAT I WAS EXPECTING, BUT NOT THIS.
I COME TO THIS BUILDING FOR LUNCH SOMETIMES-- RESTAURANTS BENEATH AN APARTMENT BUILDING.

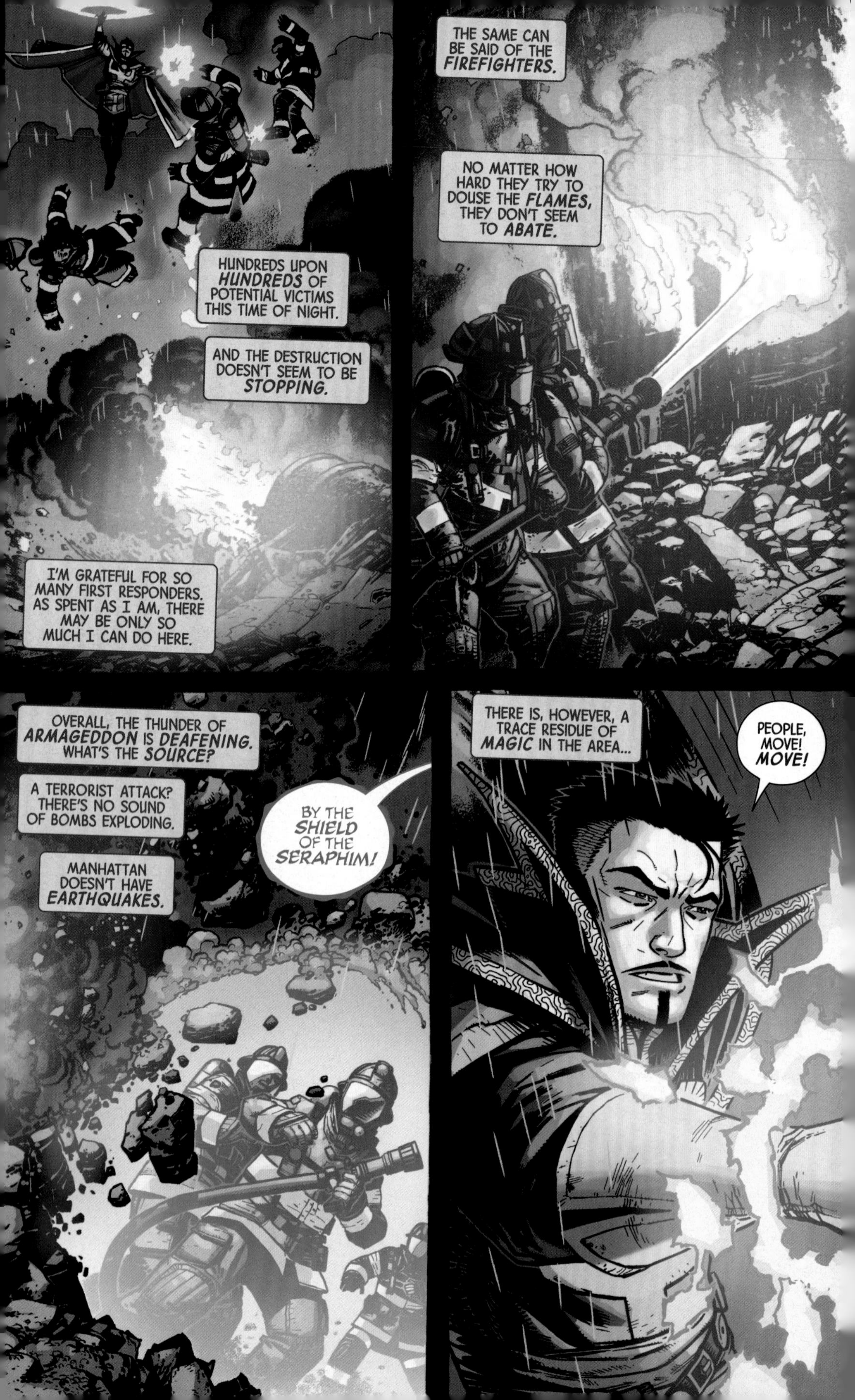
HUNDREDS UPON HUNDREDS OF POTENTIAL VICTIMS THIS TIME OF NIGHT.
AND THE DESTRUCTION DOESN'T SEEM TO BE STOPPING.
I'M GRATEFUL FOR SO MANY FIRST RESPONDERS. AS SPENT AS I AM, THERE MAY BE ONLY SO MUCH I CAN DO HERE.
THE SAME CAN BE SAID OF THE FIREFIGHTERS.
NO MATTER HOW HARD THEY TRY TO DOUSE THE FLAMES, THEY DON'T SEEM TO ABATE.
OVERALL, THE THUNDER OF ARMAGEDDON IS DEAFENING. WHAT'S THE SOURCE?
A TERRORIST ATTACK? THERE'S NO SOUND OF BOMBS EXPLODING.
MANHATTAN DOESN'T HAVE EARTHQUAKES.
BY THE SHIELD OF THE SERAPHIM!
THERE IS, HOWEVER, A TRACE RESIDUE OF MAGIC IN THE AREA...
PEOPLE, MOVE! MOVE!

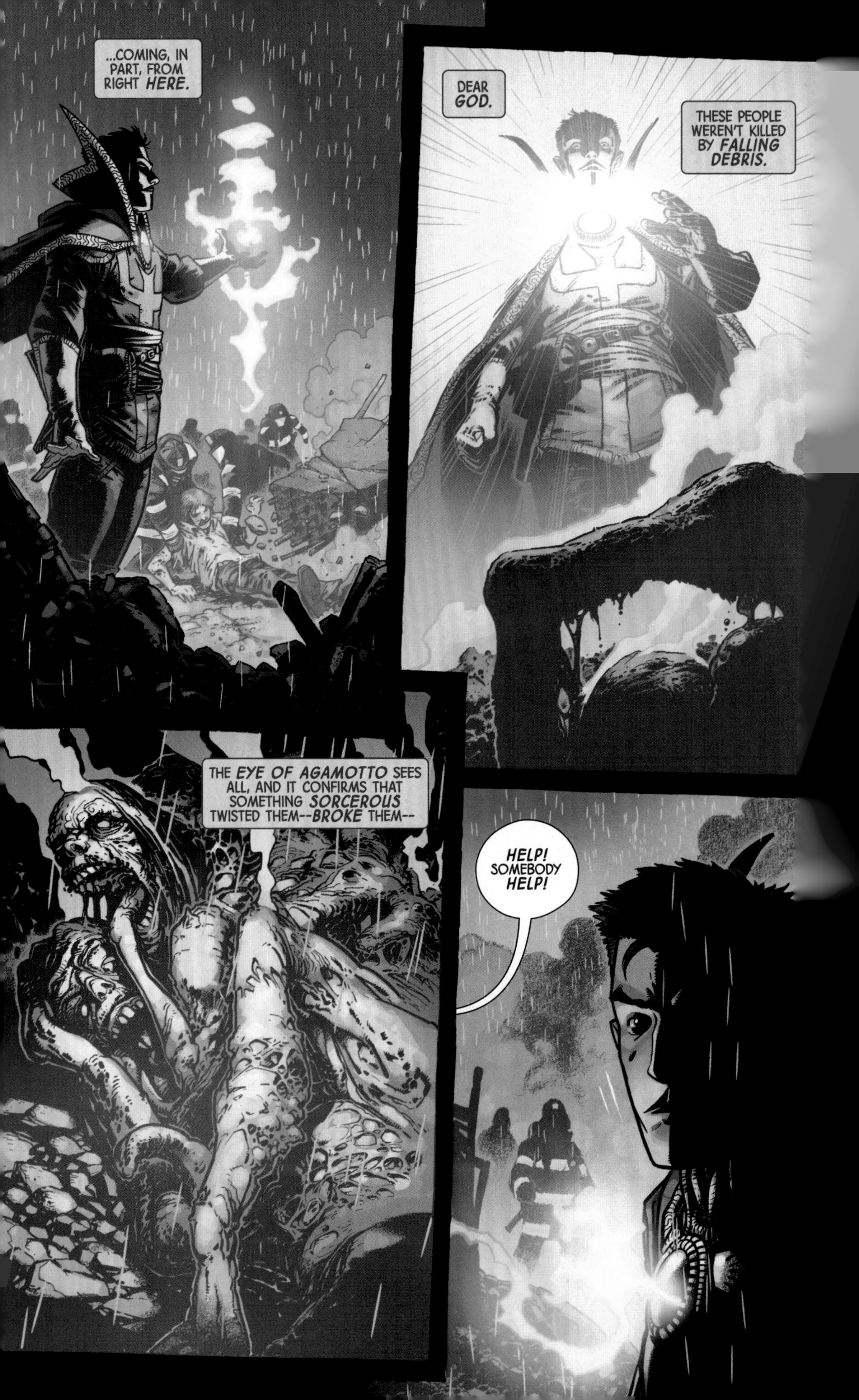
...COMING, IN PART, FROM RIGHT HERE.
DEAR GOD.
THESE PEOPLE WEREN'T KILLED BY FALLING DEBRIS.
THE EYE OF AGAMOTTO SEES ALL, AND IT CONFIRMS THAT SOMETHING SORCEROUS TWISTED THEM--BROKE THEM--
HELP! SOMEBODY HELP!

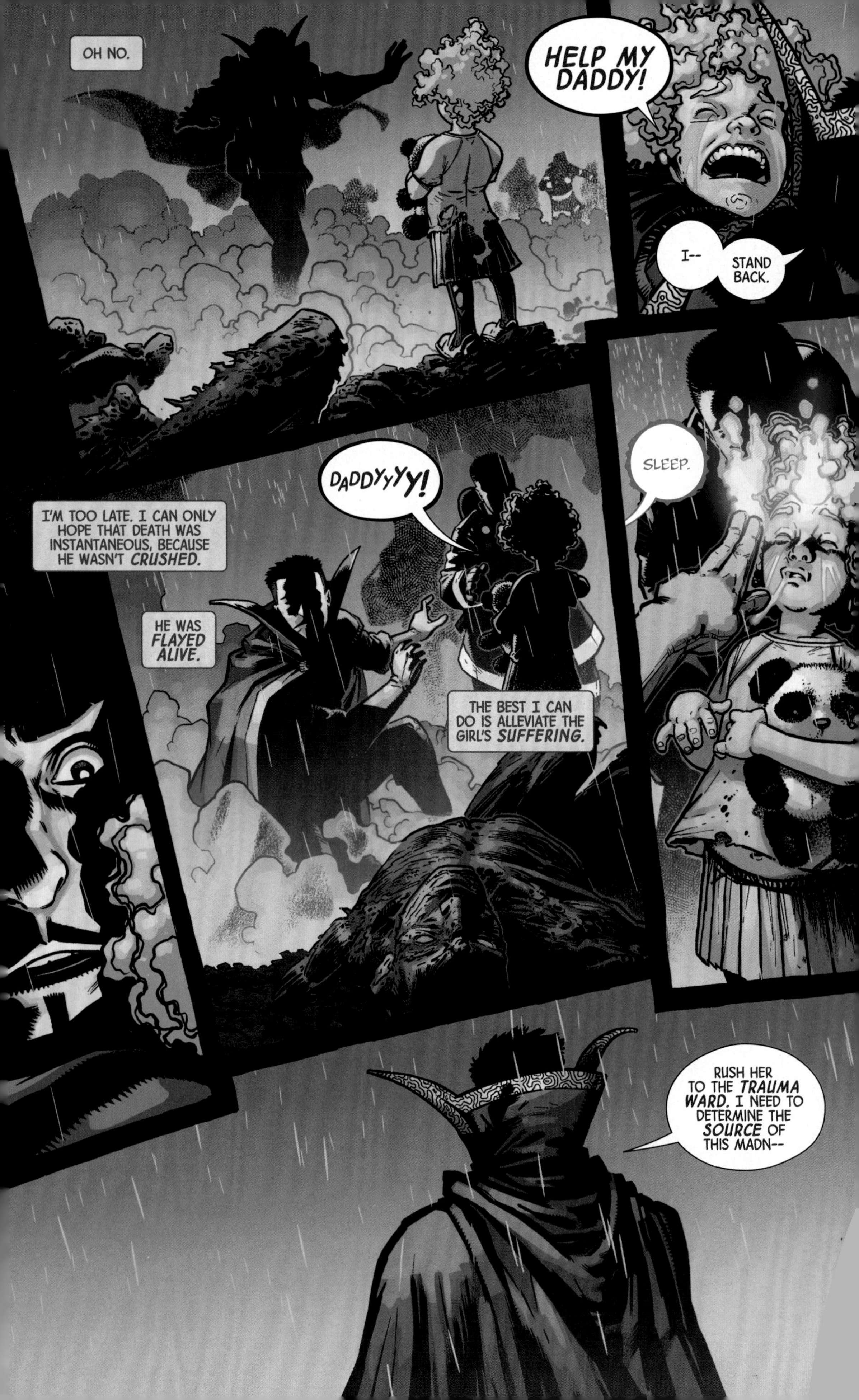
OH NO.
HELP MY DADDY!
I--
STAND BACK.
DADDYyYY!
I'M TOO LATE. I CAN ONLY HOPE THAT DEATH WAS INSTANTANEOUS, BECAUSE HE WASN'T CRUSHED.
HE WAS FLAYED ALIVE.
THE BEST I CAN DO IS ALLEVIATE THE GIRL'S SUFFERING.
SLEEP.
RUSH HER TO THE TRAUMA WARD. I NEED TO DETERMINE THE SOURCE OF THIS MADN--

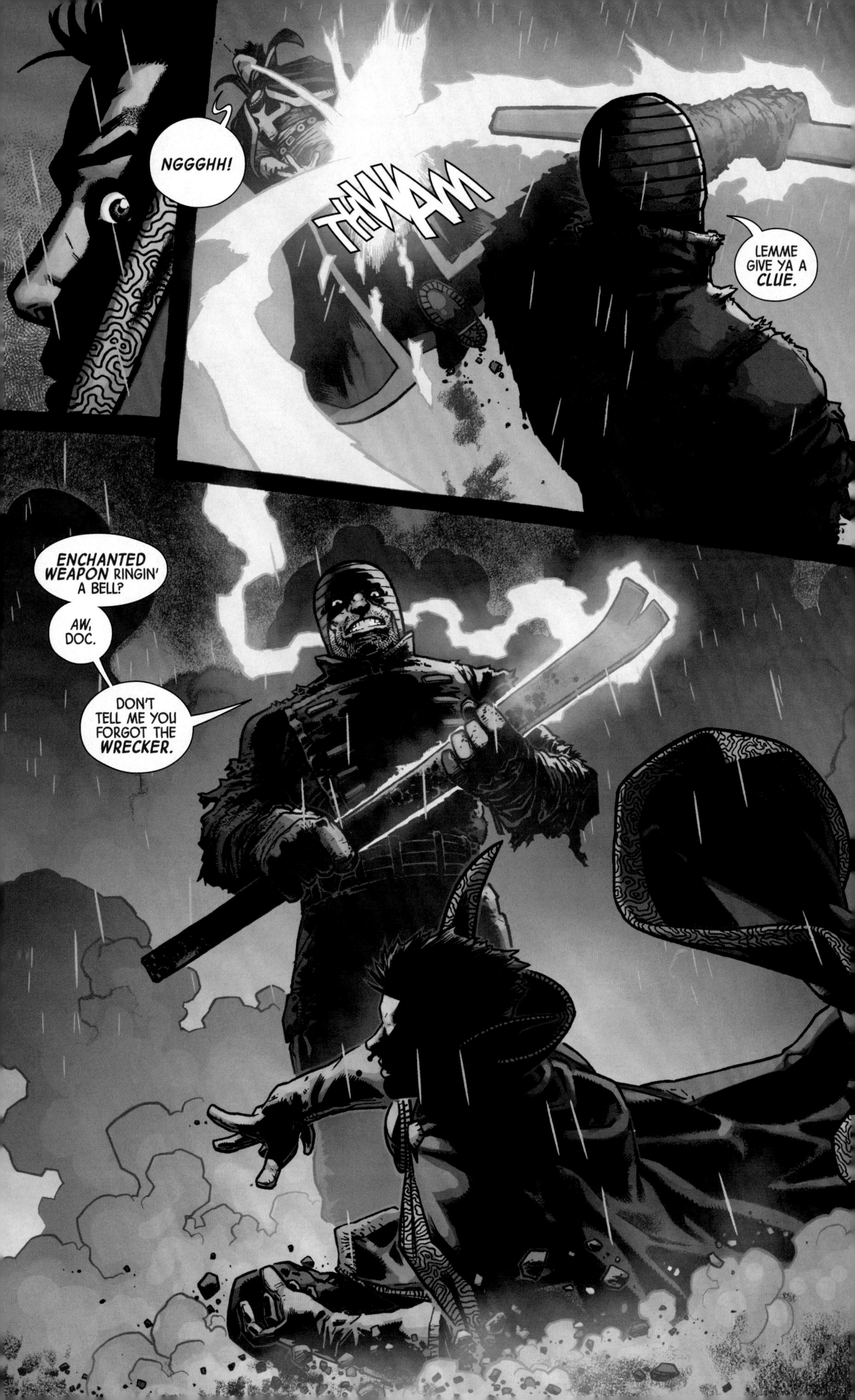
NGGGHH!
THWAM
LEMME GIVE YA A CLUE.
ENCHANTED WEAPON RINGIN' A BELL?
AW, DOC.
DON'T TELL ME YOU FORGOT THE WRECKER.

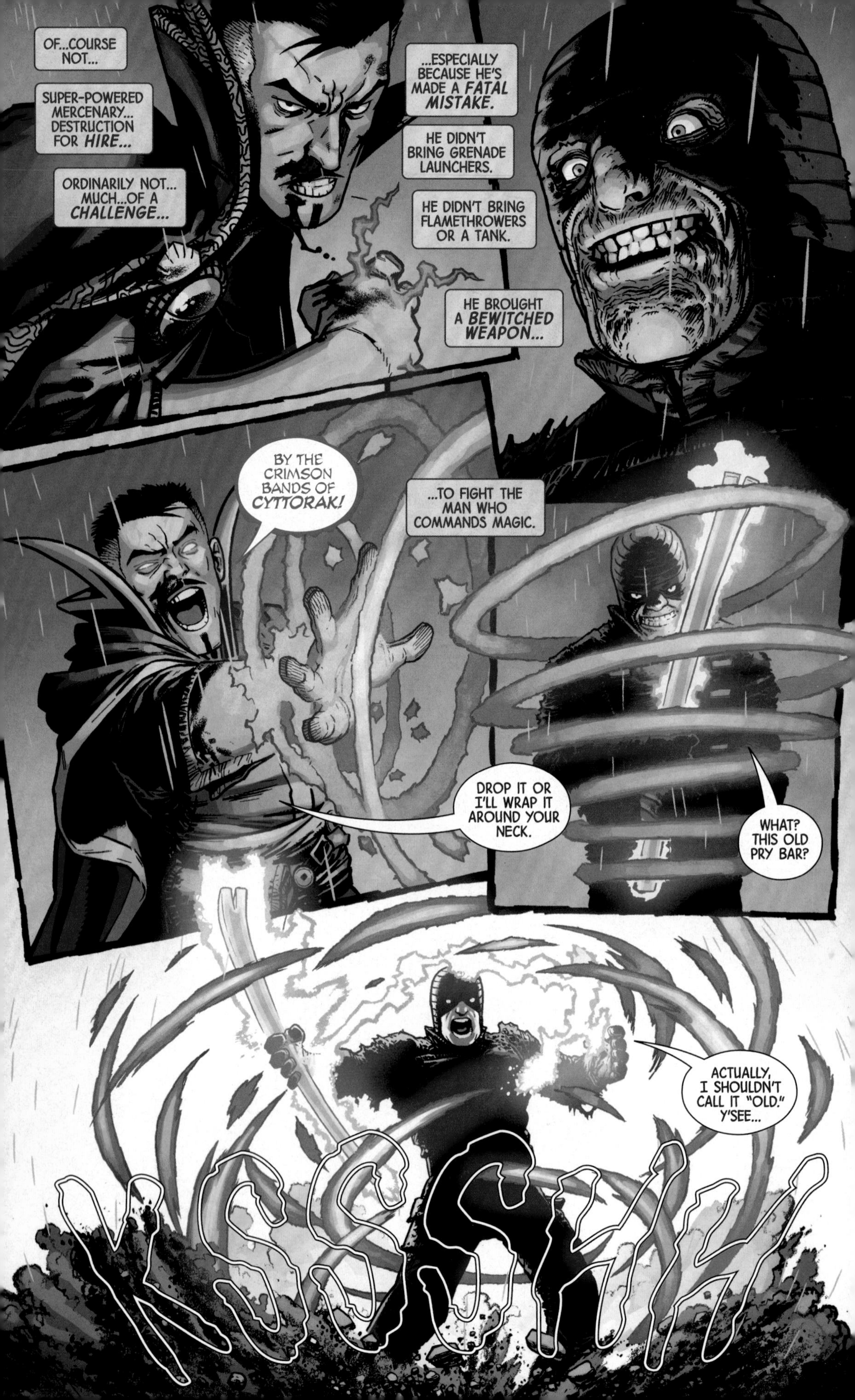
OF...COURSE NOT...
SUPER-POWERED MERCENARY... DESTRUCTION FOR HIRE...
ORDINARILY NOT... MUCH...OF A CHALLENGE...
...ESPECIALLY BECAUSE HE'S MADE A FATAL MISTAKE.
HE DIDN'T BRING GRENADE LAUNCHERS.
HE DIDN'T BRING FLAMETHROWERS OR A TANK.
HE BROUGHT A BEWITCHED WEAPON...
BY THE CRIMSON BANDS OF CYTTORAK!
...TO FIGHT THE MAN WHO COMMANDS MAGIC.
DROP IT OR I'LL WRAP IT AROUND YOUR NECK.
WHAT? THIS OLD PRY BAR?
ACTUALLY, I SHOULDN'T CALL IT "OLD." Y'SEE...
KSSSHH

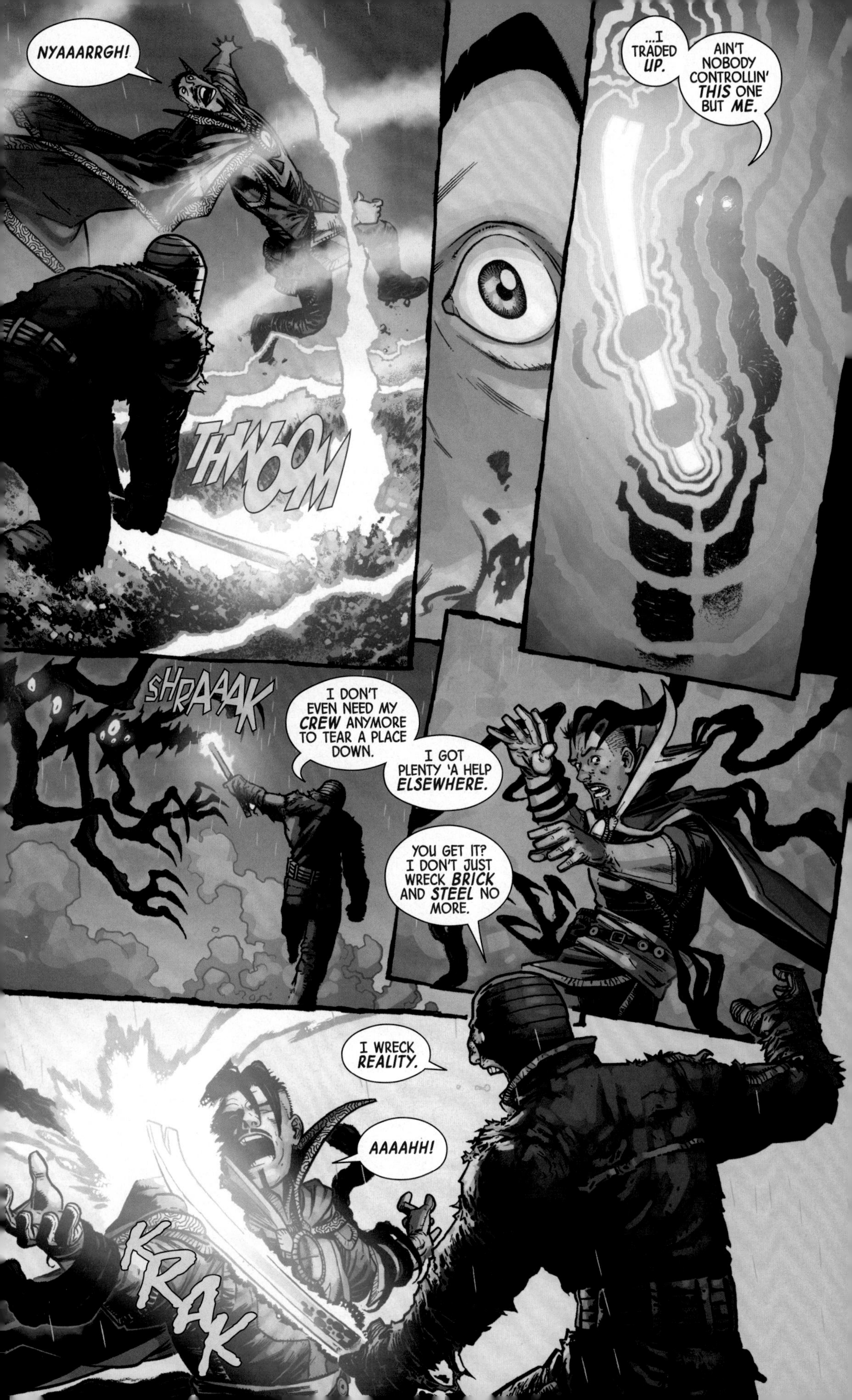
NYAAARRGH!
THWOOM
...I TRADED UP.
AIN'T NOBODY CONTROLLIN' THIS ONE BUT ME.
SHRAAAK
I DON'T EVEN NEED MY CREW ANYMORE TO TEAR A PLACE DOWN.
I GOT PLENTY 'A HELP ELSEWHERE.
YOU GET IT? I DON'T JUST WRECK BRICK AND STEEL NO MORE.
I WRECK REALITY.
AAAAHH!
KRAK

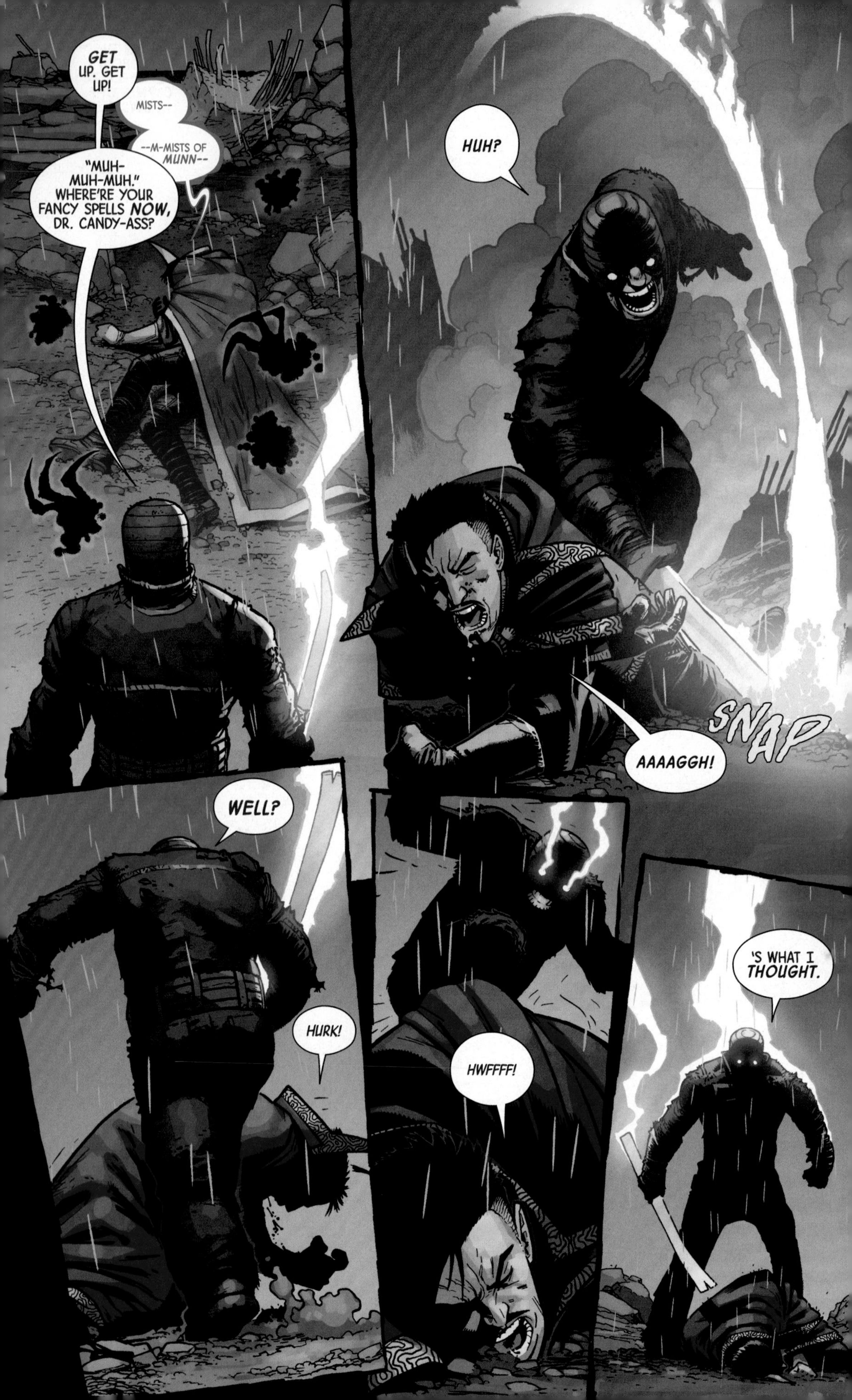
GET UP. GET UP!
MISTS--
--M-MISTS OF MUNN--
"MUH-MUH-MUH." WHERE'RE YOUR FANCY SPELLS NOW, DR. CANDY-ASS?
HUH?
SNAP
AAAAGGH!
WELL?
HURK!
HWFFFF!
'S WHAT I THOUGHT.

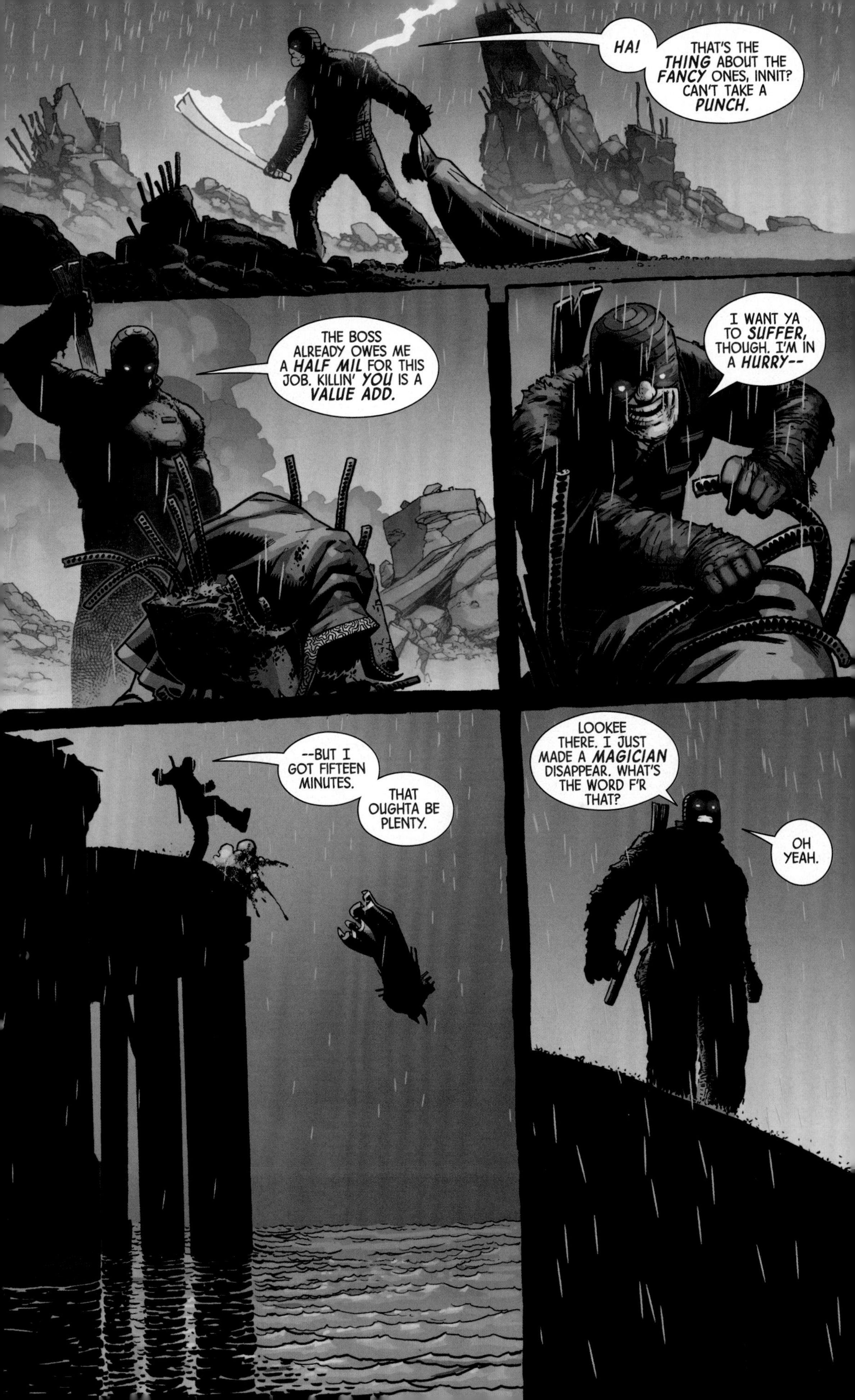
HA!
THAT'S THE THING ABOUT THE FANCY ONES, INNIT? CAN'T TAKE A PUNCH.
THE BOSS ALREADY OWES ME A HALF MIL FOR THIS JOB. KILLIN' YOU IS A VALUE ADD.
I WANT YA TO SUFFER, THOUGH. I'M IN A HURRY--
--BUT I GOT FIFTEEN MINUTES.
THAT OUGHTA BE PLENTY.
LOOKEE THERE. I JUST MADE A MAGICIAN DISAPPEAR. WHAT'S THE WORD F'R THAT?
OH YEAH.

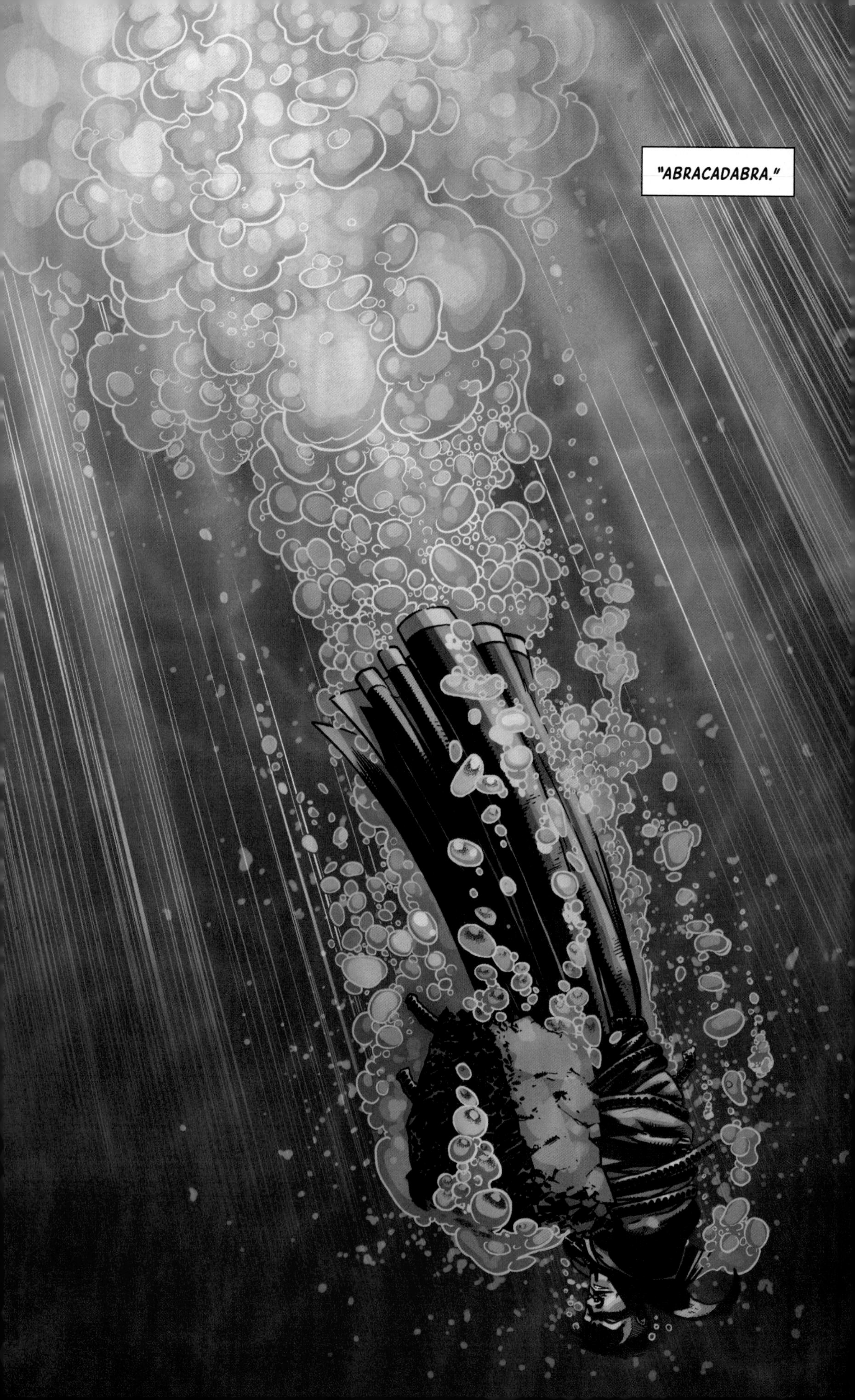
"ABRACADABRA."

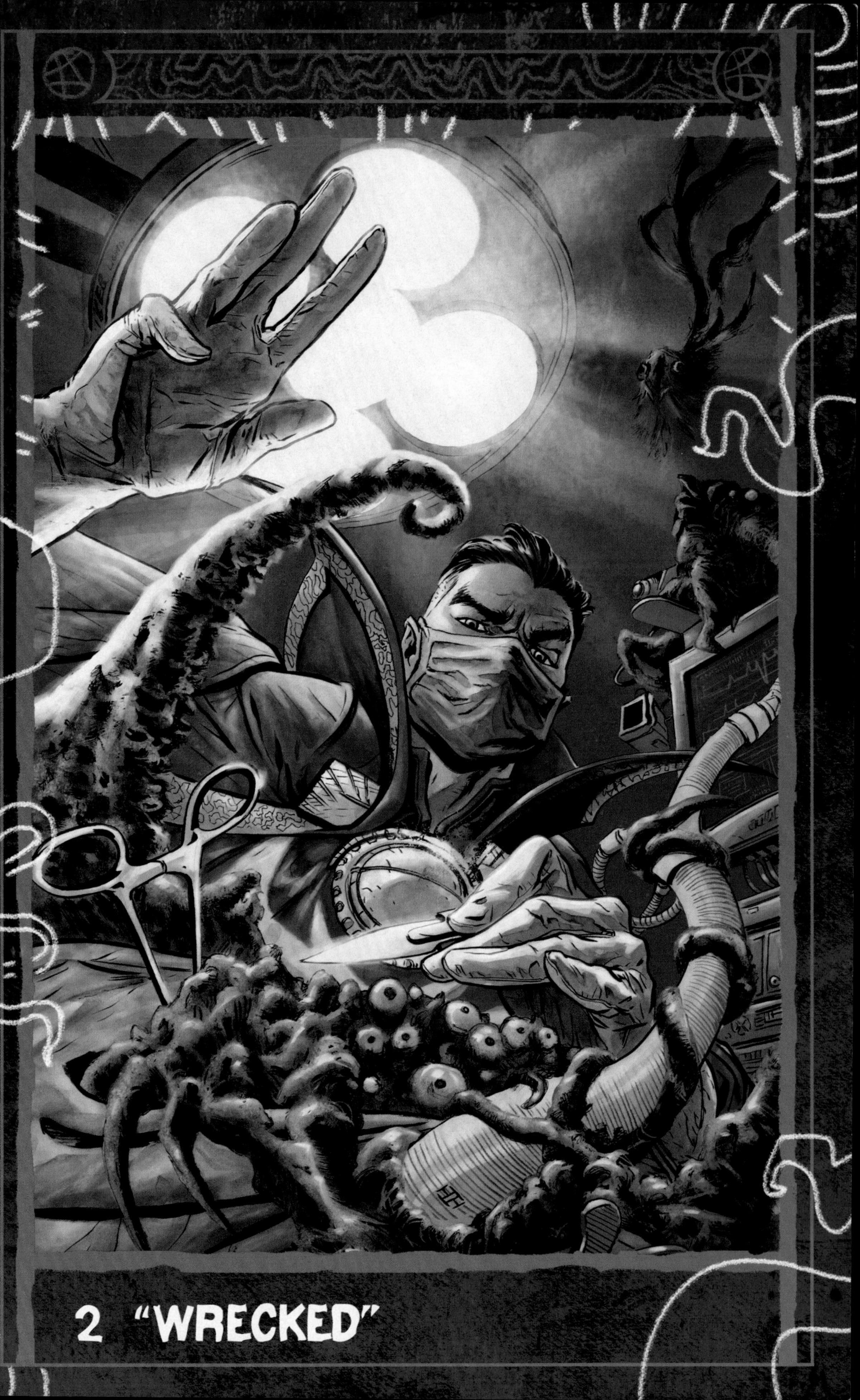

2 "WRECKED"

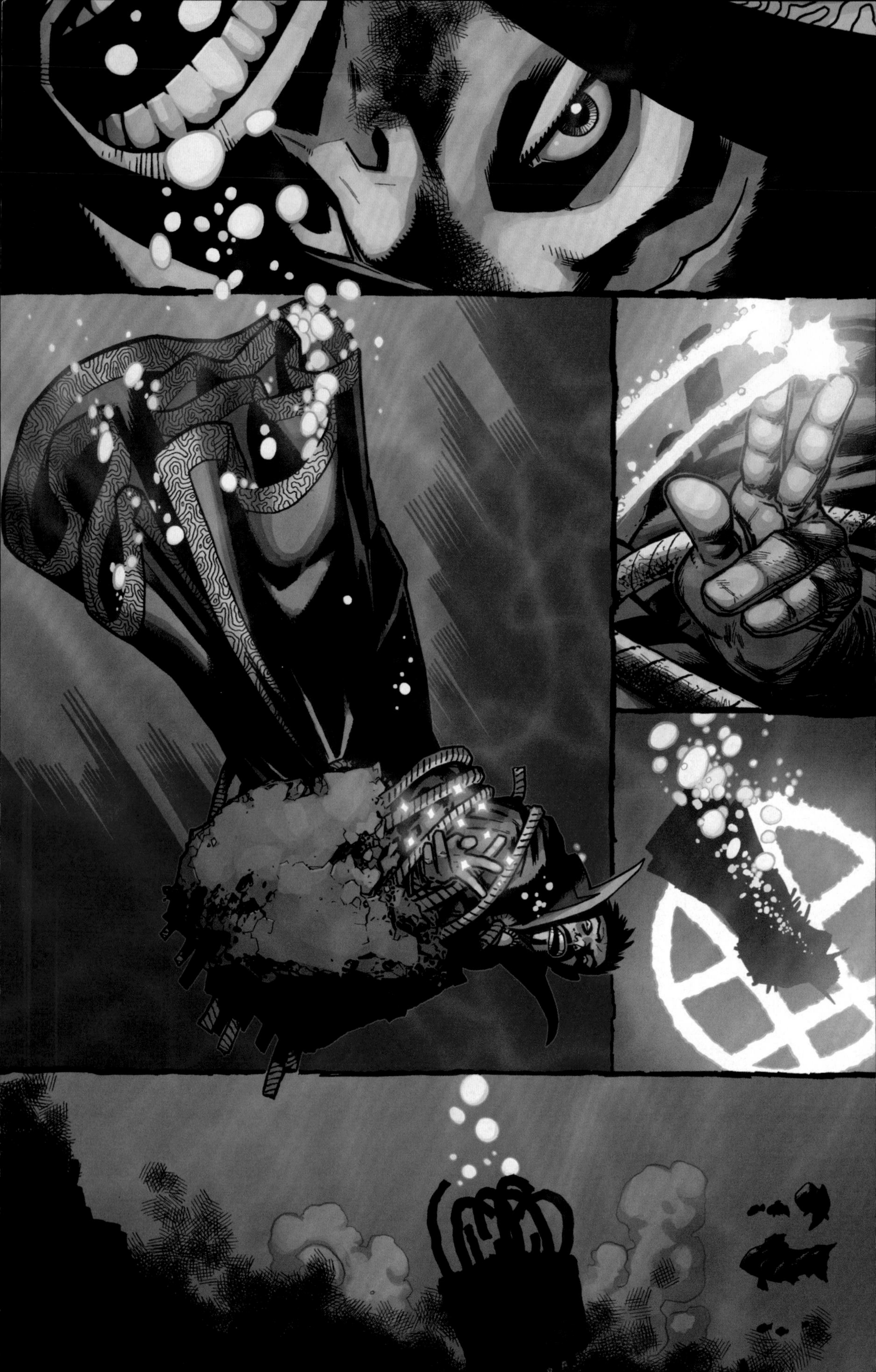

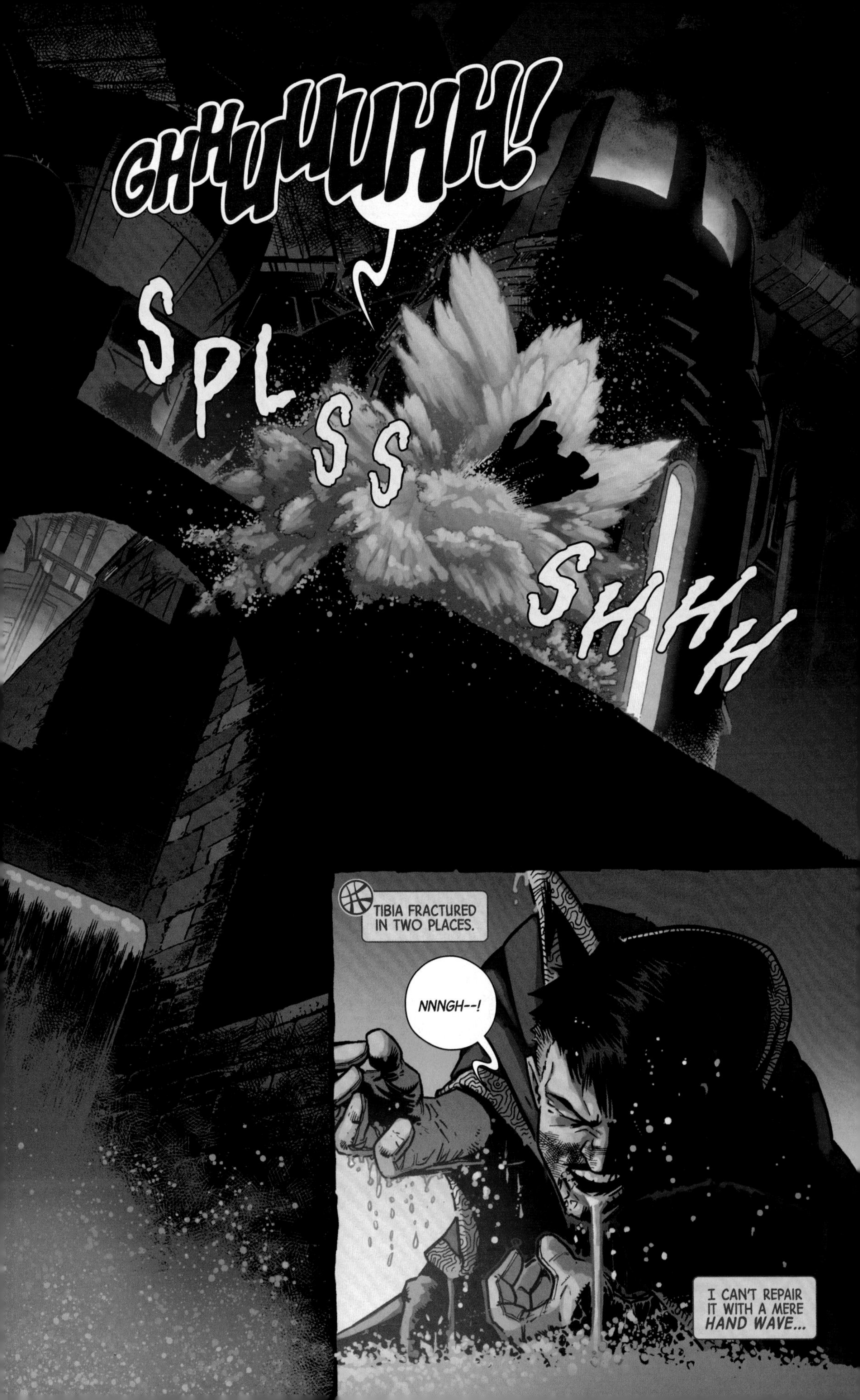
GHUUUHH!
SPLSSSHHH
TIBIA FRACTURED IN TWO PLACES.
NNNGH--!
I CAN'T REPAIR IT WITH A MERE HAND WAVE...

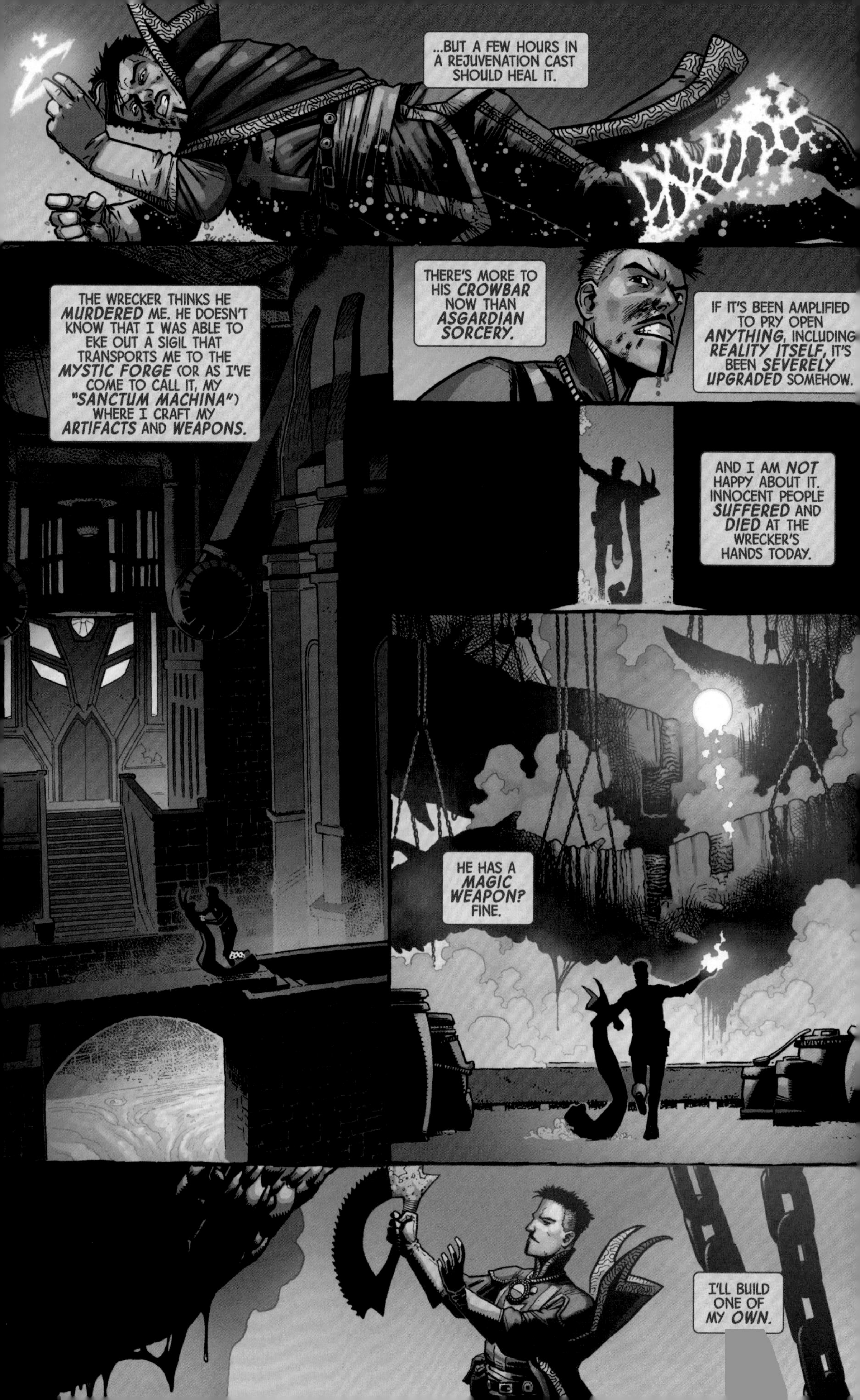
...BUT A FEW HOURS IN A REJUVENATION CAST SHOULD HEAL IT.
THE WRECKER THINKS HE MURDERED ME. HE DOESN'T KNOW THAT I WAS ABLE TO EKE OUT A SIGIL THAT TRANSPORTS ME TO THE MYSTIC FORGE (OR AS I'VE COME TO CALL IT, MY "SANCTUM MACHINA") WHERE I CRAFT MY ARTIFACTS AND WEAPONS.
THERE'S MORE TO HIS CROWBAR NOW THAN ASGARDIAN SORCERY.
IF IT'S BEEN AMPLIFIED TO PRY OPEN ANYTHING, INCLUDING REALITY ITSELF, IT'S BEEN SEVERELY UPGRADED SOMEHOW.
AND I AM NOT HAPPY ABOUT IT. INNOCENT PEOPLE SUFFERED AND DIED AT THE WRECKER'S HANDS TODAY.
HE HAS A MAGIC WEAPON? FINE.
I'LL BUILD ONE OF MY OWN.

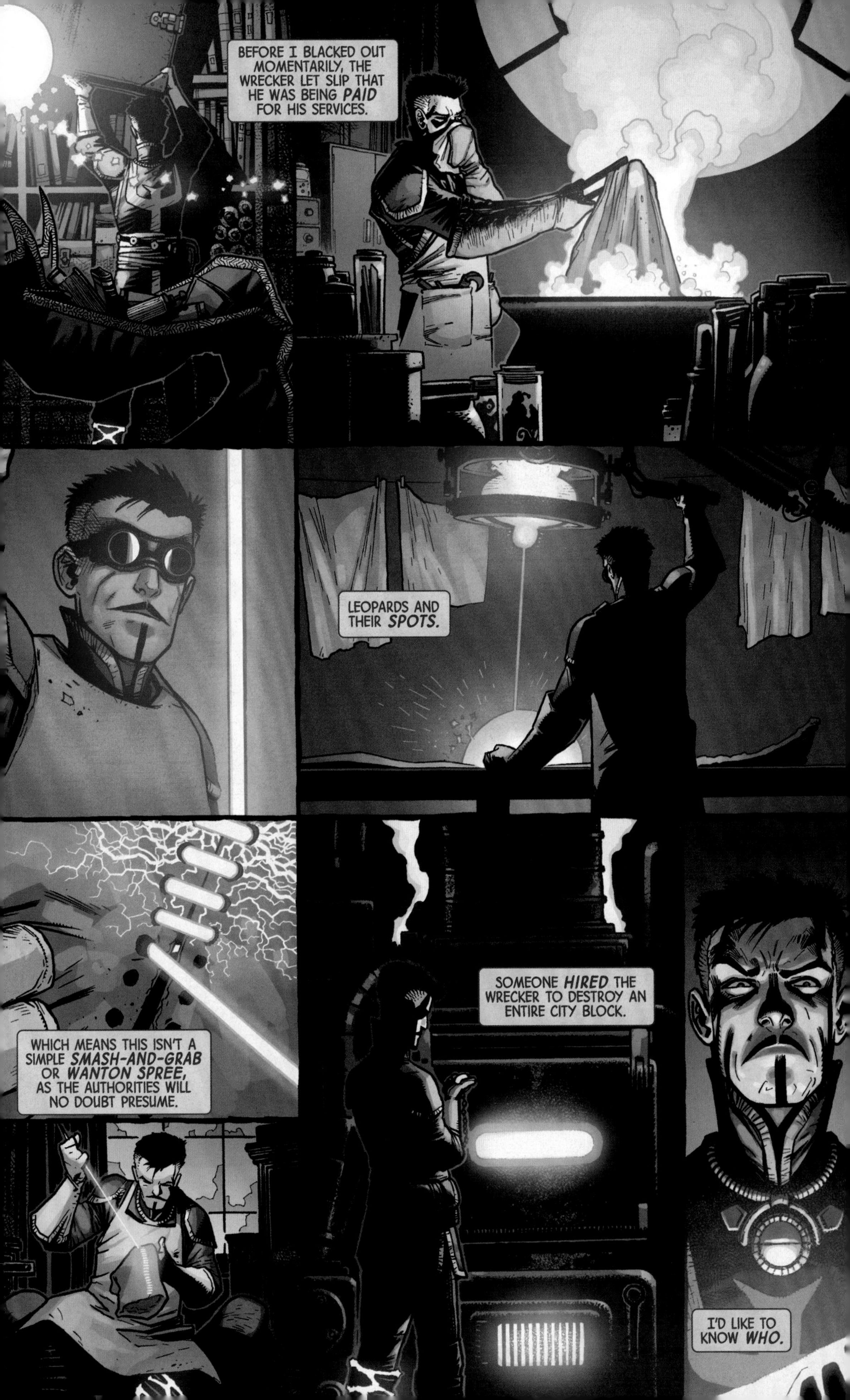
BEFORE I BLACKED OUT MOMENTARILY, THE WRECKER LET SLIP THAT HE WAS BEING PAID FOR HIS SERVICES.
LEOPARDS AND THEIR SPOTS.
WHICH MEANS THIS ISN'T A SIMPLE SMASH-AND-GRAB OR WANTON SPREE, AS THE AUTHORITIES WILL NO DOUBT PRESUME.
SOMEONE HIRED THE WRECKER TO DESTROY AN ENTIRE CITY BLOCK.
I'D LIKE TO KNOW WHO.

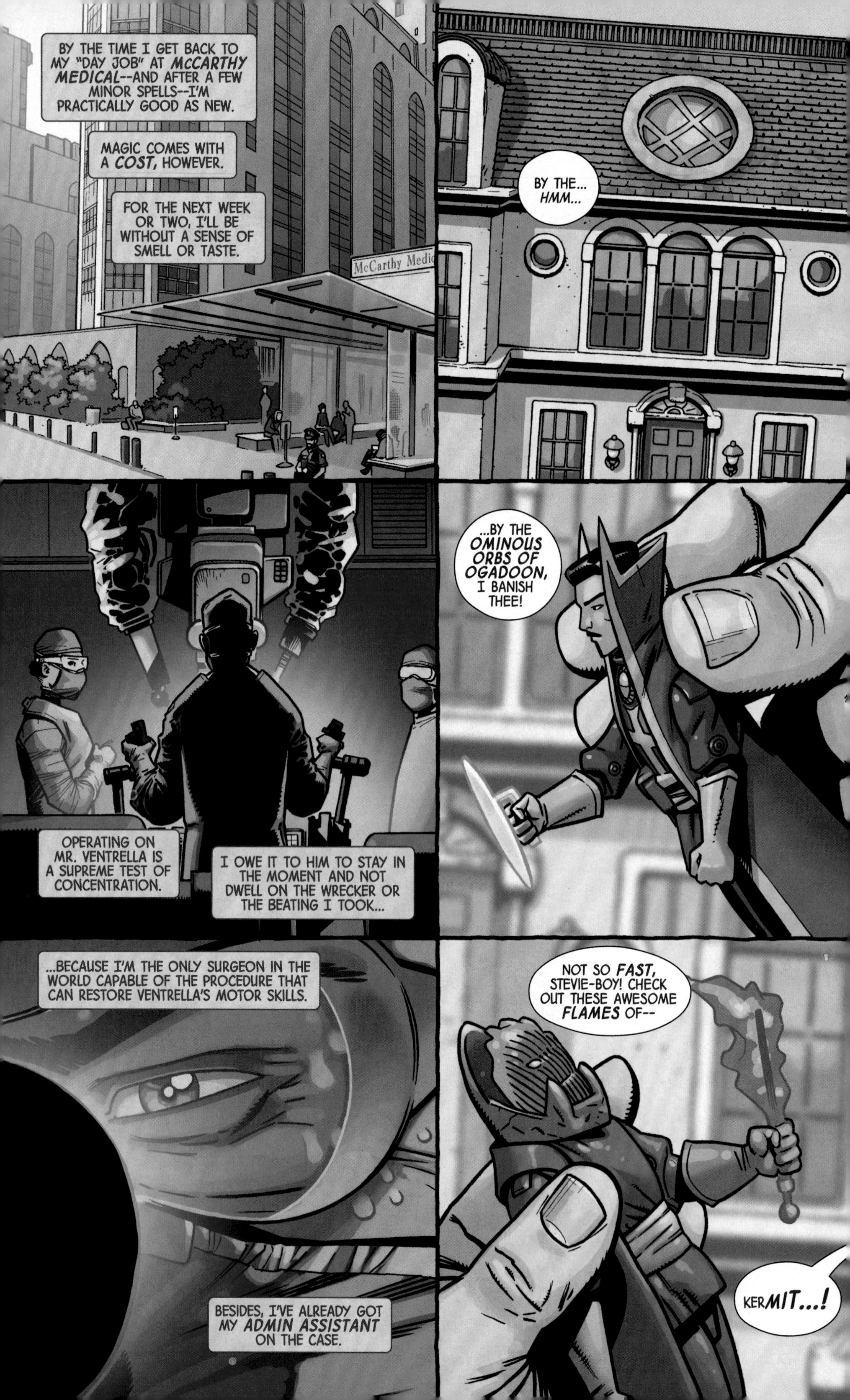
BY THE TIME I GET BACK TO MY "DAY JOB" AT McCARTHY MEDICAL--AND AFTER A FEW MINOR SPELLS--I'M PRACTICALLY GOOD AS NEW.
MAGIC COMES WITH A COST, HOWEVER.
FOR THE NEXT WEEK OR TWO, I'LL BE WITHOUT A SENSE OF SMELL OR TASTE.
McCarthy Medic
BY THE... HMM...
OPERATING ON MR. VENTRELLA IS A SUPREME TEST OF CONCENTRATION.
I OWE IT TO HIM TO STAY IN THE MOMENT AND NOT DWELL ON THE WRECKER OR THE BEATING I TOOK...
...BY THE OMINOUS ORBS OF OGADOON, I BANISH THEE!
...BECAUSE I'M THE ONLY SURGEON IN THE WORLD CAPABLE OF THE PROCEDURE THAT CAN RESTORE VENTRELLA'S MOTOR SKILLS.
BESIDES, I'VE ALREADY GOT MY ADMIN ASSISTANT ON THE CASE.
NOT SO FAST, STEVIE-BOY! CHECK OUT THESE AWESOME FLAMES OF--
KERMIT...!

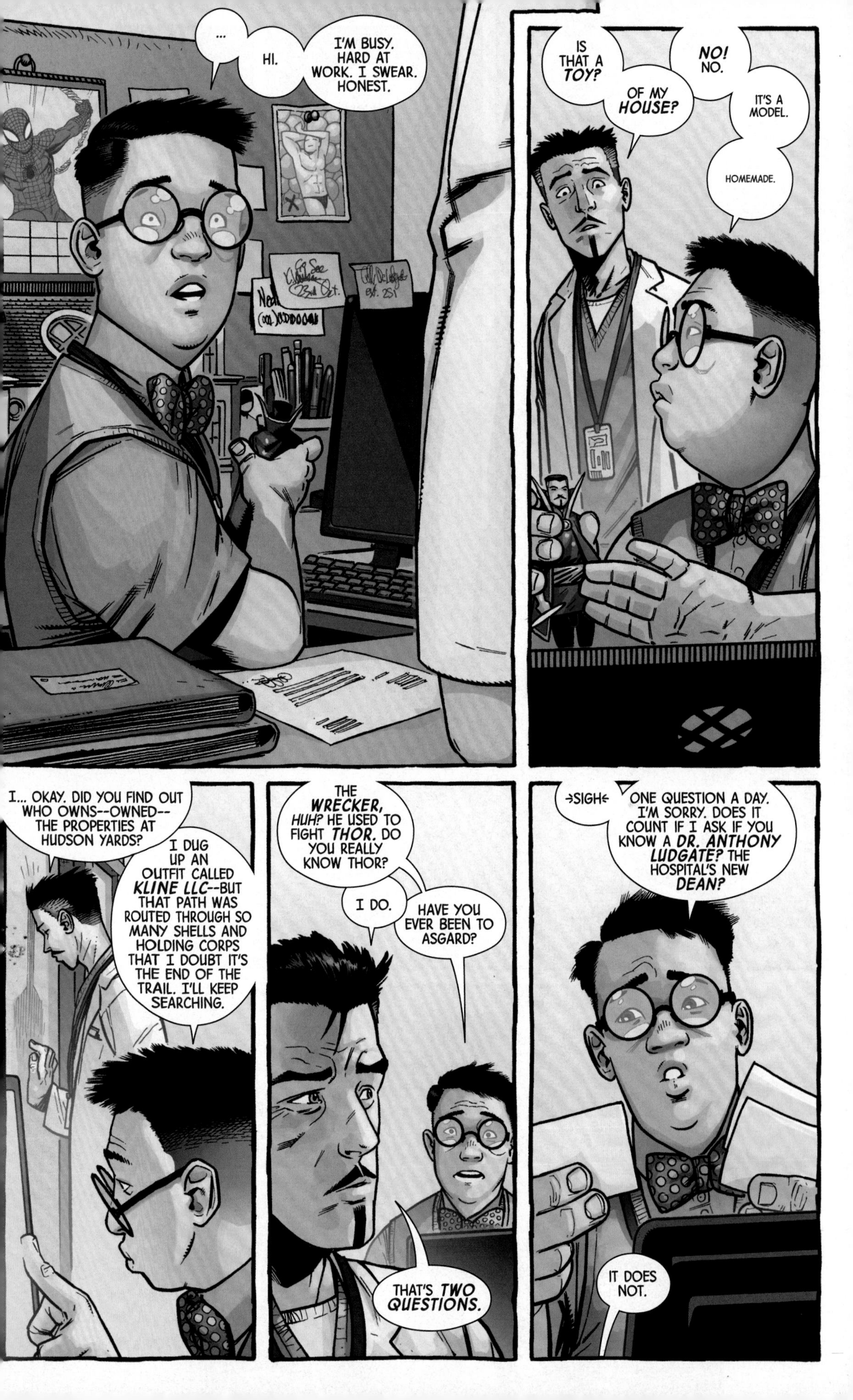

...
HI.
I'M BUSY. HARD AT WORK. I SWEAR. HONEST.
IS THAT A TOY?
OF MY HOUSE?
NO! NO.
IT'S A MODEL.
HOMEMADE.
I... OKAY. DID YOU FIND OUT WHO OWNS--OWNED-- THE PROPERTIES AT HUDSON YARDS?
I DUG UP AN OUTFIT CALLED KLINE LLC--BUT THAT PATH WAS ROUTED THROUGH SO MANY SHELLS AND HOLDING CORPS THAT I DOUBT IT'S THE END OF THE TRAIL. I'LL KEEP SEARCHING.
THE WRECKER, HUH? HE USED TO FIGHT THOR. DO YOU REALLY KNOW THOR?
I DO.
HAVE YOU EVER BEEN TO ASGARD?
THAT'S TWO QUESTIONS.
→SIGH←
ONE QUESTION A DAY. I'M SORRY. DOES IT COUNT IF I ASK IF YOU KNOW A DR. ANTHONY LUDGATE? THE HOSPITAL'S NEW DEAN?
IT DOES NOT.

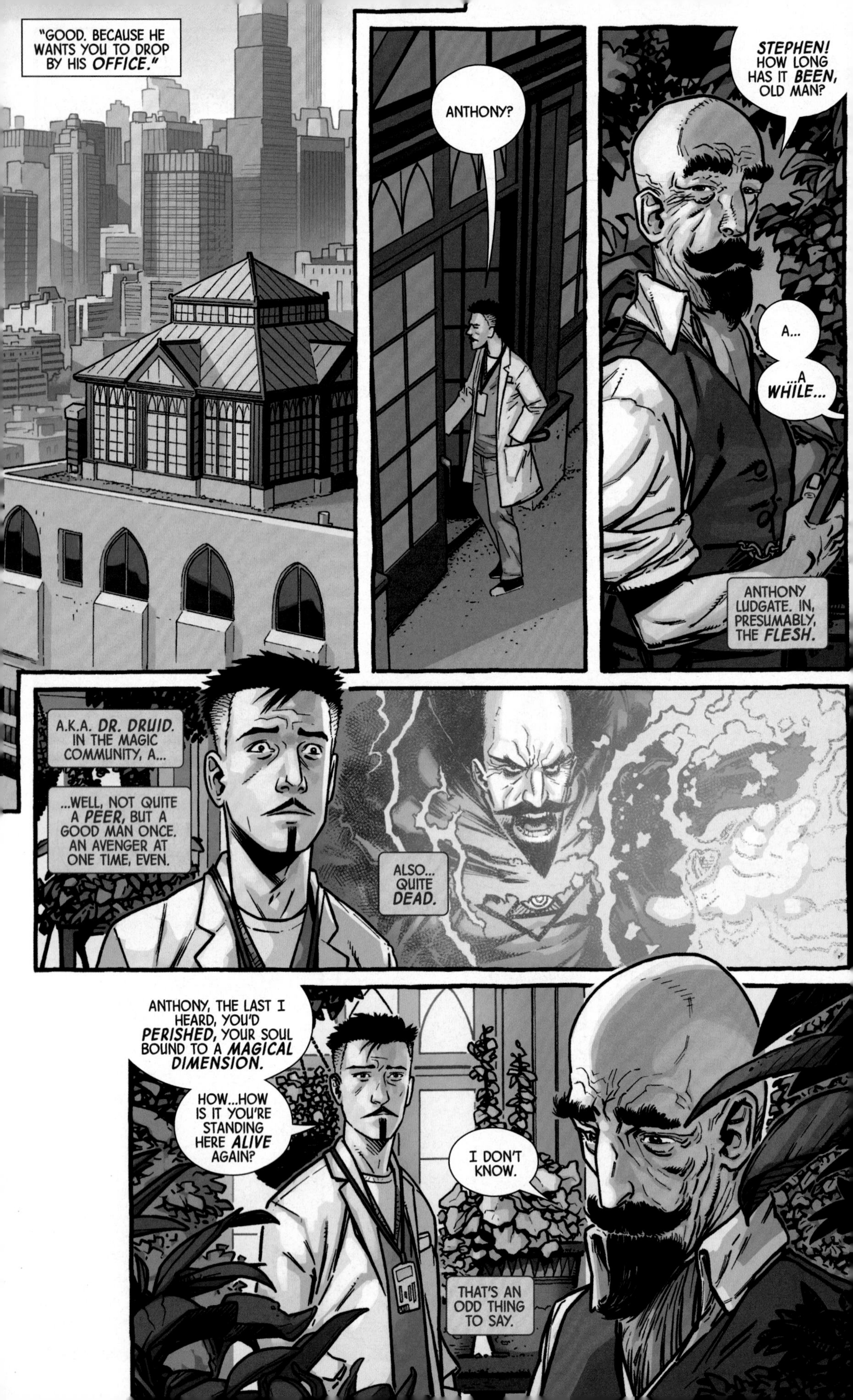
"GOOD. BECAUSE HE WANTS YOU TO DROP BY HIS OFFICE."
ANTHONY?
STEPHEN! HOW LONG HAS IT BEEN, OLD MAN?
A...
...A WHILE...
ANTHONY LUDGATE. IN, PRESUMABLY, THE FLESH.
A.K.A. DR. DRUID. IN THE MAGIC COMMUNITY, A...
...WELL, NOT QUITE A PEER, BUT A GOOD MAN ONCE. AN AVENGER AT ONE TIME, EVEN.
ALSO... QUITE DEAD.
ANTHONY, THE LAST I HEARD, YOU'D PERISHED, YOUR SOUL BOUND TO A MAGICAL DIMENSION.
HOW...HOW IS IT YOU'RE STANDING HERE ALIVE AGAIN?
I DON'T KNOW.
THAT'S AN ODD THING TO SAY.

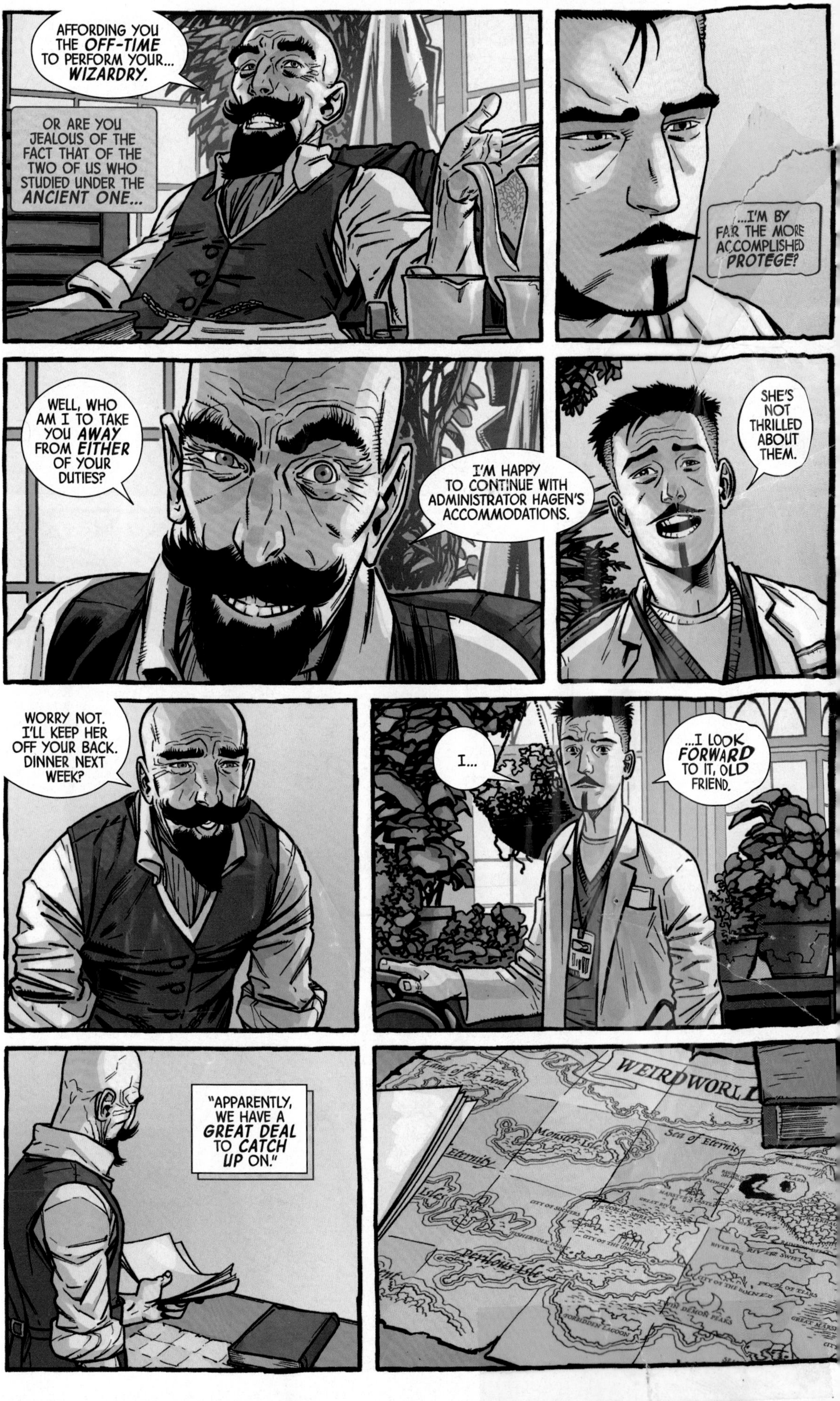
AFFORDING YOU THE OFF-TIME TO PERFORM YOUR... WIZARDRY.
OR ARE YOU JEALOUS OF THE FACT THAT OF THE TWO OF US WHO STUDIED UNDER THE ANCIENT ONE...
...I'M BY FAR THE MORE ACCOMPLISHED PROTEGE?
WELL, WHO AM I TO TAKE YOU AWAY FROM EITHER OF YOUR DUTIES?
I'M HAPPY TO CONTINUE WITH ADMINISTRATOR HAGEN'S ACCOMMODATIONS.
SHE'S NOT THRILLED ABOUT THEM.
WORRY NOT. I'LL KEEP HER OFF YOUR BACK. DINNER NEXT WEEK?
I...
...I LOOK FORWARD TO IT, OLD FRIEND.
"APPARENTLY, WE HAVE A GREAT DEAL TO CATCH UP ON."
WEIRDWORLD
Land of the Dead
Monster Isle
Sea of Eternity
Eternity
Perilous Isle

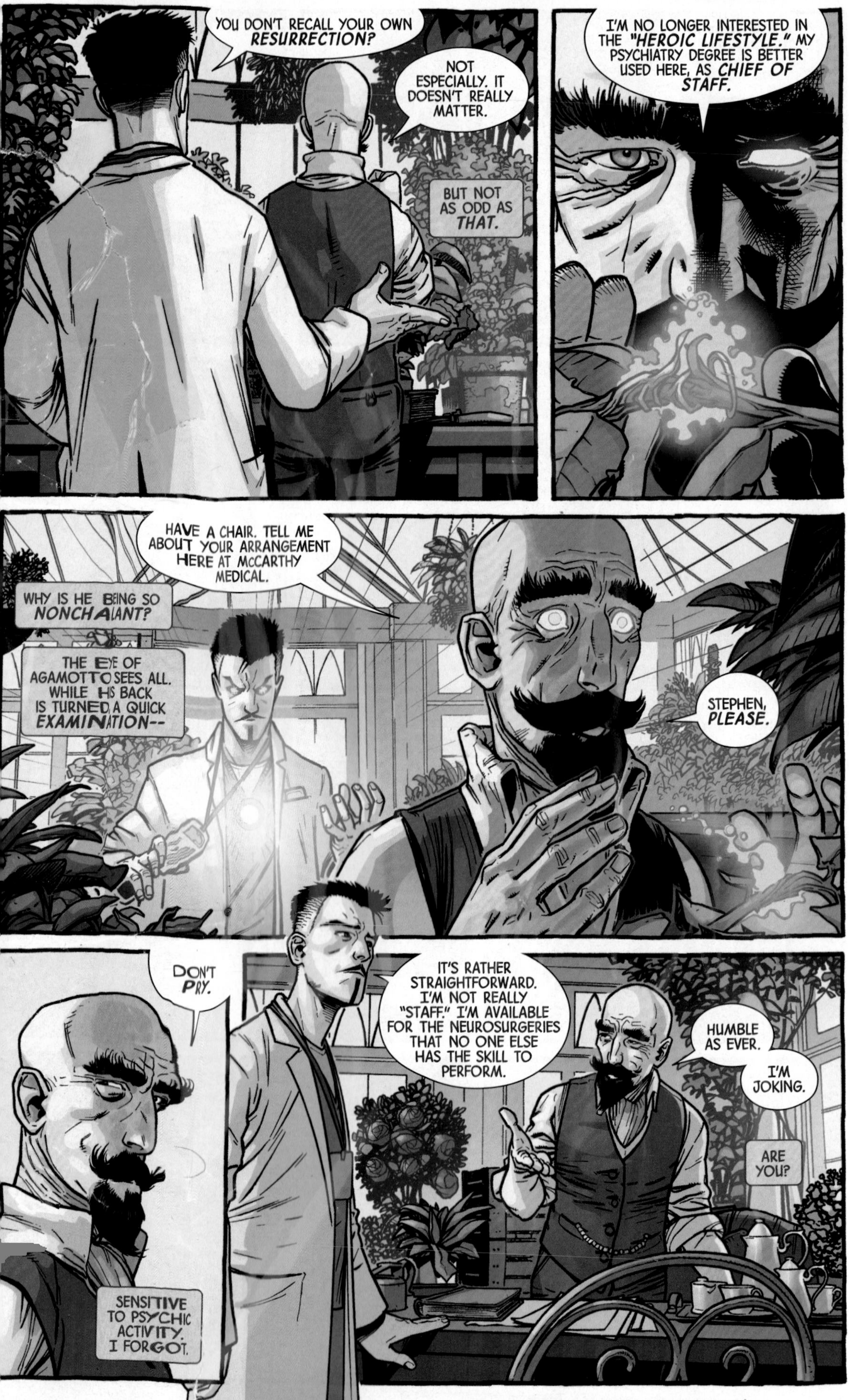
YOU DON'T RECALL YOUR OWN RESURRECTION?
NOT ESPECIALLY. IT DOESN'T REALLY MATTER.
BUT NOT AS ODD AS THAT.
I'M NO LONGER INTERESTED IN THE "HEROIC LIFESTYLE." MY PSYCHIATRY DEGREE IS BETTER USED HERE, AS CHIEF OF STAFF.
HAVE A CHAIR. TELL ME ABOUT YOUR ARRANGEMENT HERE AT McCARTHY MEDICAL.
WHY IS HE BEING SO NONCHALANT?
THE EYE OF AGAMOTTO SEES ALL. WHILE HIS BACK IS TURNED, A QUICK EXAMINATION--
STEPHEN, PLEASE.
DON'T PRY.
SENSITIVE TO PSYCHIC ACTIVITY. I FORGOT.
IT'S RATHER STRAIGHTFORWARD. I'M NOT REALLY "STAFF." I'M AVAILABLE FOR THE NEUROSURGERIES THAT NO ONE ELSE HAS THE SKILL TO PERFORM.
HUMBLE AS EVER.
I'M JOKING.
ARE YOU?

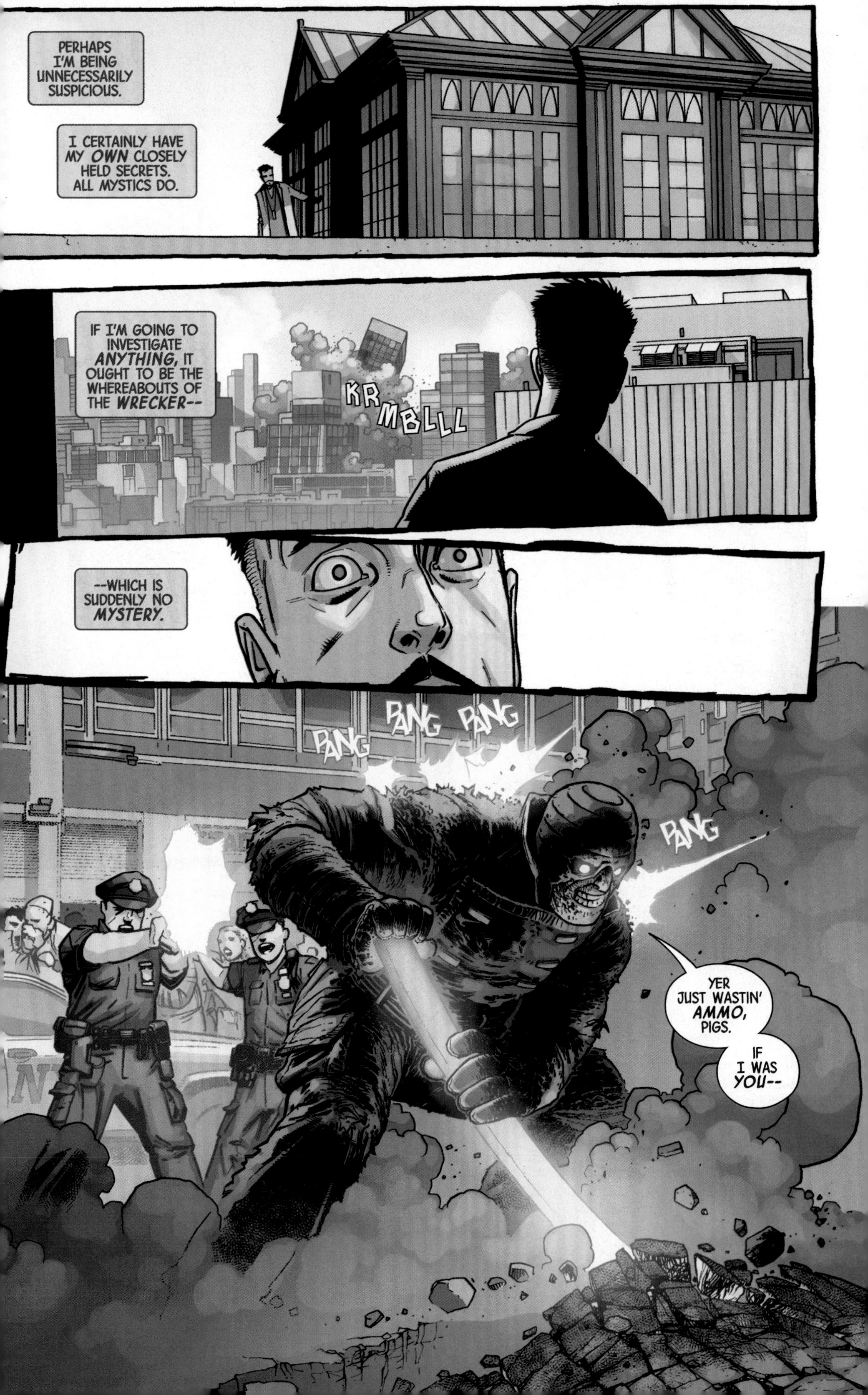
PERHAPS I'M BEING UNNECESSARILY SUSPICIOUS.
I CERTAINLY HAVE MY OWN CLOSELY HELD SECRETS. ALL MYSTICS DO.
IF I'M GOING TO INVESTIGATE ANYTHING, IT OUGHT TO BE THE WHEREABOUTS OF THE WRECKER--
KRMBLLL
--WHICH IS SUDDENLY NO MYSTERY.
PANG
PANG
PANG
PANG
YER JUST WASTIN' AMMO, PIGS.
IF I WAS YOU--

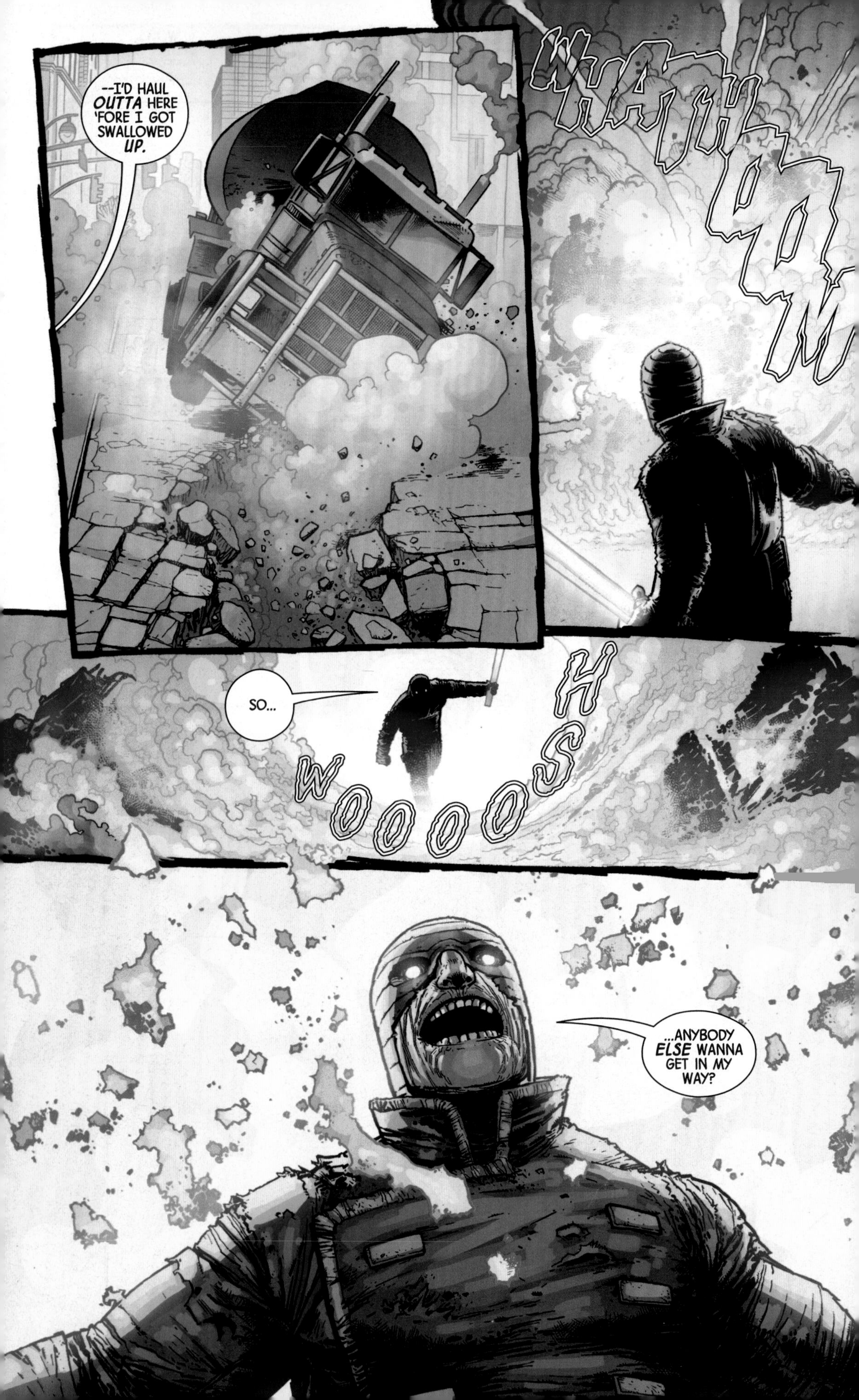
--I'D HAUL OUTTA HERE 'FORE I GOT SWALLOWED UP.
SO...
WOOOOSH
...ANYBODY ELSE WANNA GET IN MY WAY?

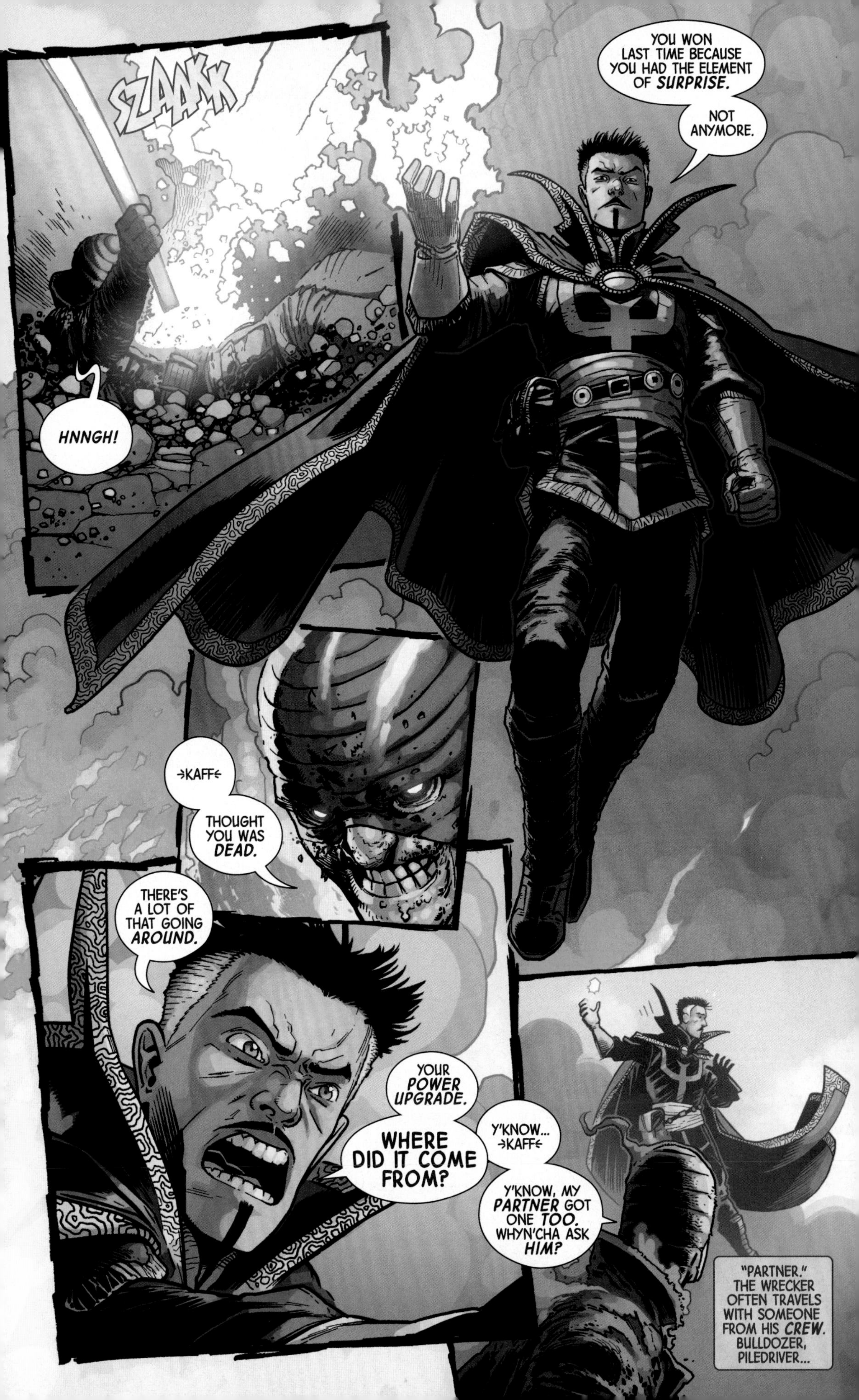
SZAAKK
YOU WON LAST TIME BECAUSE YOU HAD THE ELEMENT OF SURPRISE.
NOT ANYMORE.
HNNGH!
KAFF
THOUGHT YOU WAS DEAD.
THERE'S A LOT OF THAT GOING AROUND.
YOUR POWER UPGRADE.
WHERE DID IT COME FROM?
Y'KNOW... *KAFF*
Y'KNOW, MY PARTNER GOT ONE TOO. WHYN'CHA ASK HIM?
"PARTNER." THE WRECKER OFTEN TRAVELS WITH SOMEONE FROM HIS CREW. BULLDOZER, PILEDRIVER...

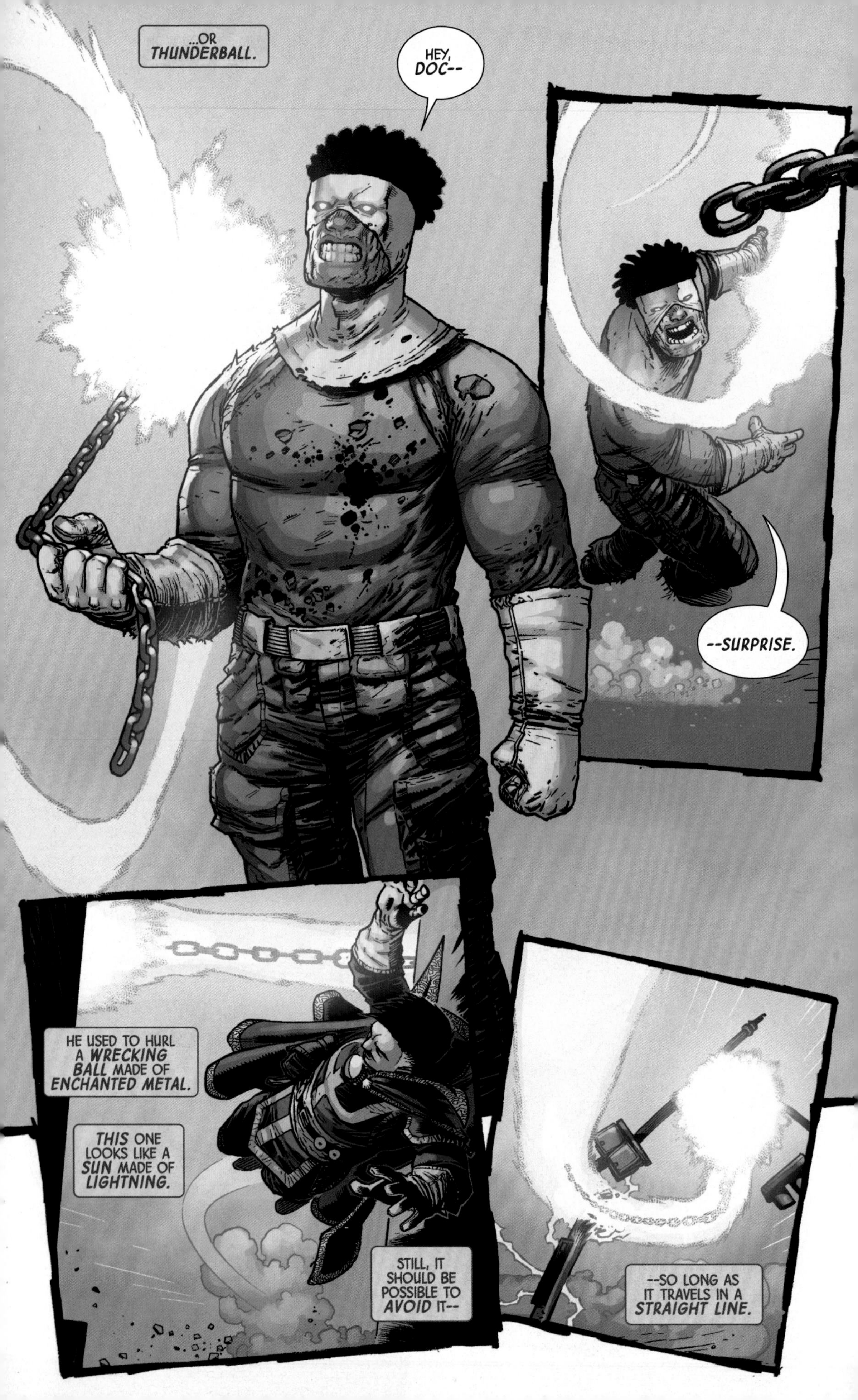
...OR THUNDERBALL.
HEY, DOC--
--SURPRISE.
HE USED TO HURL A WRECKING BALL MADE OF ENCHANTED METAL.
THIS ONE LOOKS LIKE A SUN MADE OF LIGHTNING.
STILL, IT SHOULD BE POSSIBLE TO AVOID IT--
--SO LONG AS IT TRAVELS IN A STRAIGHT LINE.

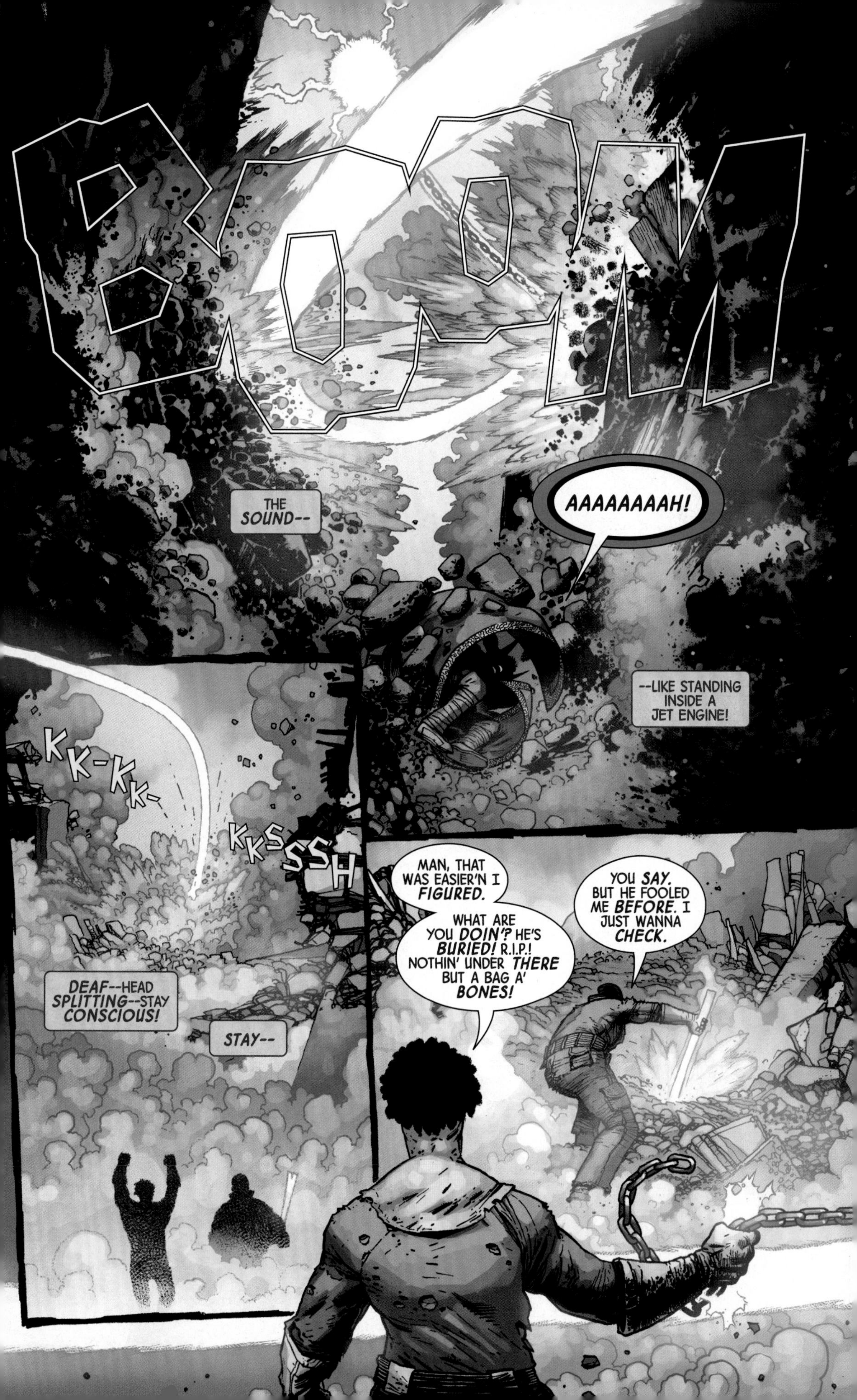
BOOM
THE SOUND--
AAAAAAAAH!
--LIKE STANDING INSIDE A JET ENGINE!
KK-KK-
KKSSSH
DEAF--HEAD SPLITTING--STAY CONSCIOUS!
STAY--
MAN, THAT WAS EASIER'N I FIGURED.
WHAT ARE YOU DOIN'? HE'S BURIED! R.I.P.! NOTHIN' UNDER THERE BUT A BAG A' BONES!
YOU SAY. BUT HE FOOLED ME BEFORE. I JUST WANNA CHECK.

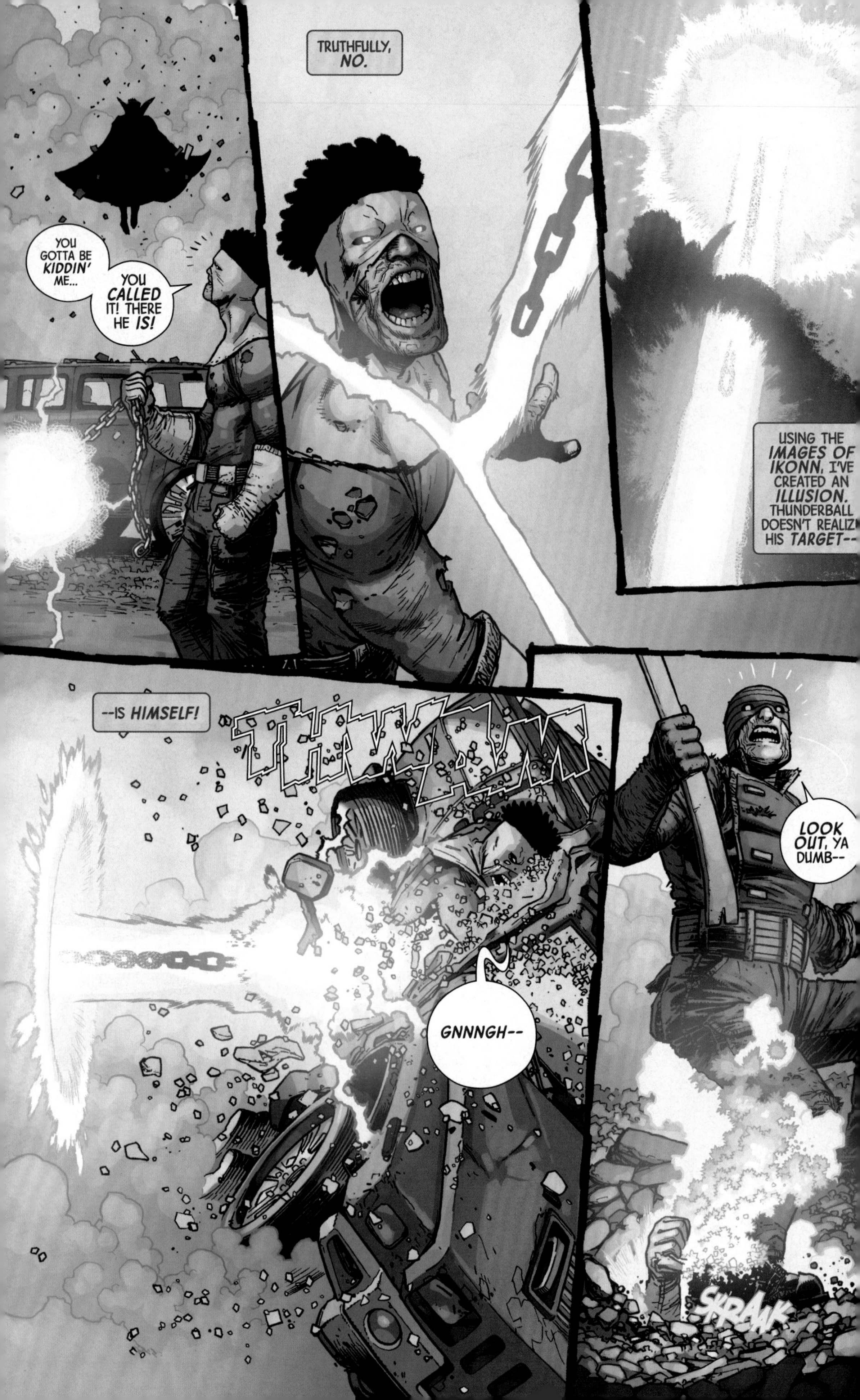
YOU GOTTA BE KIDDIN' ME...
YOU CALLED IT! THERE HE IS!
TRUTHFULLY, NO.
USING THE IMAGES OF IKONN, I'VE CREATED AN ILLUSION. THUNDERBALL DOESN'T REALIZ HIS TARGET--
--IS HIMSELF!
THWAM
GNNNGH--
LOOK OUT, YA DUMB--
SKRAAK

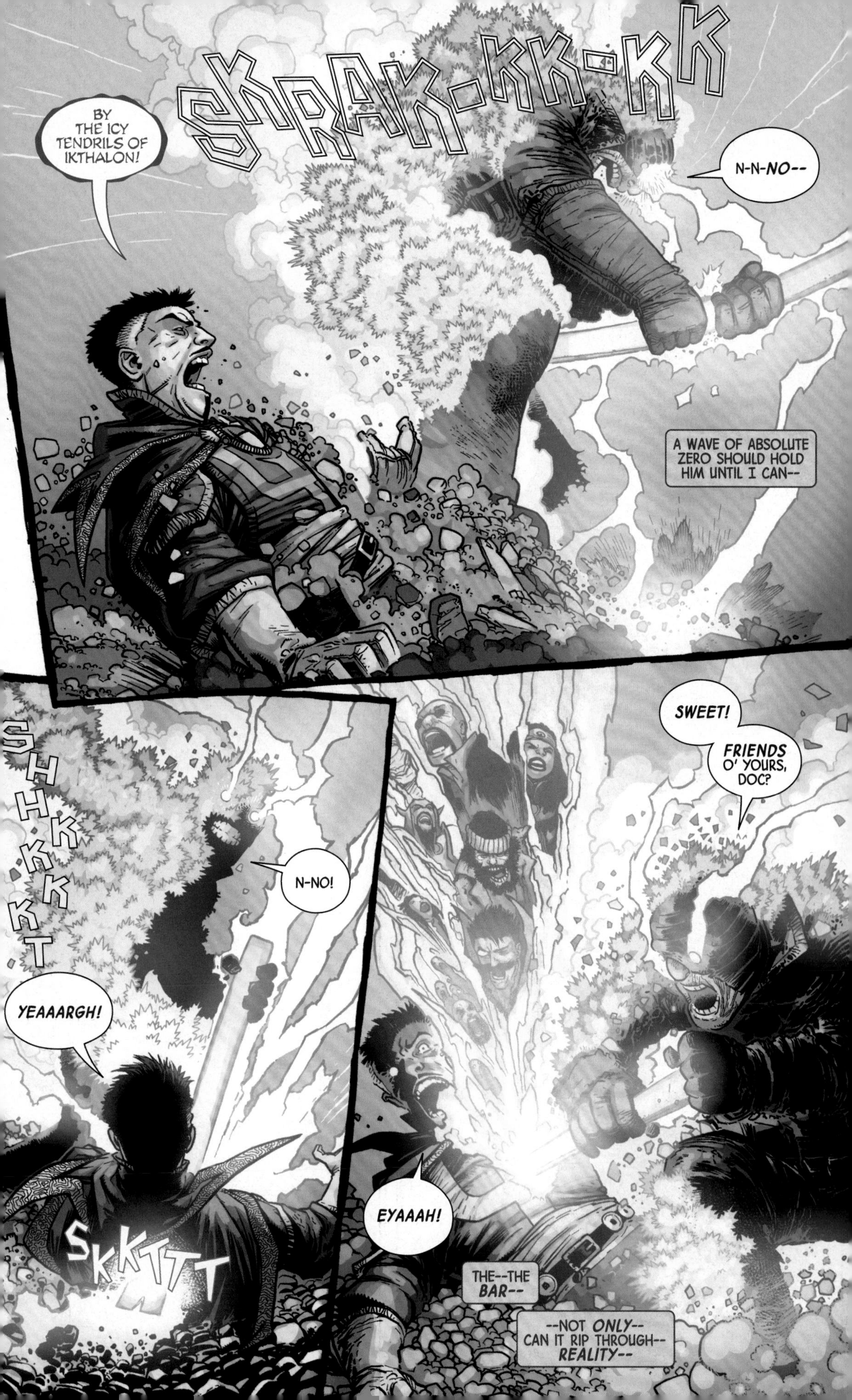

SHRAK-KK-KK
BY THE ICY TENDRILS OF IKTHALON!
N-N-NO--
A WAVE OF ABSOLUTE ZERO SHOULD HOLD HIM UNTIL I CAN--
SHHKKKKT
N-NO!
YEAAARGH!
SKKTTT
SWEET!
FRIENDS O' YOURS, DOC?
EYAAAH!
THE--THE BAR--
--NOT ONLY-- CAN IT RIP THROUGH-- REALITY--

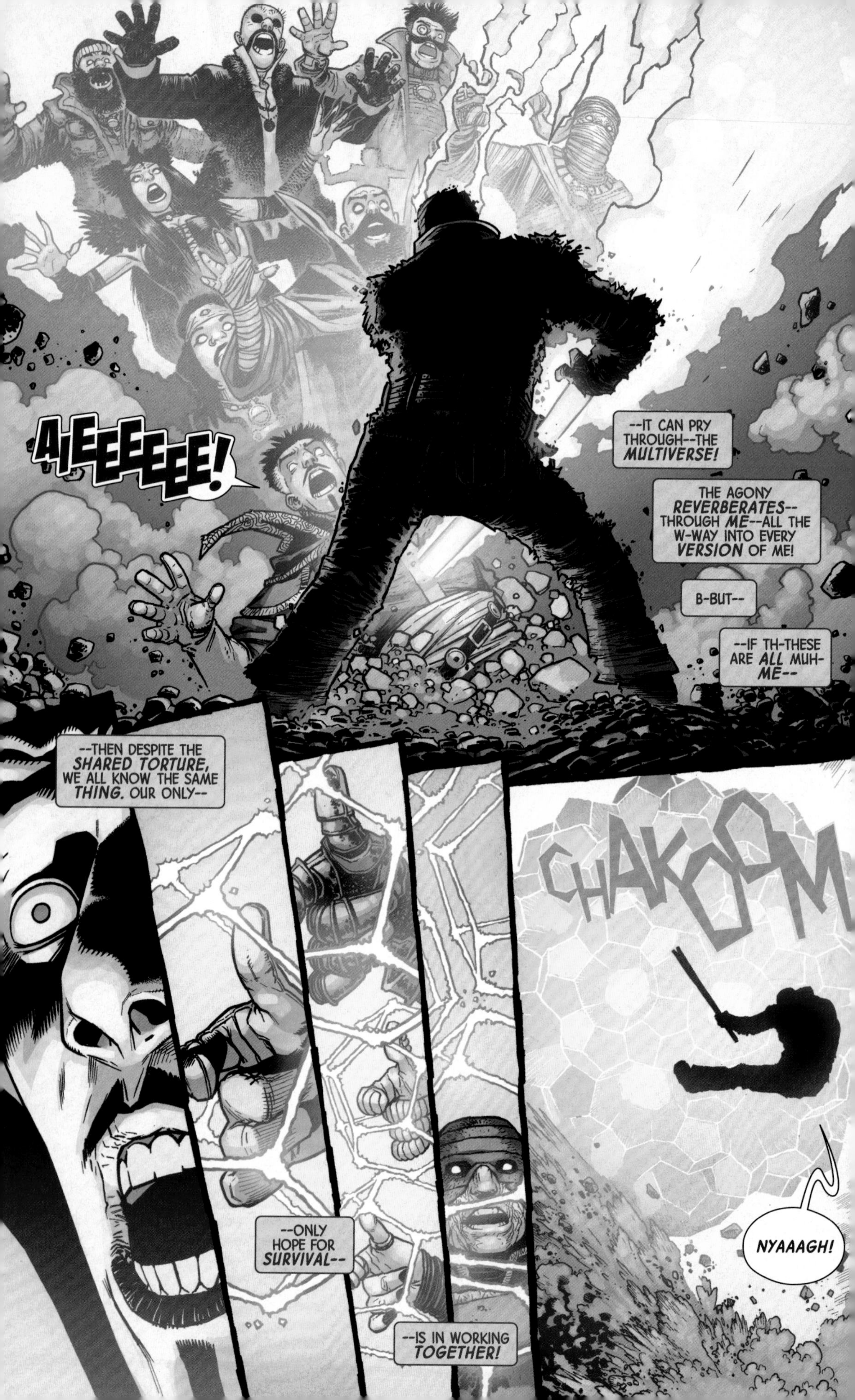
AIEEEEEEE!
--IT CAN PRY THROUGH--THE MULTIVERSE!
THE AGONY REVERBERATES--THROUGH ME--ALL THE W-WAY INTO EVERY VERSION OF ME!
B-BUT--
--IF TH-THESE ARE ALL MUH-ME--
--THEN DESPITE THE SHARED TORTURE, WE ALL KNOW THE SAME THING. OUR ONLY--
--ONLY HOPE FOR SURVIVAL--
--IS IN WORKING TOGETHER!
CHAKOOM
NYAAAGH!

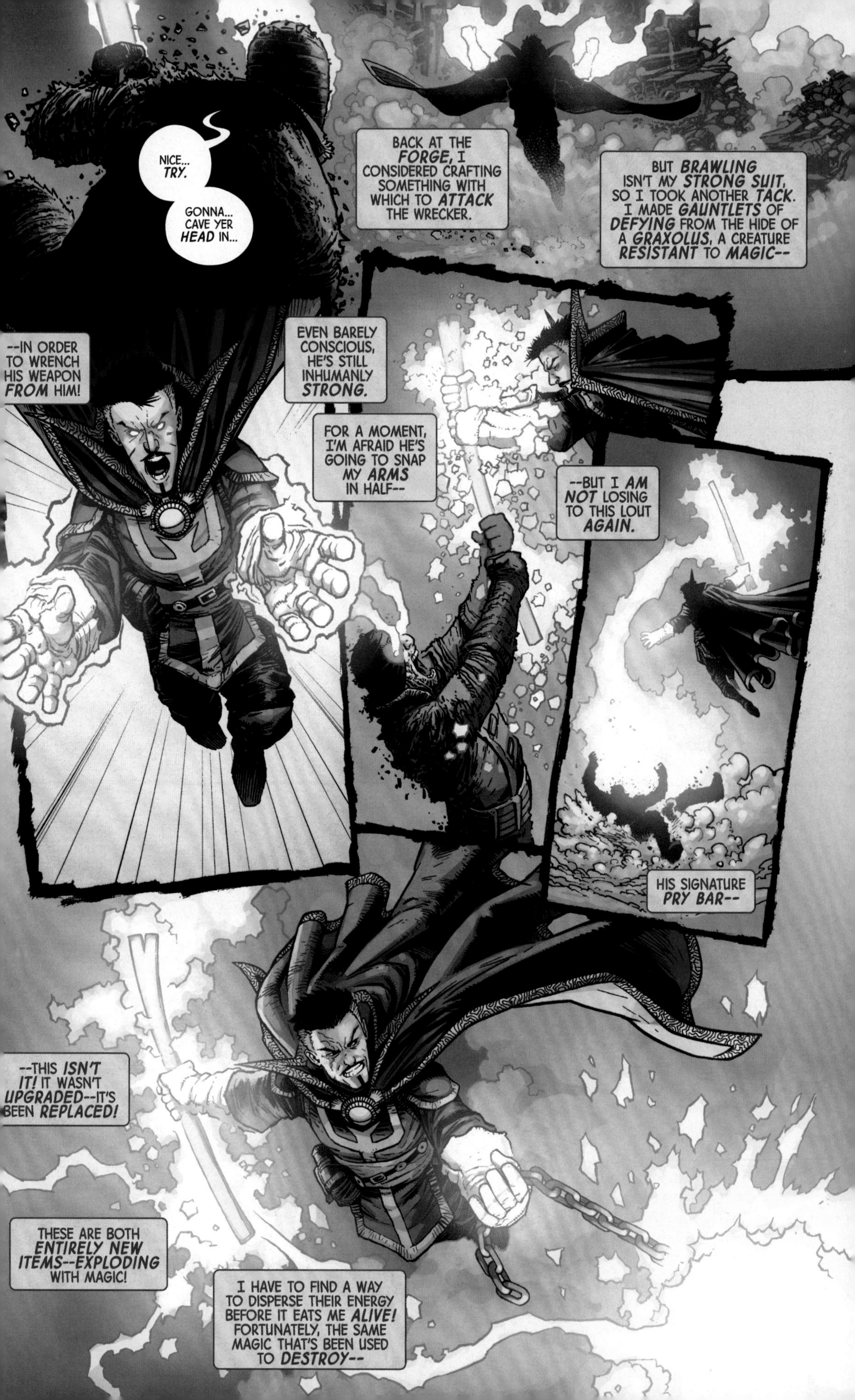
NICE... TRY.
GONNA... CAVE YER HEAD IN...
BACK AT THE FORGE, I CONSIDERED CRAFTING SOMETHING WITH WHICH TO ATTACK THE WRECKER.
BUT BRAWLING ISN'T MY STRONG SUIT, SO I TOOK ANOTHER TACK. I MADE GAUNTLETS OF DEFYING FROM THE HIDE OF A GRAXOLUS, A CREATURE RESISTANT TO MAGIC--
--IN ORDER TO WRENCH HIS WEAPON FROM HIM!
EVEN BARELY CONSCIOUS, HE'S STILL INHUMANLY STRONG.
FOR A MOMENT, I'M AFRAID HE'S GOING TO SNAP MY ARMS IN HALF--
--BUT I AM NOT LOSING TO THIS LOUT AGAIN.
HIS SIGNATURE PRY BAR--
--THIS ISN'T IT! IT WASN'T UPGRADED--IT'S BEEN REPLACED!
THESE ARE BOTH ENTIRELY NEW ITEMS--EXPLODING WITH MAGIC!
I HAVE TO FIND A WAY TO DISPERSE THEIR ENERGY BEFORE IT EATS ME ALIVE! FORTUNATELY, THE SAME MAGIC THAT'S BEEN USED TO DESTROY--

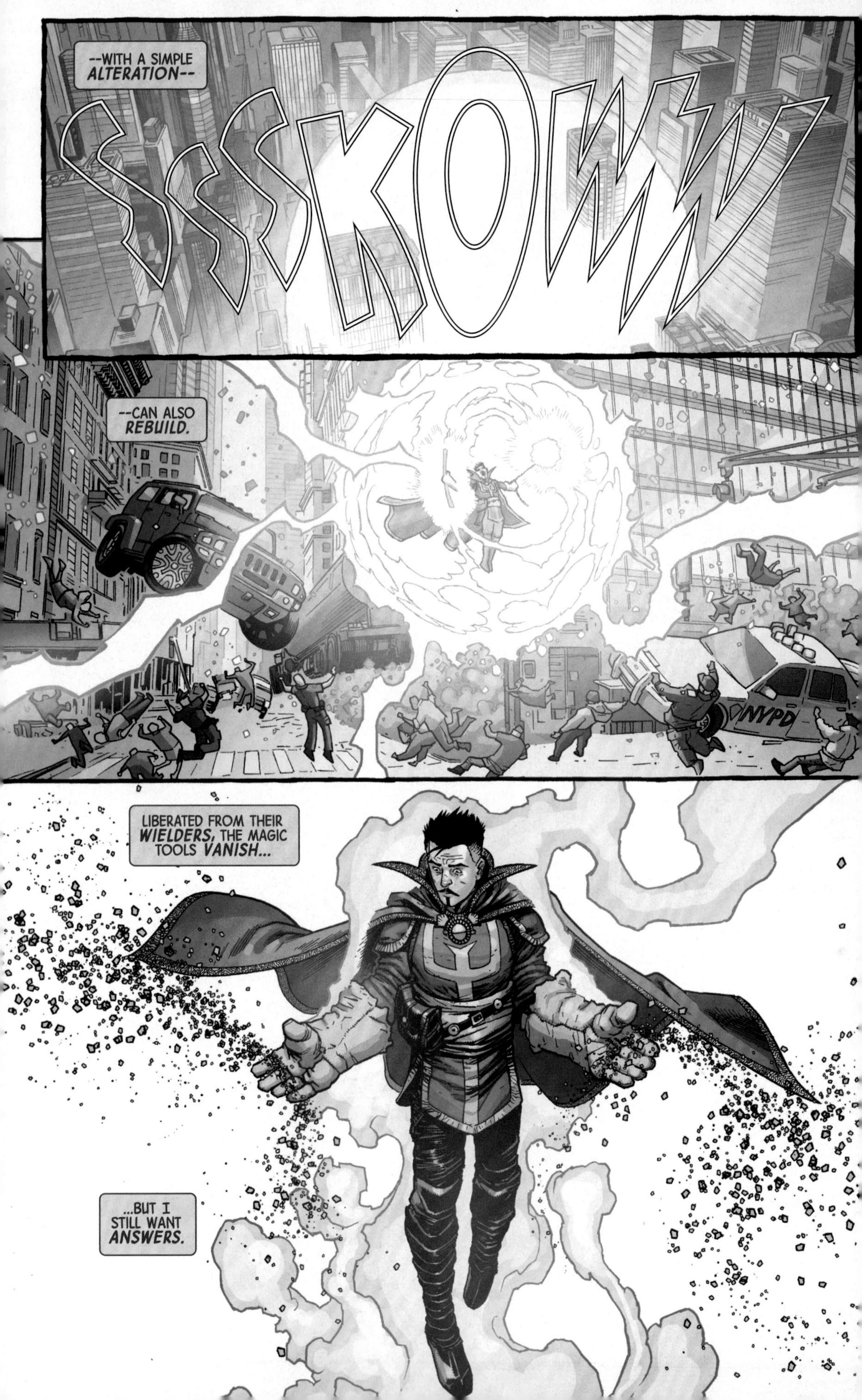
--WITH A SIMPLE ALTERATION--
SSSKOWW
--CAN ALSO REBUILD.
NYPD
LIBERATED FROM THEIR WIELDERS, THE MAGIC TOOLS VANISH...
...BUT I STILL WANT ANSWERS.

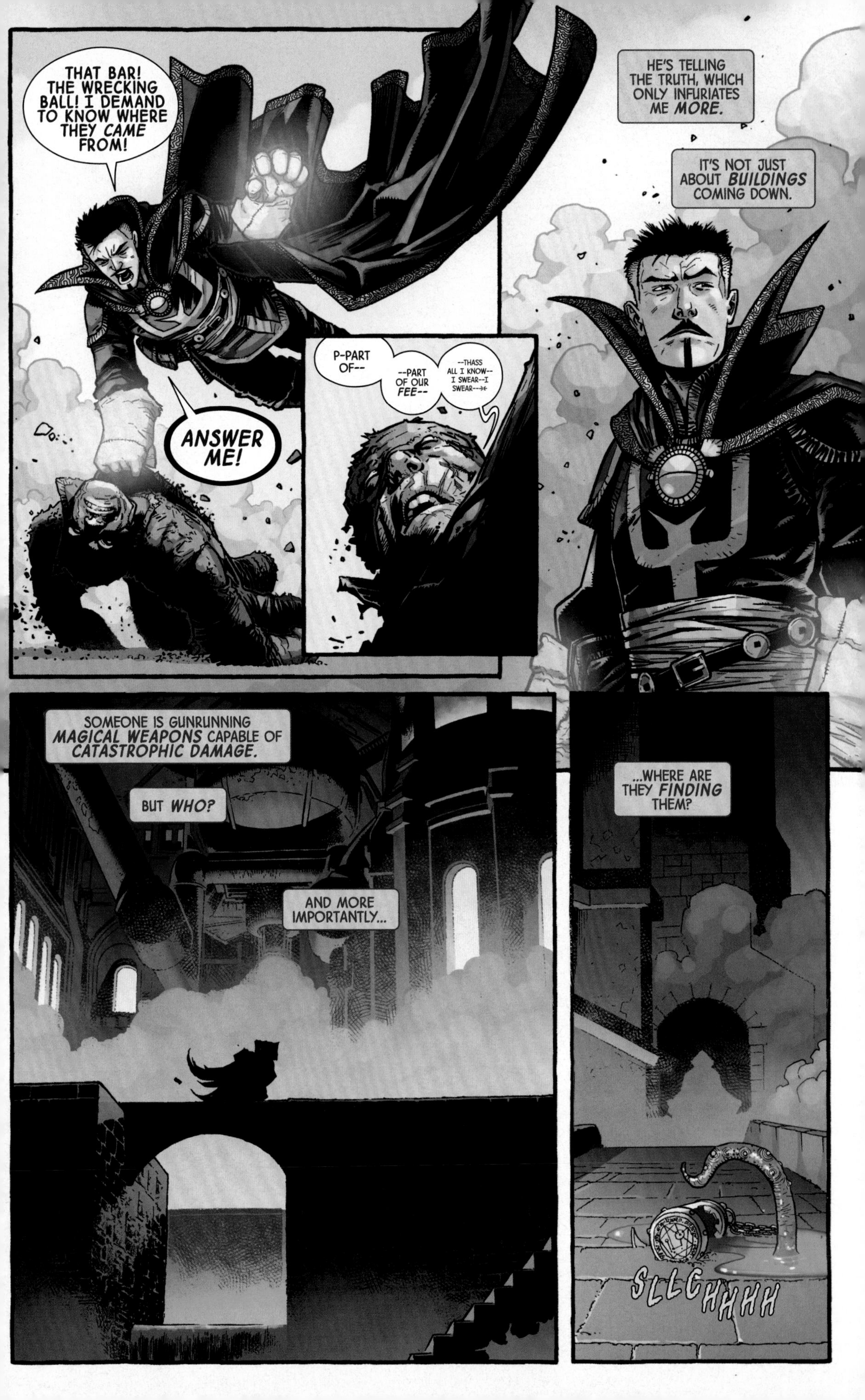
THAT BAR! THE WRECKING BALL! I DEMAND TO KNOW WHERE THEY CAME FROM!
ANSWER ME!
P-PART OF--
--PART OF OUR FEE--
--THASS ALL I KNOW-- I SWEAR--I SWEAR--
HE'S TELLING THE TRUTH, WHICH ONLY INFURIATES ME MORE.
IT'S NOT JUST ABOUT BUILDINGS COMING DOWN.
SOMEONE IS GUNRUNNING MAGICAL WEAPONS CAPABLE OF CATASTROPHIC DAMAGE.
BUT WHO?
AND MORE IMPORTANTLY...
...WHERE ARE THEY FINDING THEM?
SLLCHHHH

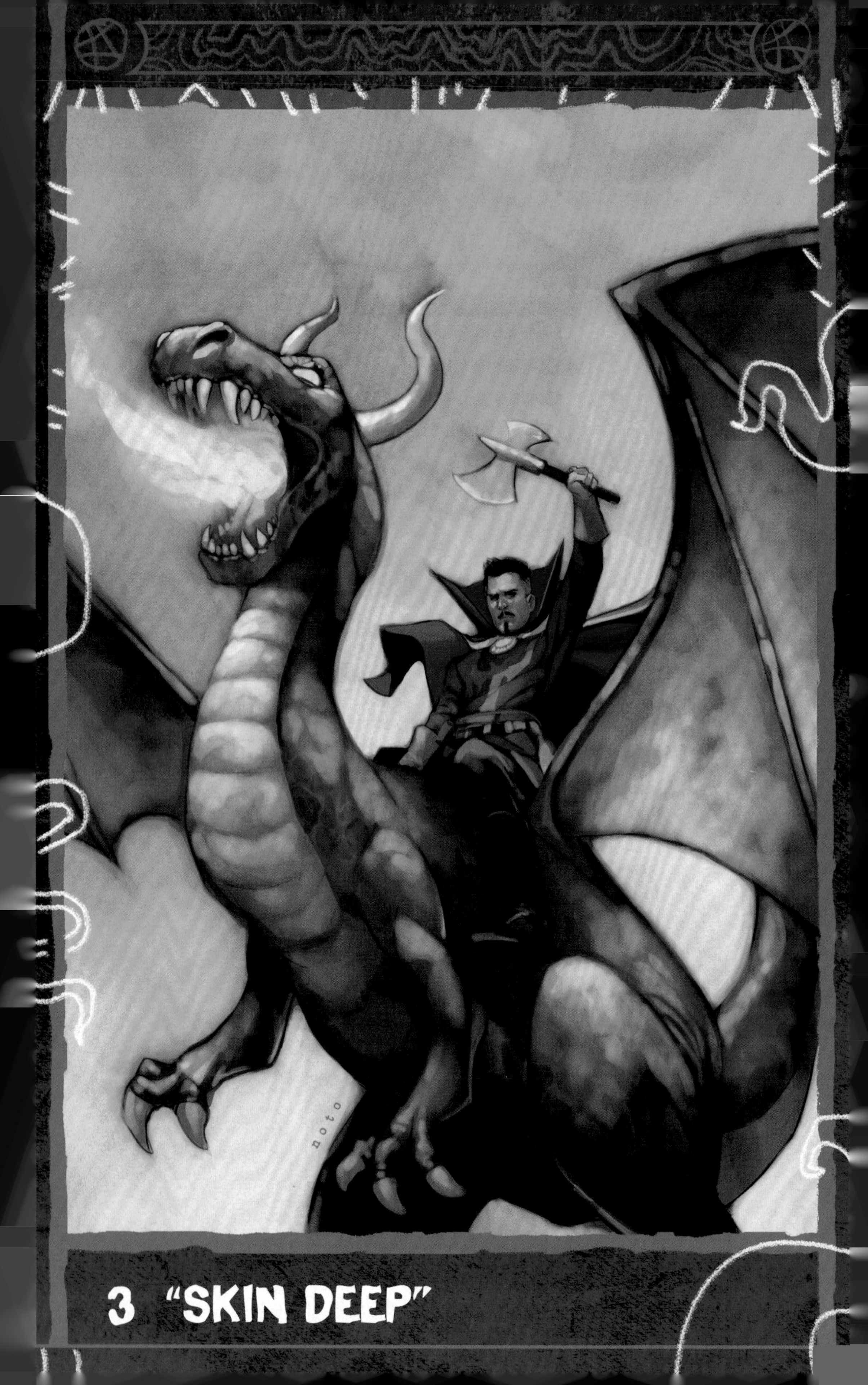
noto

3 "SKIN DEEP"

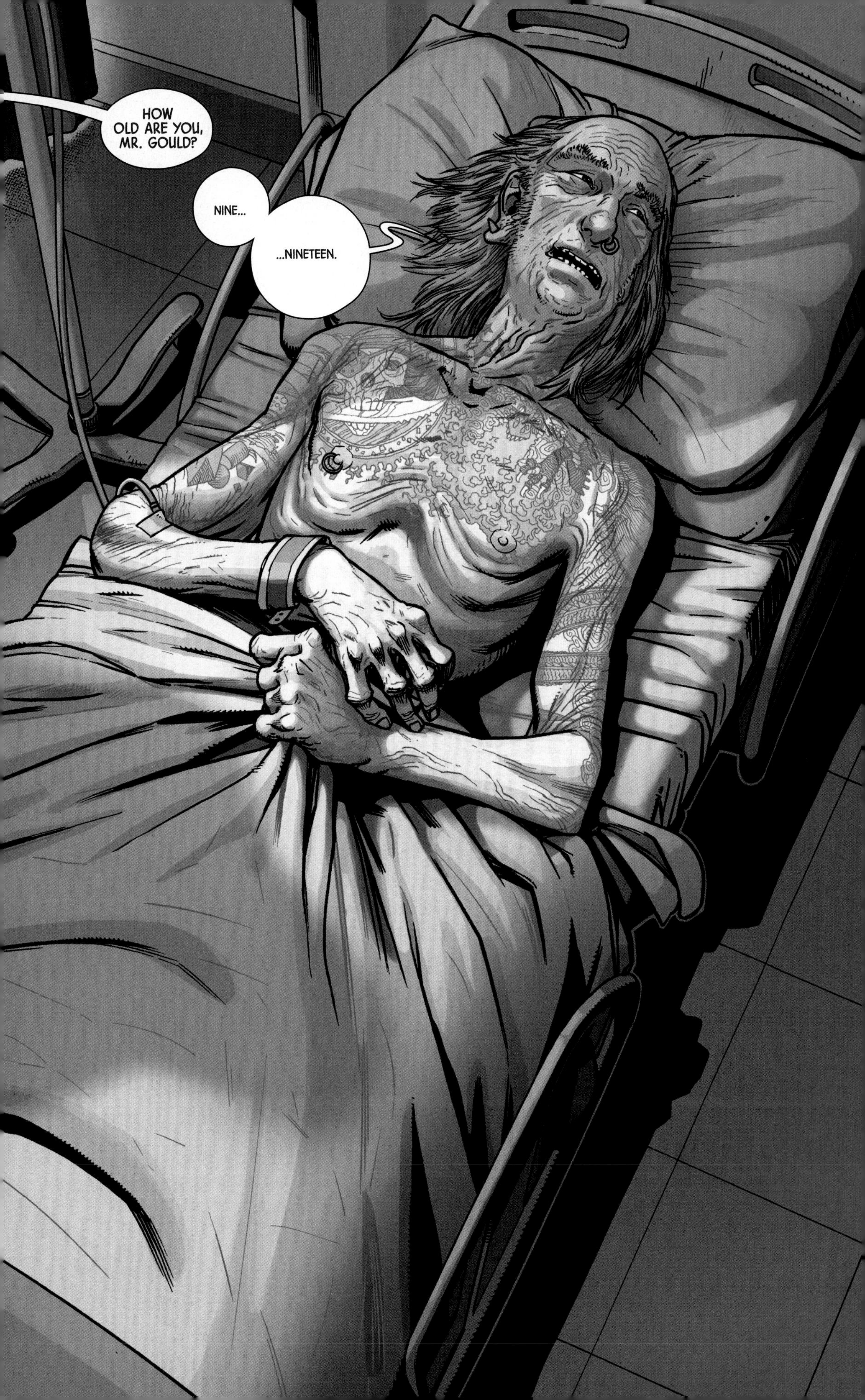
HOW OLD ARE YOU, MR. GOULD?
NINE...
...NINETEEN.

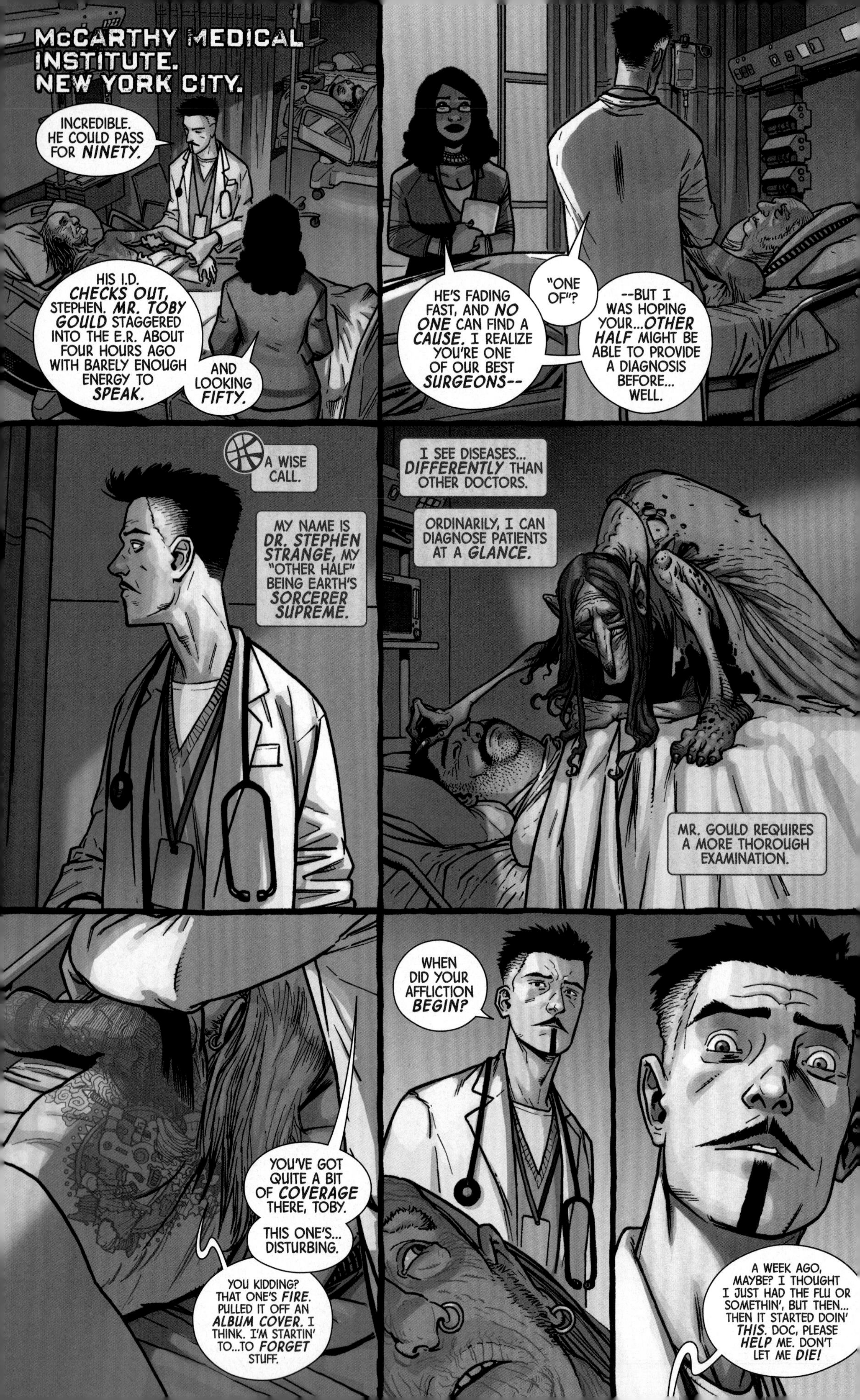
McCARTHY MEDICAL INSTITUTE. NEW YORK CITY.
INCREDIBLE. HE COULD PASS FOR NINETY.
HIS I.D. CHECKS OUT, STEPHEN. MR. TOBY GOULD STAGGERED INTO THE E.R. ABOUT FOUR HOURS AGO WITH BARELY ENOUGH ENERGY TO SPEAK.
AND LOOKING FIFTY.
HE'S FADING FAST, AND NO ONE CAN FIND A CAUSE. I REALIZE YOU'RE ONE OF OUR BEST SURGEONS--
"ONE OF"?
--BUT I WAS HOPING YOUR...OTHER HALF MIGHT BE ABLE TO PROVIDE A DIAGNOSIS BEFORE... WELL.
A WISE CALL.
MY NAME IS DR. STEPHEN STRANGE, MY "OTHER HALF" BEING EARTH'S SORCERER SUPREME.
I SEE DISEASES... DIFFERENTLY THAN OTHER DOCTORS.
ORDINARILY, I CAN DIAGNOSE PATIENTS AT A GLANCE.
MR. GOULD REQUIRES A MORE THOROUGH EXAMINATION.
YOU'VE GOT QUITE A BIT OF COVERAGE THERE, TOBY.
THIS ONE'S... DISTURBING.
YOU KIDDING? THAT ONE'S FIRE. PULLED IT OFF AN ALBUM COVER. I THINK. I'M STARTIN' TO...TO FORGET STUFF.
WHEN DID YOUR AFFLICTION BEGIN?
A WEEK AGO, MAYBE? I THOUGHT I JUST HAD THE FLU OR SOMETHIN', BUT THEN... THEN IT STARTED DOIN' THIS. DOC, PLEASE HELP ME. DON'T LET ME DIE!

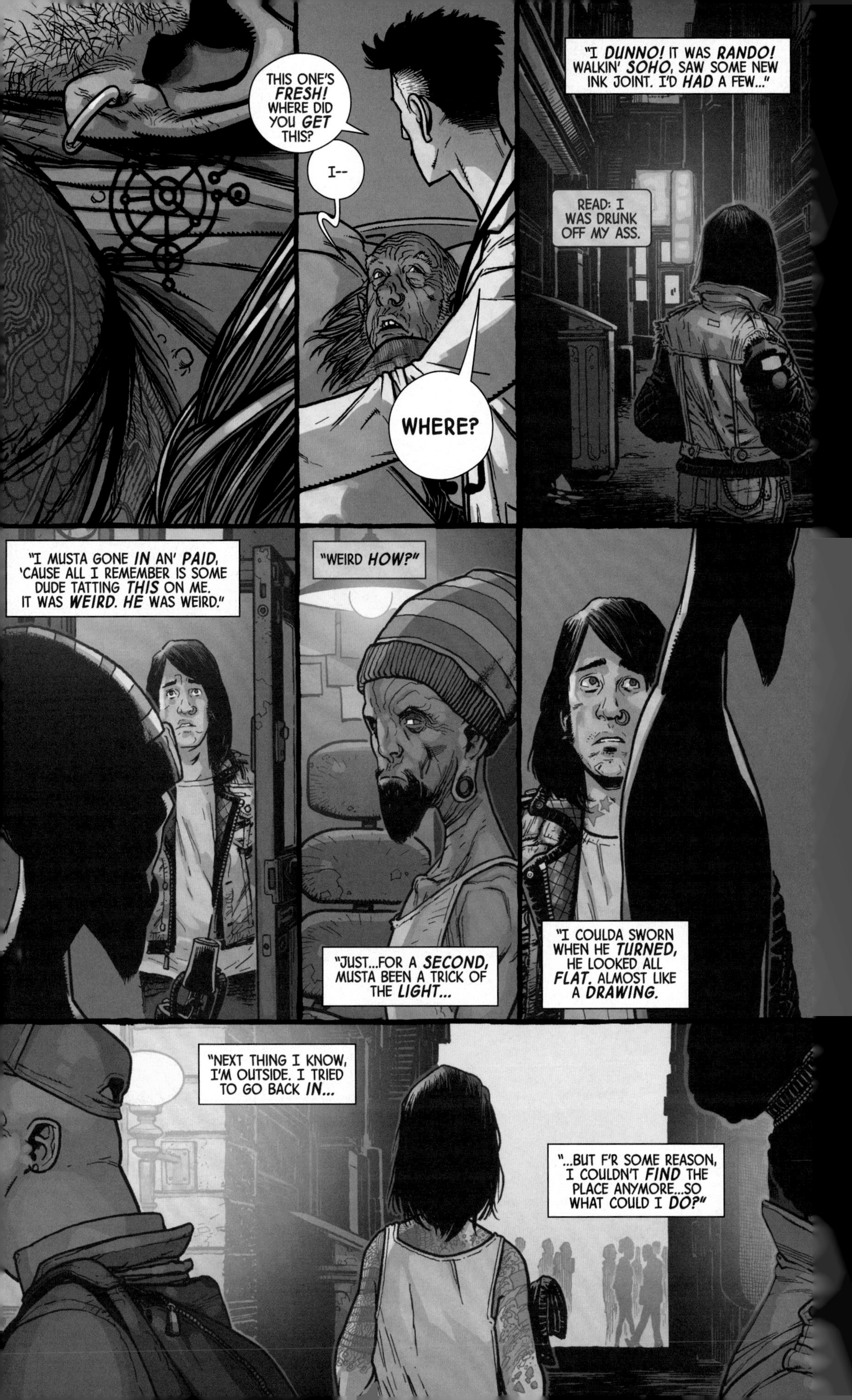

THIS ONE'S FRESH! WHERE DID YOU GET THIS?
I--
WHERE?
"I DUNNO! IT WAS RANDO! WALKIN' SOHO, SAW SOME NEW INK JOINT. I'D HAD A FEW..."
READ: I WAS DRUNK OFF MY ASS.
"I MUSTA GONE IN AN' PAID, 'CAUSE ALL I REMEMBER IS SOME DUDE TATTING THIS ON ME. IT WAS WEIRD. HE WAS WEIRD."
"WEIRD HOW?"
"JUST...FOR A SECOND, MUSTA BEEN A TRICK OF THE LIGHT...
"I COULDA SWORN WHEN HE TURNED, HE LOOKED ALL FLAT. ALMOST LIKE A DRAWING.
"NEXT THING I KNOW, I'M OUTSIDE. I TRIED TO GO BACK IN...
"...BUT F'R SOME REASON, I COULDN'T FIND THE PLACE ANYMORE...SO WHAT COULD I DO?"

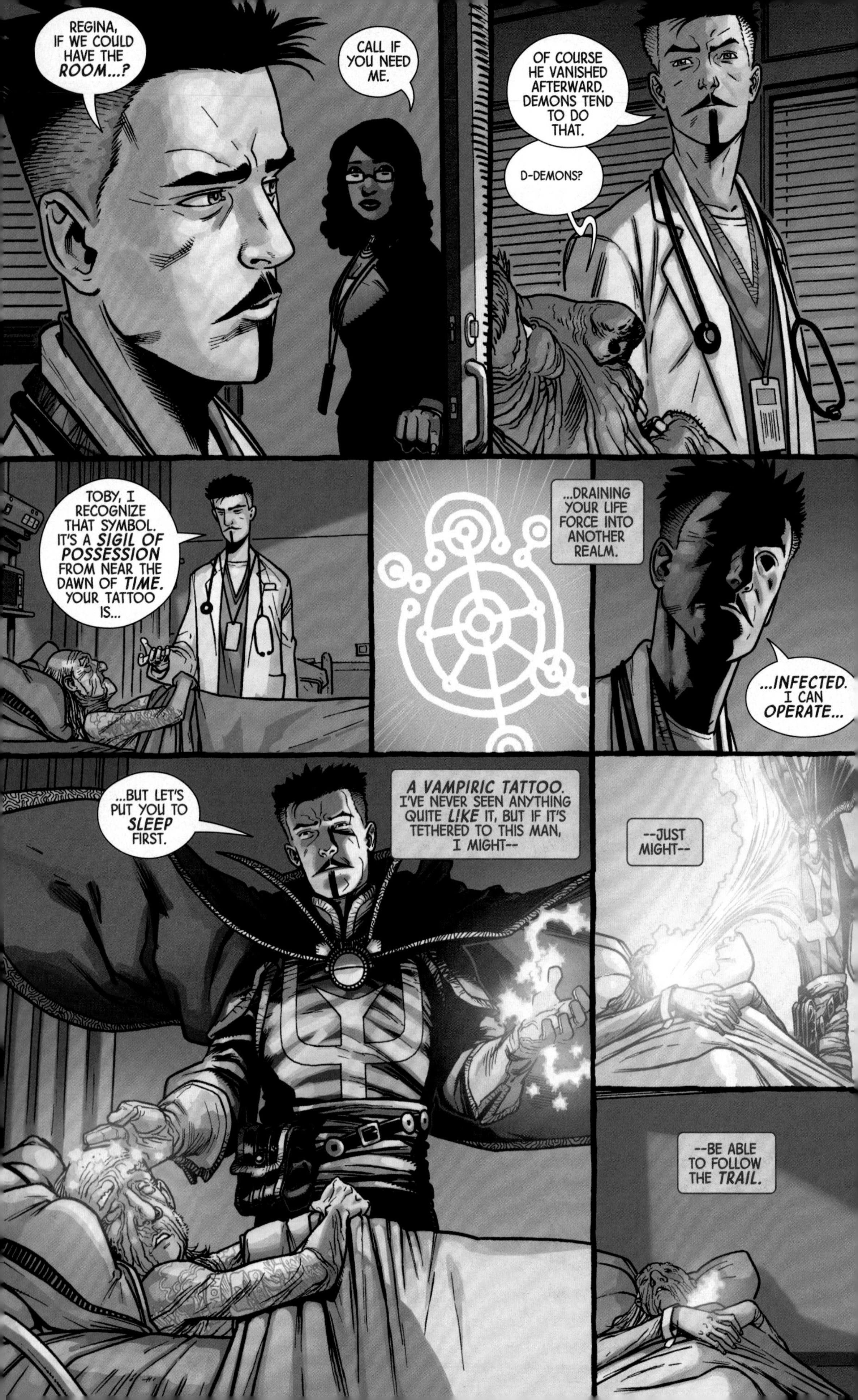
REGINA, IF WE COULD HAVE THE ROOM...?
CALL IF YOU NEED ME.
OF COURSE HE VANISHED AFTERWARD. DEMONS TEND TO DO THAT.
D-DEMONS?
TOBY, I RECOGNIZE THAT SYMBOL. IT'S A SIGIL OF POSSESSION FROM NEAR THE DAWN OF TIME. YOUR TATTOO IS...
...DRAINING YOUR LIFE FORCE INTO ANOTHER REALM.
...INFECTED. I CAN OPERATE...
...BUT LET'S PUT YOU TO SLEEP FIRST.
A VAMPIRIC TATTOO. I'VE NEVER SEEN ANYTHING QUITE LIKE IT, BUT IF IT'S TETHERED TO THIS MAN, I MIGHT--
--JUST MIGHT--
--BE ABLE TO FOLLOW THE TRAIL.

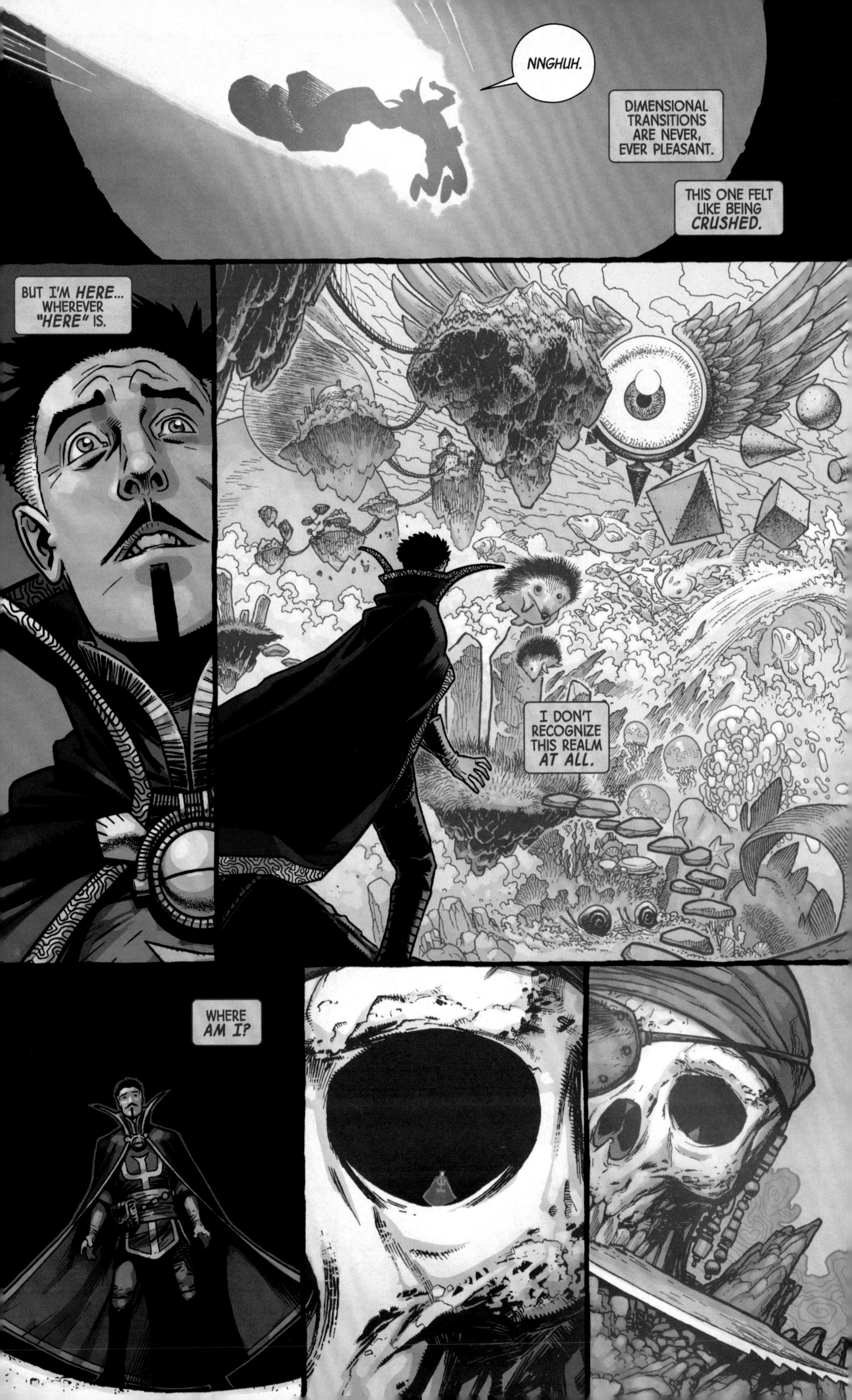
NNGHUH.
DIMENSIONAL TRANSITIONS ARE NEVER, EVER PLEASANT.
THIS ONE FELT LIKE BEING CRUSHED.
BUT I'M HERE... WHEREVER "HERE" IS.
I DON'T RECOGNIZE THIS REALM AT ALL.
WHERE AM I?

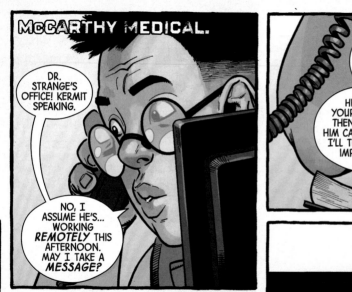

McCARTHY MEDICAL.

DR. STRANGE'S OFFICE! KERMIT SPEAKING.

NO, I ASSUME HE'S... WORKING *REMOTELY* THIS AFTERNOON. MAY I TAKE A *MESSAGE*?

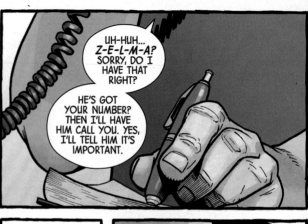

UH-HUH... Z-E-L-M-A? SORRY, DO I HAVE THAT RIGHT?

HE'S GOT YOUR NUMBER? THEN I'LL HAVE HIM CALL YOU. YES, I'LL TELL HIM IT'S IMPORTANT.

STOP *INTERRUPTING*, PEOPLE. I'M ON A *MISSION.*

DOC'S COUNTING ON ME TO FIGURE OUT WHO MIGHT HAVE HIRED THE *WRECKER* TO DO HIS DIRTY WORK.*

*LAST ISSUE. --DS

!

WHAT THE *HELL...?*

SSSKKK

?

ADNIERAUOTNE
PETSREGNADKO
OLCEHTHCTAWI
COLCEHTKCOLC
HTKCOLCEHTK

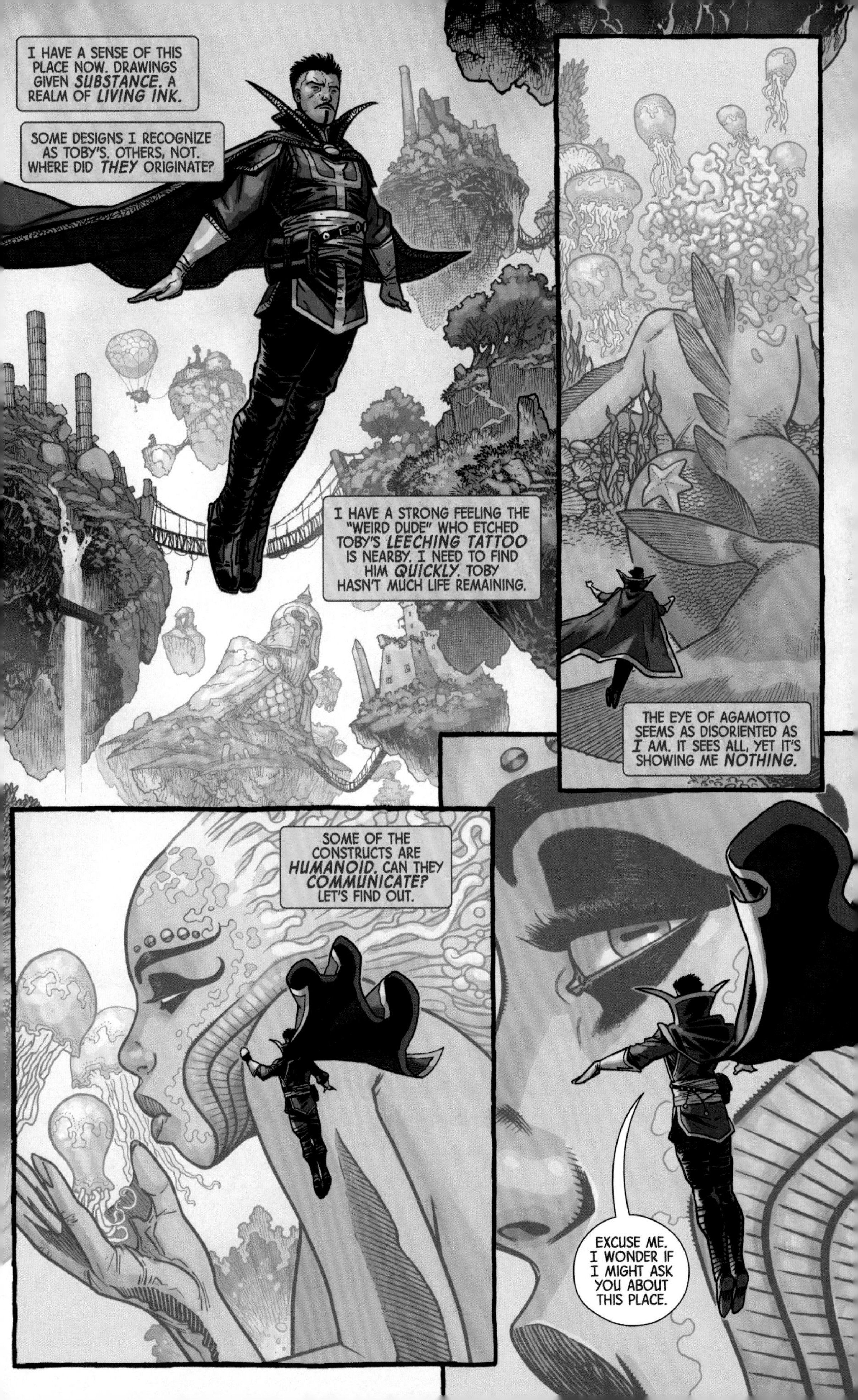
I HAVE A SENSE OF THIS PLACE NOW. DRAWINGS GIVEN SUBSTANCE. A REALM OF LIVING INK.
SOME DESIGNS I RECOGNIZE AS TOBY'S. OTHERS, NOT. WHERE DID THEY ORIGINATE?
I HAVE A STRONG FEELING THE "WEIRD DUDE" WHO ETCHED TOBY'S LEECHING TATTOO IS NEARBY. I NEED TO FIND HIM QUICKLY. TOBY HASN'T MUCH LIFE REMAINING.
THE EYE OF AGAMOTTO SEEMS AS DISORIENTED AS I AM. IT SEES ALL, YET IT'S SHOWING ME NOTHING.
SOME OF THE CONSTRUCTS ARE HUMANOID. CAN THEY COMMUNICATE? LET'S FIND OUT.
EXCUSE ME. I WONDER IF I MIGHT ASK YOU ABOUT THIS PLACE.

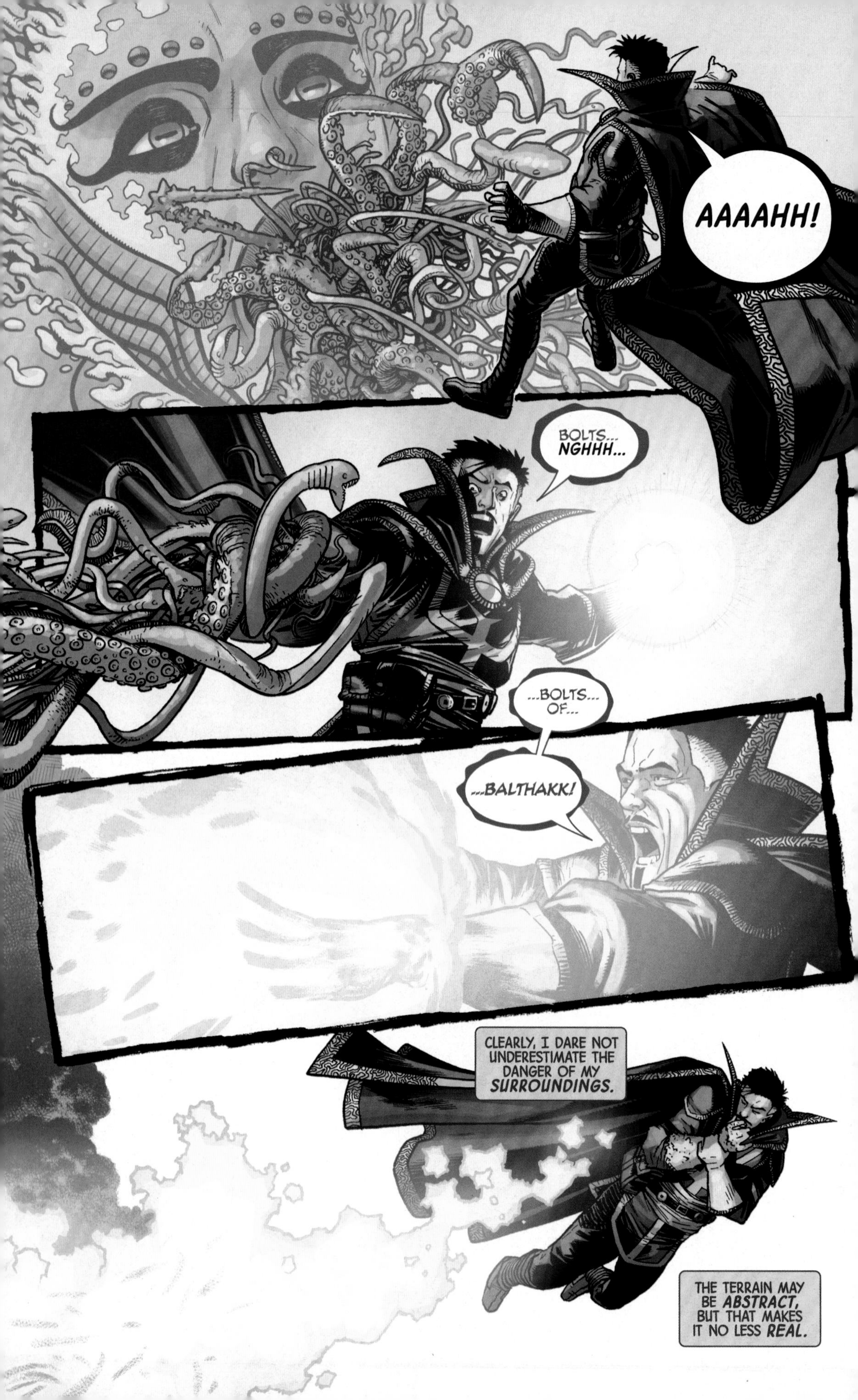
AAAAHH!
BOLTS... NGHHH...
...BOLTS... OF...
...BALTHAKK!
CLEARLY, I DARE NOT UNDERESTIMATE THE DANGER OF MY SURROUNDINGS.
THE TERRAIN MAY BE ABSTRACT, BUT THAT MAKES IT NO LESS REAL.

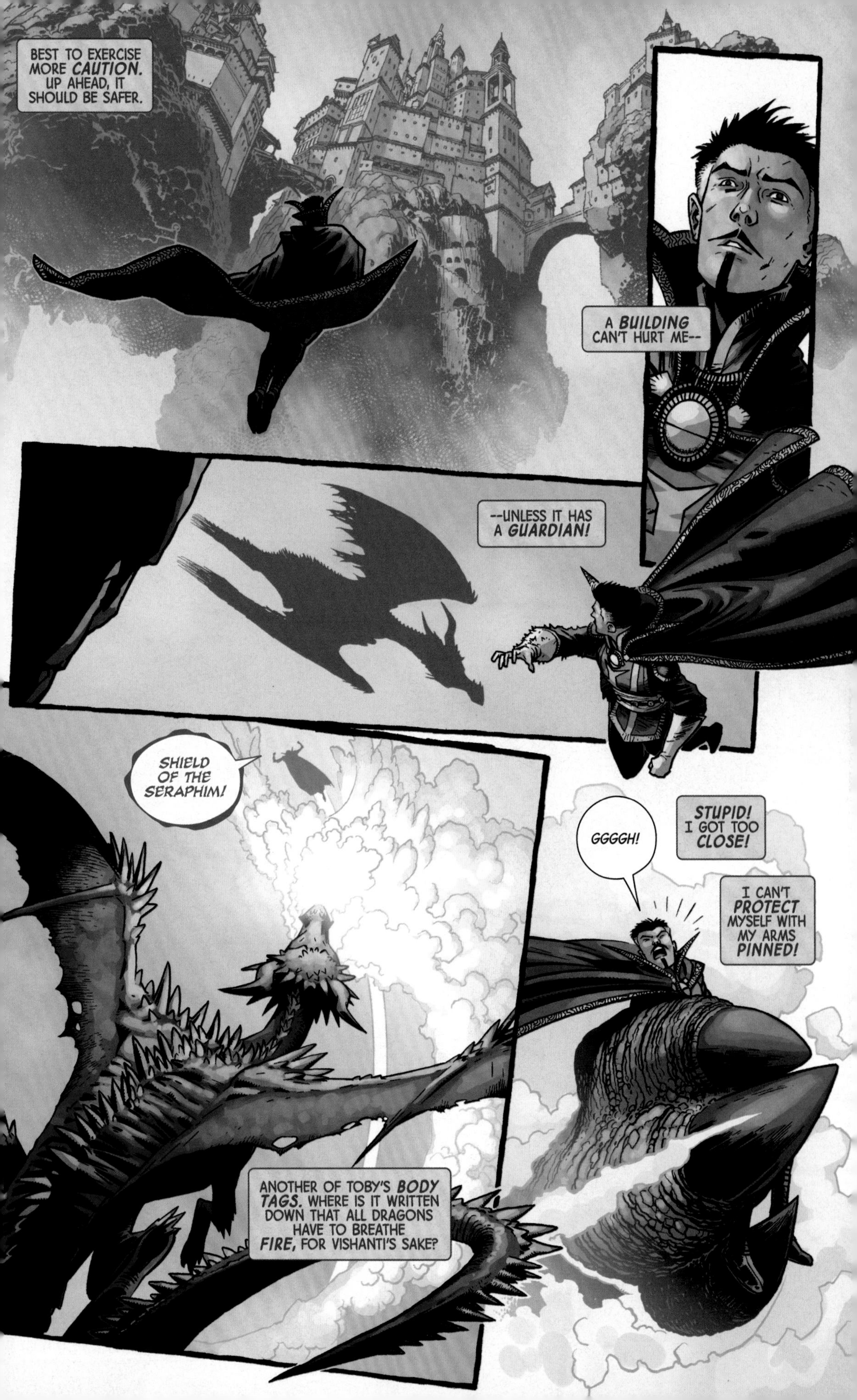
BEST TO EXERCISE MORE CAUTION. UP AHEAD, IT SHOULD BE SAFER.
A BUILDING CAN'T HURT ME--
--UNLESS IT HAS A GUARDIAN!
SHIELD OF THE SERAPHIM!
GGGGH!
STUPID! I GOT TOO CLOSE!
I CAN'T PROTECT MYSELF WITH MY ARMS PINNED!
ANOTHER OF TOBY'S BODY TAGS. WHERE IS IT WRITTEN DOWN THAT ALL DRAGONS HAVE TO BREATHE FIRE, FOR VISHANTI'S SAKE?

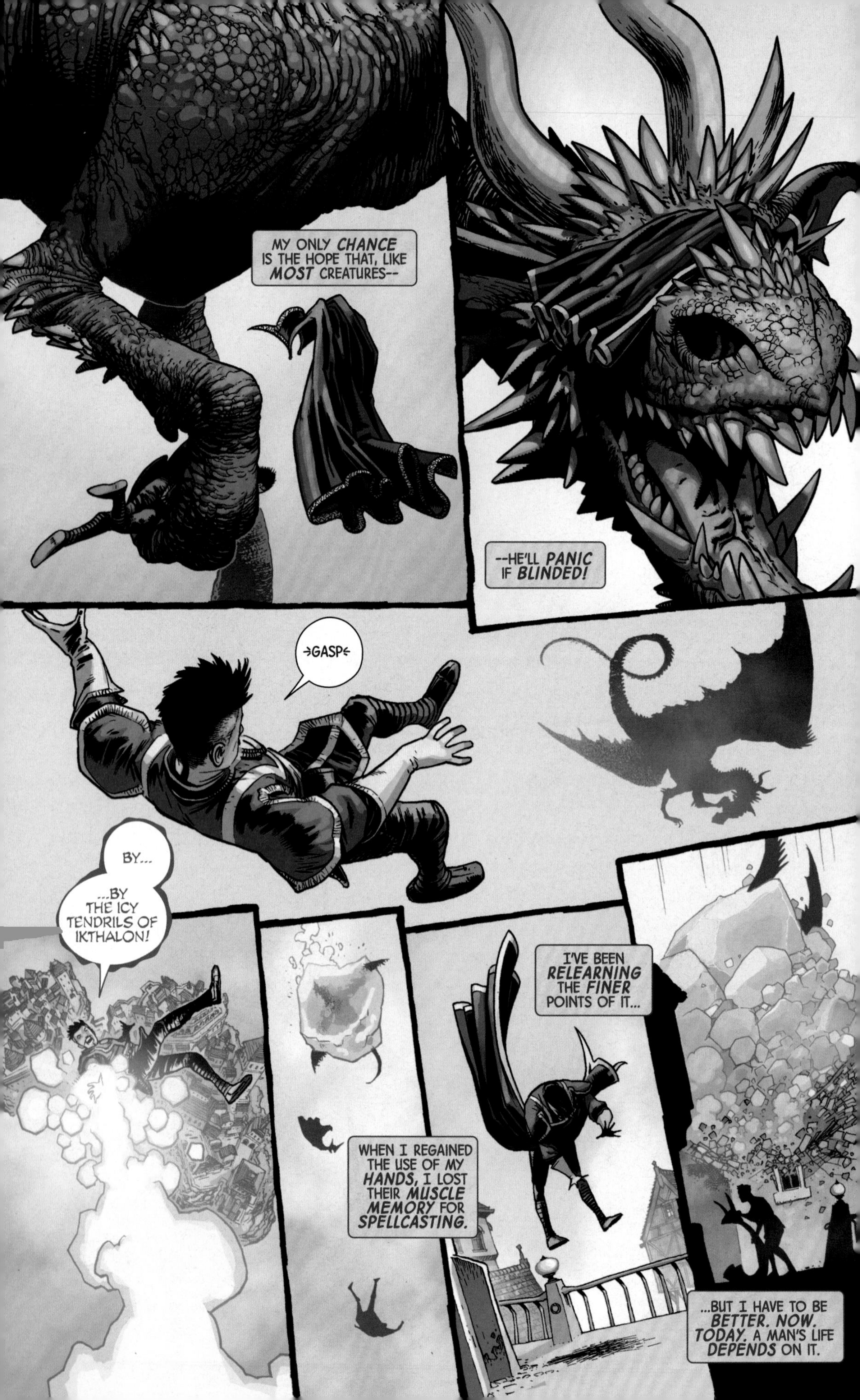
MY ONLY CHANCE IS THE HOPE THAT, LIKE MOST CREATURES--
--HE'LL PANIC IF BLINDED!
GASP
BY...
...BY THE ICY TENDRILS OF IKTHALON!
WHEN I REGAINED THE USE OF MY HANDS, I LOST THEIR MUSCLE MEMORY FOR SPELLCASTING.
I'VE BEEN RELEARNING THE FINER POINTS OF IT...
...BUT I HAVE TO BE BETTER. NOW. TODAY. A MAN'S LIFE DEPENDS ON IT.

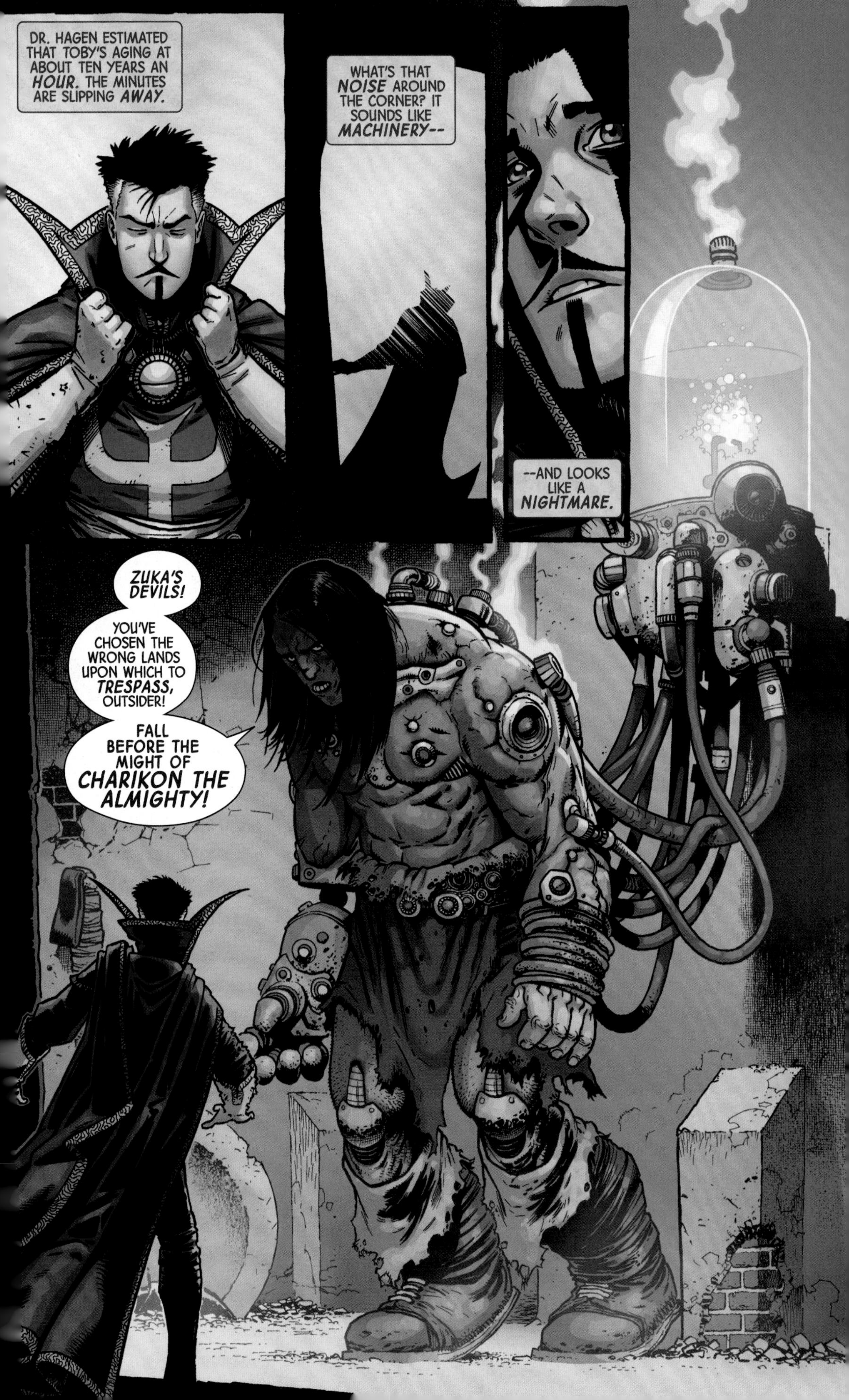
DR. HAGEN ESTIMATED THAT TOBY'S AGING AT ABOUT TEN YEARS AN HOUR. THE MINUTES ARE SLIPPING AWAY.
WHAT'S THAT NOISE AROUND THE CORNER? IT SOUNDS LIKE MACHINERY--
--AND LOOKS LIKE A NIGHTMARE.
ZUKA'S DEVILS!
YOU'VE CHOSEN THE WRONG LANDS UPON WHICH TO TRESPASS, OUTSIDER!
FALL BEFORE THE MIGHT OF CHARIKON THE ALMIGHTY!

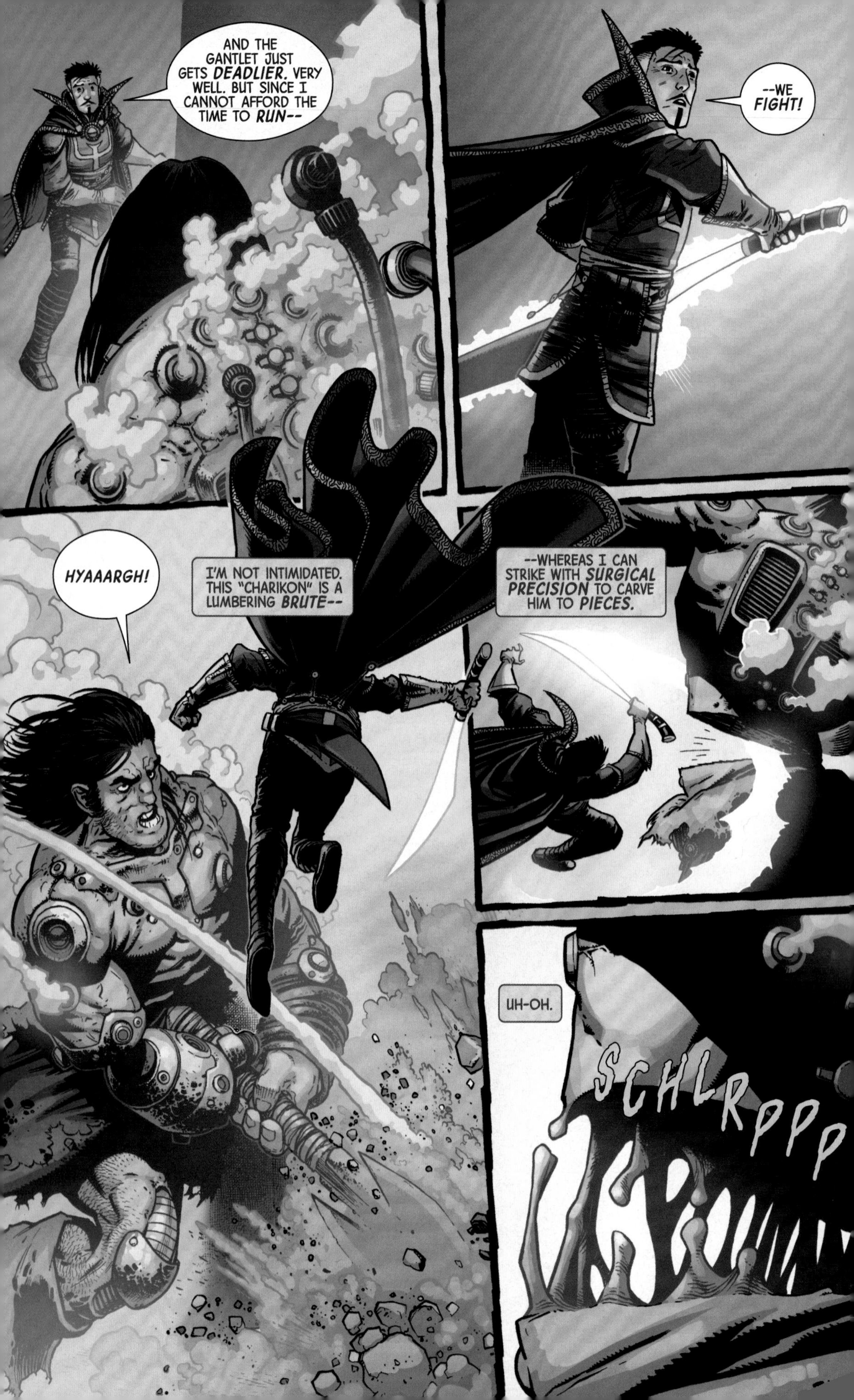
AND THE GANTLET JUST GETS DEADLIER. VERY WELL. BUT SINCE I CANNOT AFFORD THE TIME TO RUN--
--WE FIGHT!
HYAAARGH!
I'M NOT INTIMIDATED. THIS "CHARIKON" IS A LUMBERING BRUTE--
--WHEREAS I CAN STRIKE WITH SURGICAL PRECISION TO CARVE HIM TO PIECES.
UH-OH.
SCHLRPPPP

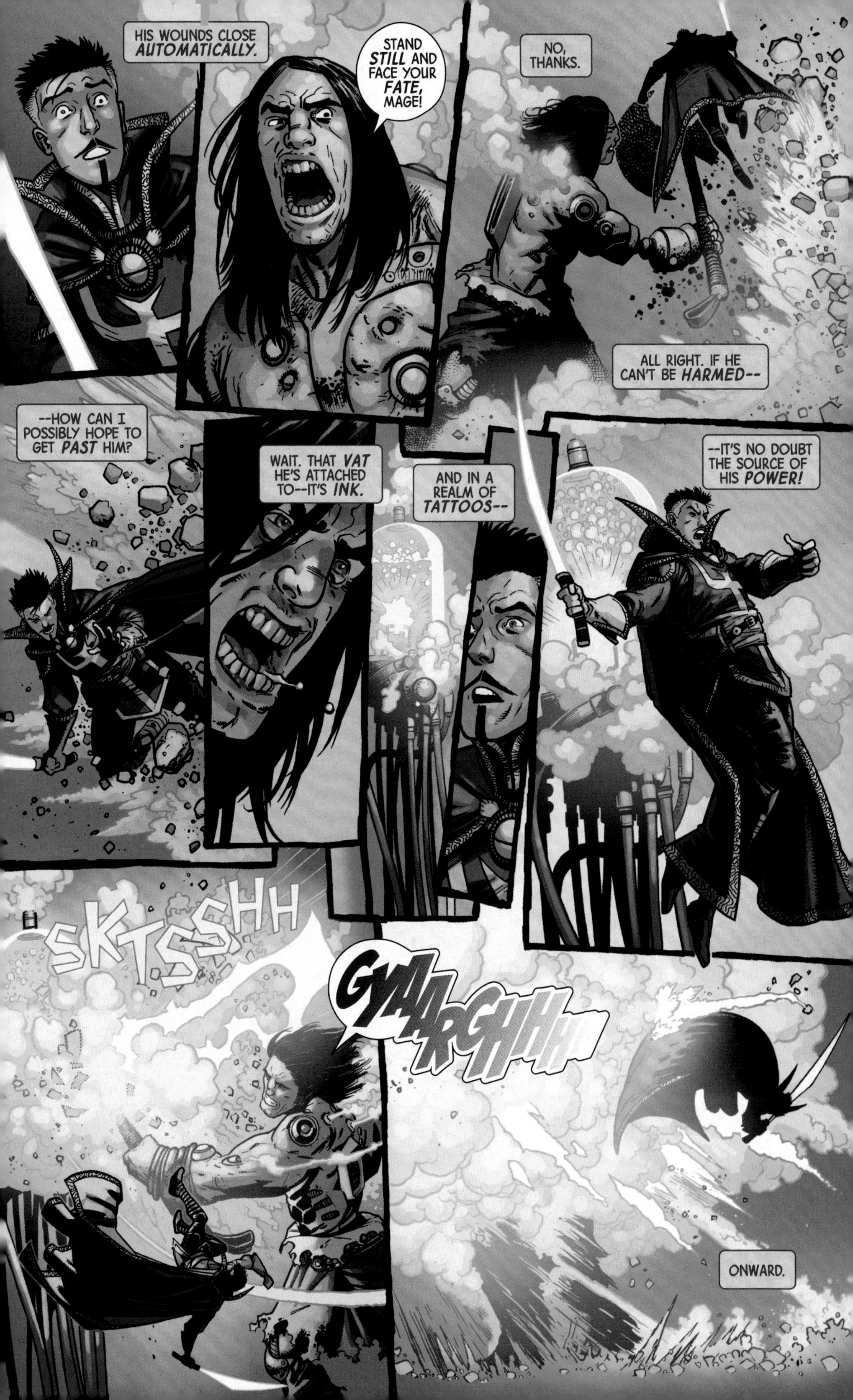
HIS WOUNDS CLOSE *AUTOMATICALLY.*
STAND *STILL* AND FACE YOUR *FATE,* MAGE!
NO, THANKS.
ALL RIGHT. IF HE CAN'T BE *HARMED--*
--HOW CAN I POSSIBLY HOPE TO GET *PAST* HIM?
WAIT. THAT *VAT* HE'S ATTACHED TO--IT'S *INK.*
AND IN A REALM OF *TATTOOS--*
--IT'S NO DOUBT THE SOURCE OF HIS *POWER!*
SKTSSHH
GYAARGHHHH
ONWARD.

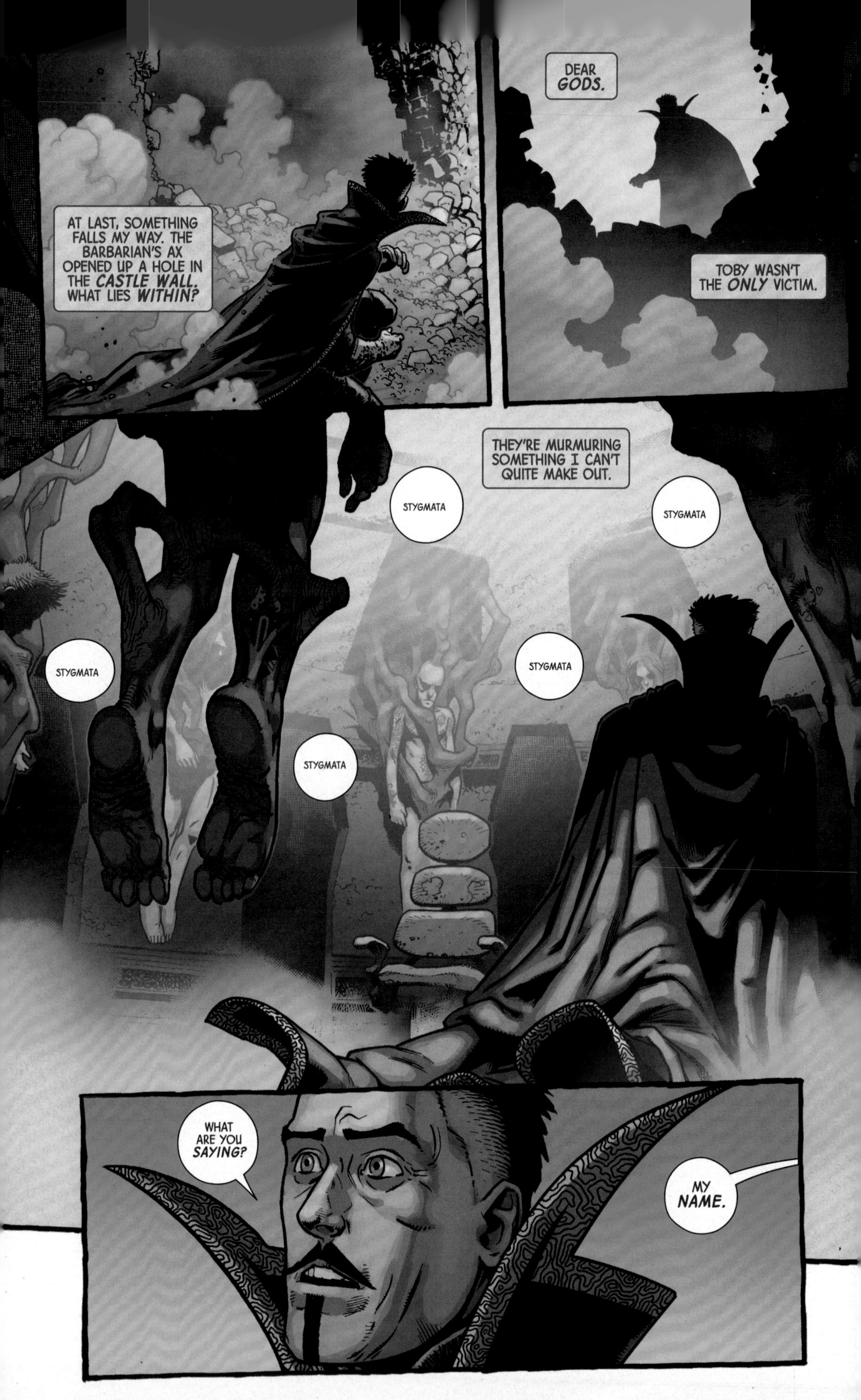
AT LAST, SOMETHING FALLS MY WAY. THE BARBARIAN'S AX OPENED UP A HOLE IN THE CASTLE WALL. WHAT LIES WITHIN?
DEAR GODS.
TOBY WASN'T THE ONLY VICTIM.
THEY'RE MURMURING SOMETHING I CAN'T QUITE MAKE OUT.
STYGMATA
STYGMATA
STYGMATA
STYGMATA
STYGMATA
WHAT ARE YOU SAYING?
MY NAME.

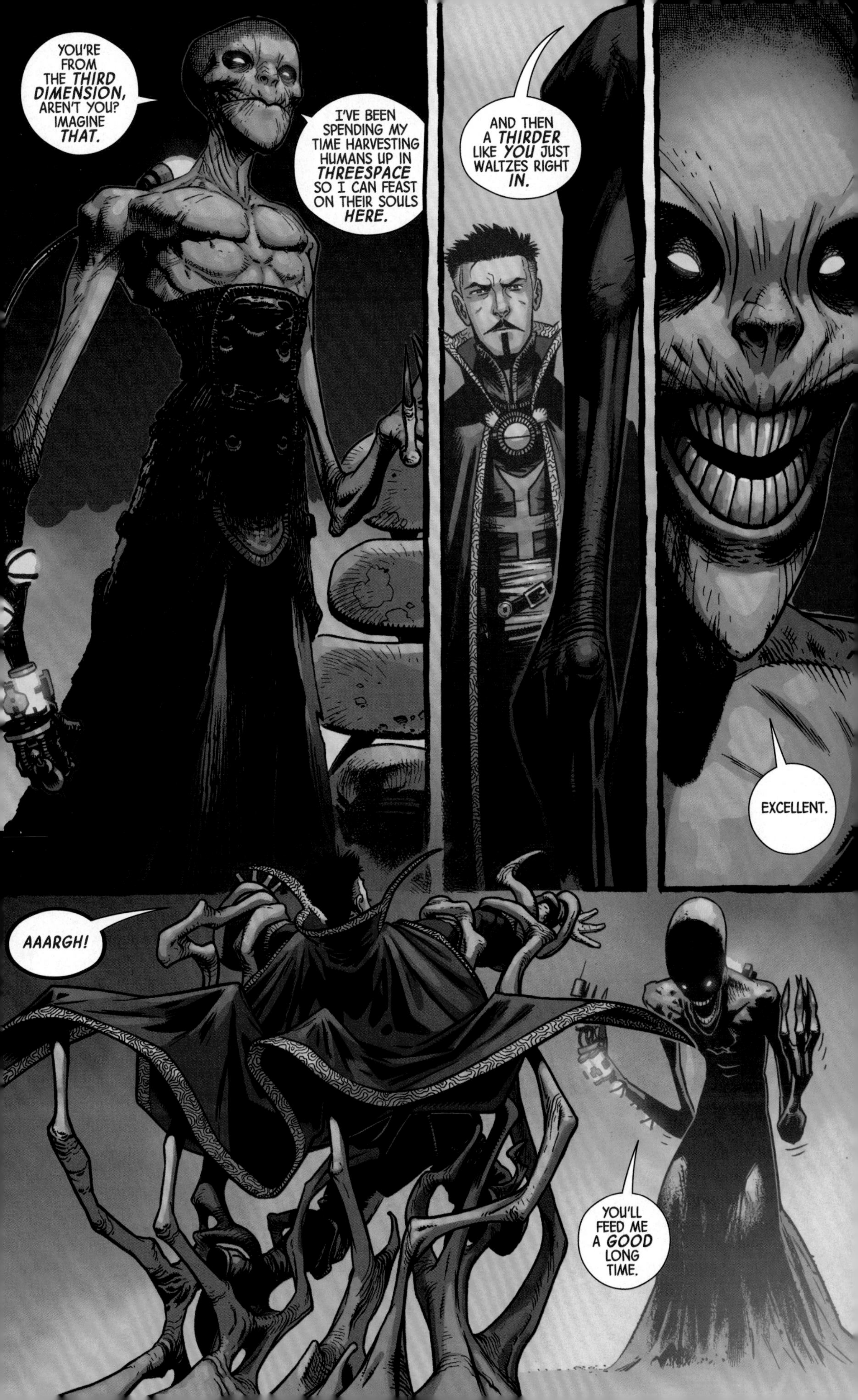
YOU'RE FROM THE THIRD DIMENSION, AREN'T YOU? IMAGINE THAT.
I'VE BEEN SPENDING MY TIME HARVESTING HUMANS UP IN THREESPACE SO I CAN FEAST ON THEIR SOULS HERE.
AND THEN A THIRDER LIKE YOU JUST WALTZES RIGHT IN.
EXCELLENT.
AAARGH!
YOU'LL FEED ME A GOOD LONG TIME.

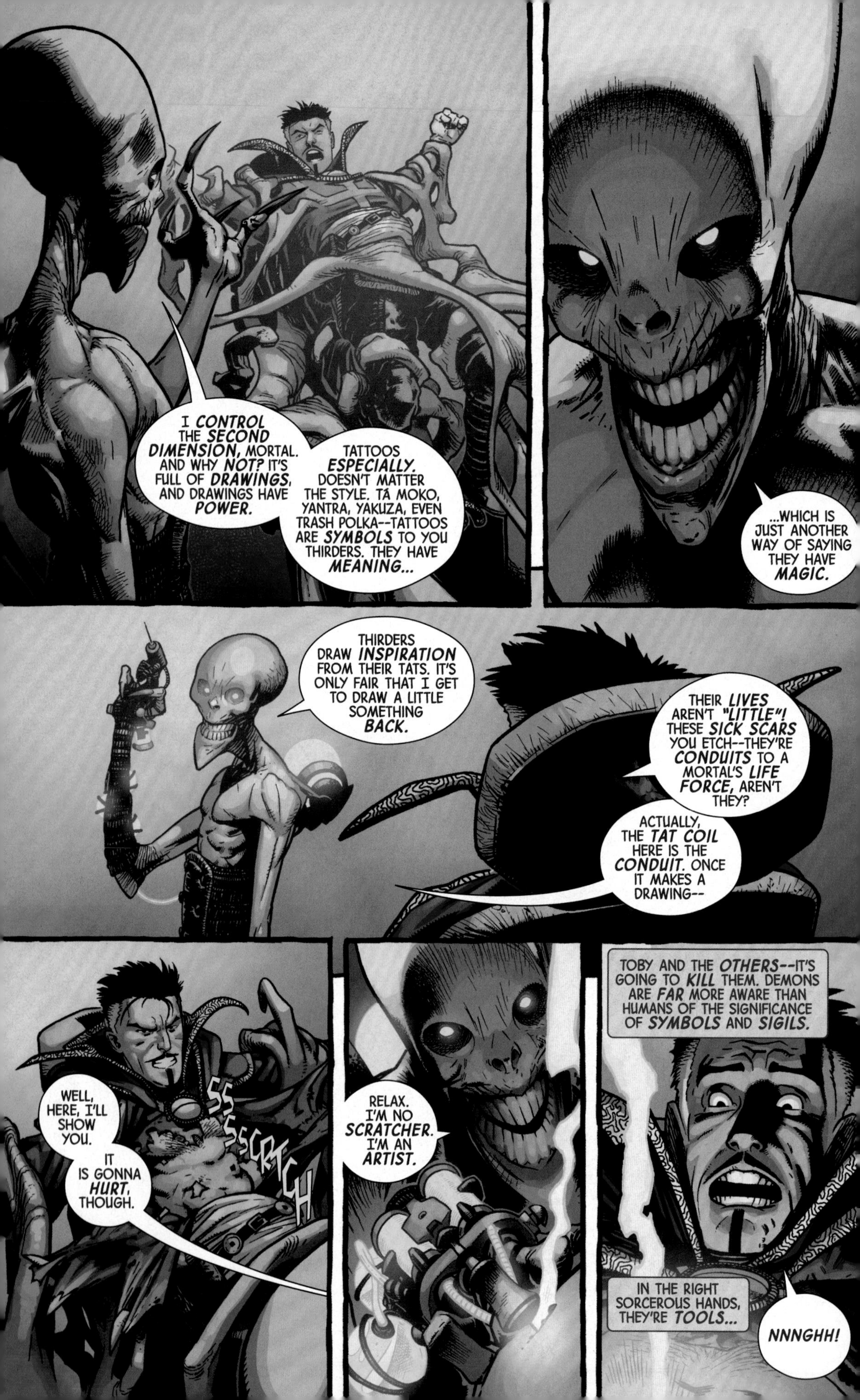
I CONTROL THE SECOND DIMENSION, MORTAL. AND WHY NOT? IT'S FULL OF DRAWINGS, AND DRAWINGS HAVE POWER.
TATTOOS ESPECIALLY. DOESN'T MATTER THE STYLE. TĀ MOKO, YANTRA, YAKUZA, EVEN TRASH POLKA--TATTOOS ARE SYMBOLS TO YOU THIRDERS. THEY HAVE MEANING...
...WHICH IS JUST ANOTHER WAY OF SAYING THEY HAVE MAGIC.
THIRDERS DRAW INSPIRATION FROM THEIR TATS. IT'S ONLY FAIR THAT I GET TO DRAW A LITTLE SOMETHING BACK.
THEIR LIVES AREN'T "LITTLE"! THESE SICK SCARS YOU ETCH--THEY'RE CONDUITS TO A MORTAL'S LIFE FORCE, AREN'T THEY?
ACTUALLY, THE TAT COIL HERE IS THE CONDUIT. ONCE IT MAKES A DRAWING--
WELL, HERE, I'LL SHOW YOU.
IT IS GONNA HURT, THOUGH.
SSSSCRTCH
RELAX. I'M NO SCRATCHER. I'M AN ARTIST.
TOBY AND THE OTHERS--IT'S GOING TO KILL THEM. DEMONS ARE FAR MORE AWARE THAN HUMANS OF THE SIGNIFICANCE OF SYMBOLS AND SIGILS.
IN THE RIGHT SORCEROUS HANDS, THEY'RE TOOLS...
NNNGHH!

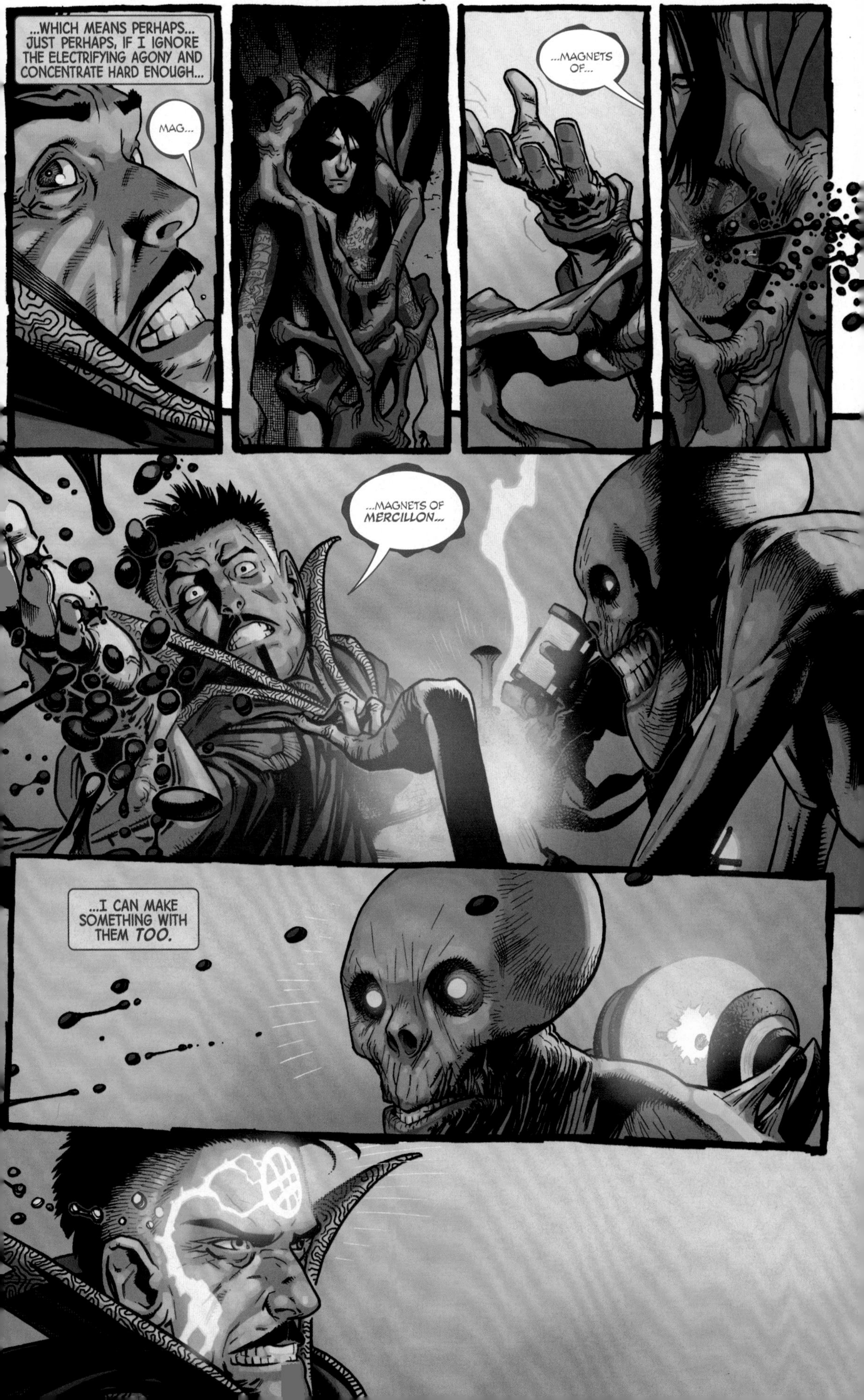
...WHICH MEANS PERHAPS... JUST PERHAPS, IF I IGNORE THE ELECTRIFYING AGONY AND CONCENTRATE HARD ENOUGH...
MAG...
...MAGNETS OF...
...MAGNETS OF MERCILLON...
...I CAN MAKE SOMETHING WITH THEM TOO.

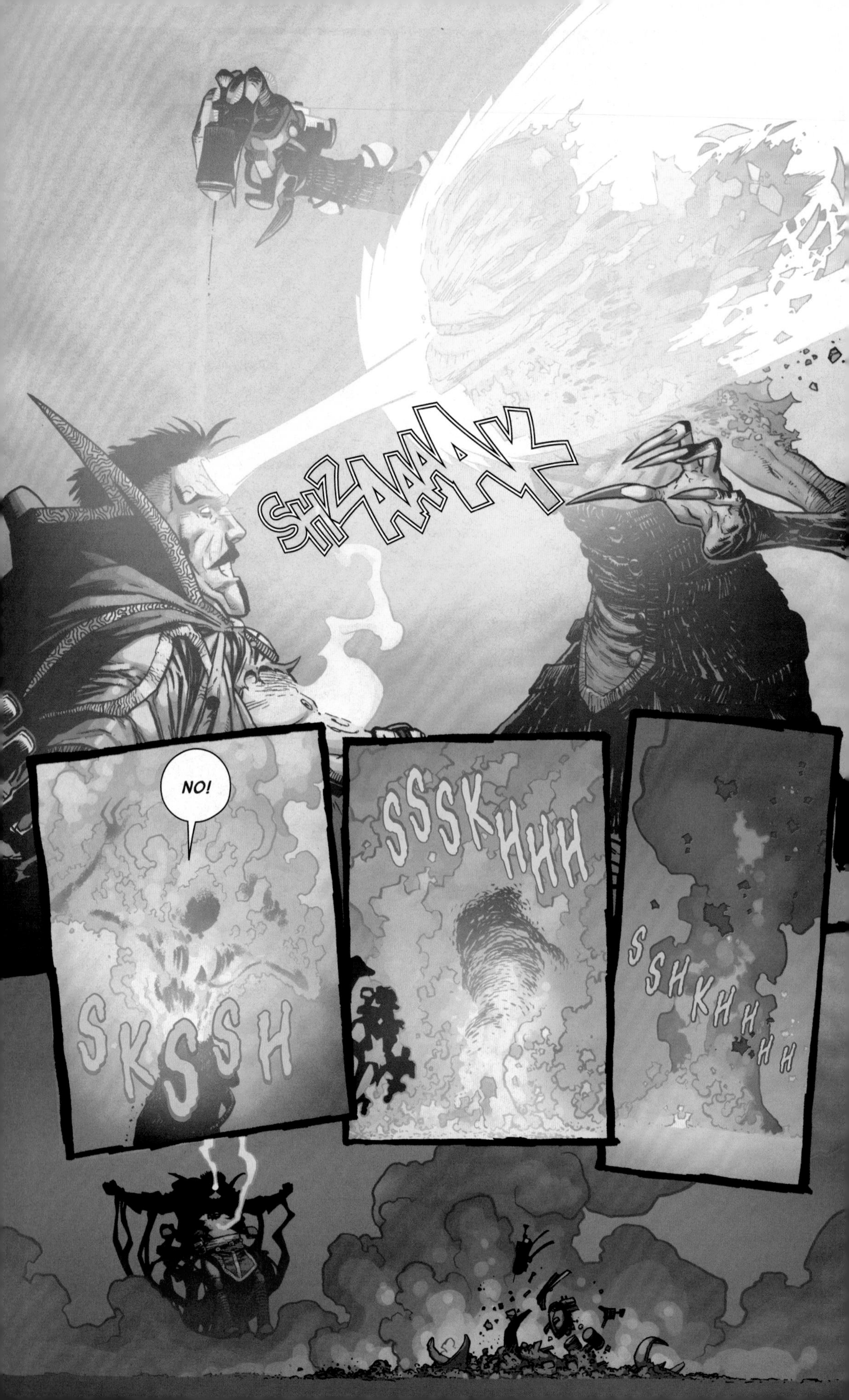
SHZAAAAK
NO!
SKSSH
SSSKHHH
SSHKHHHH

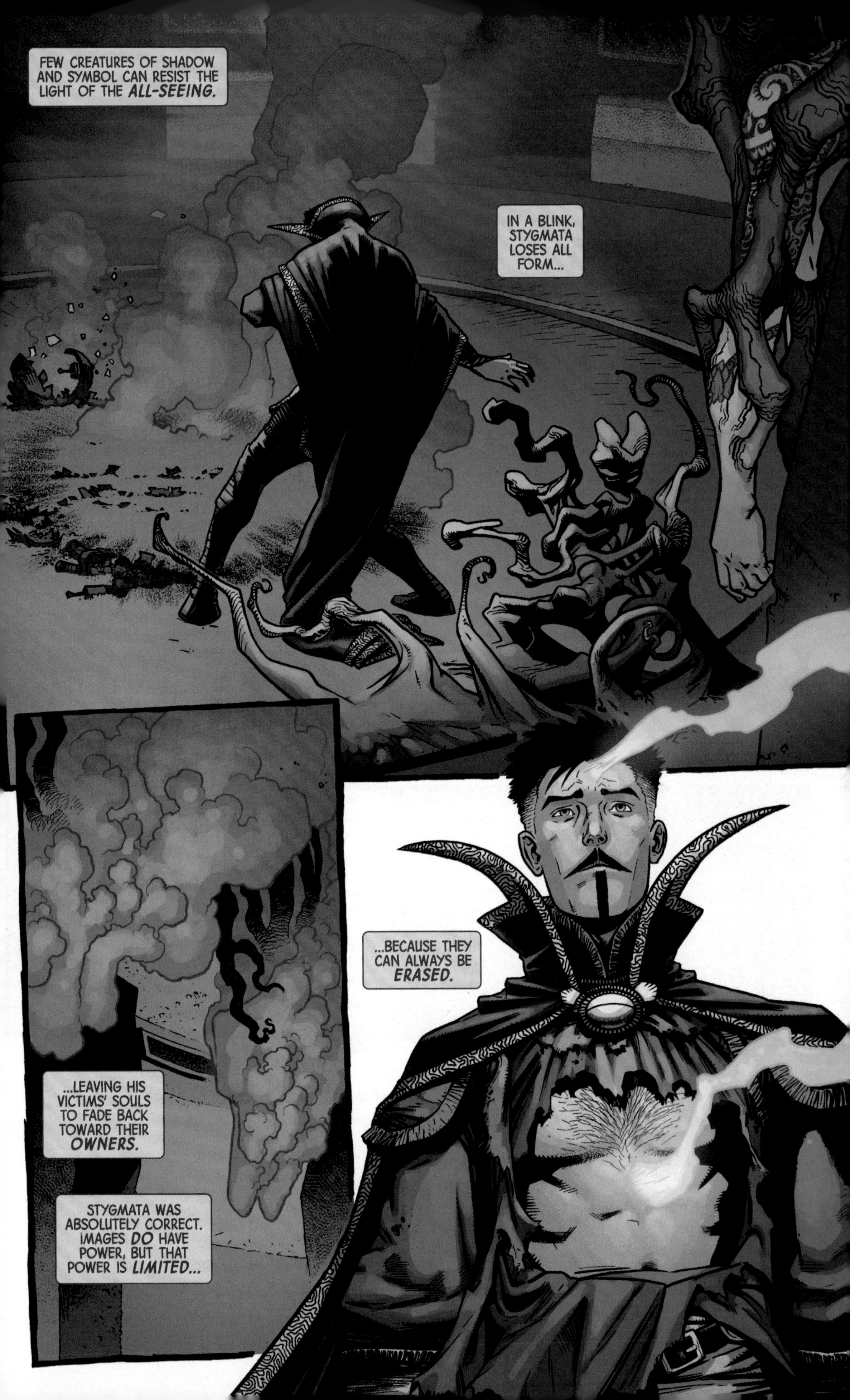
FEW CREATURES OF SHADOW AND SYMBOL CAN RESIST THE LIGHT OF THE ALL-SEEING.
IN A BLINK, STYGMATA LOSES ALL FORM...
...LEAVING HIS VICTIMS' SOULS TO FADE BACK TOWARD THEIR OWNERS.
STYGMATA WAS ABSOLUTELY CORRECT. IMAGES DO HAVE POWER, BUT THAT POWER IS LIMITED...
...BECAUSE THEY CAN ALWAYS BE ERASED.

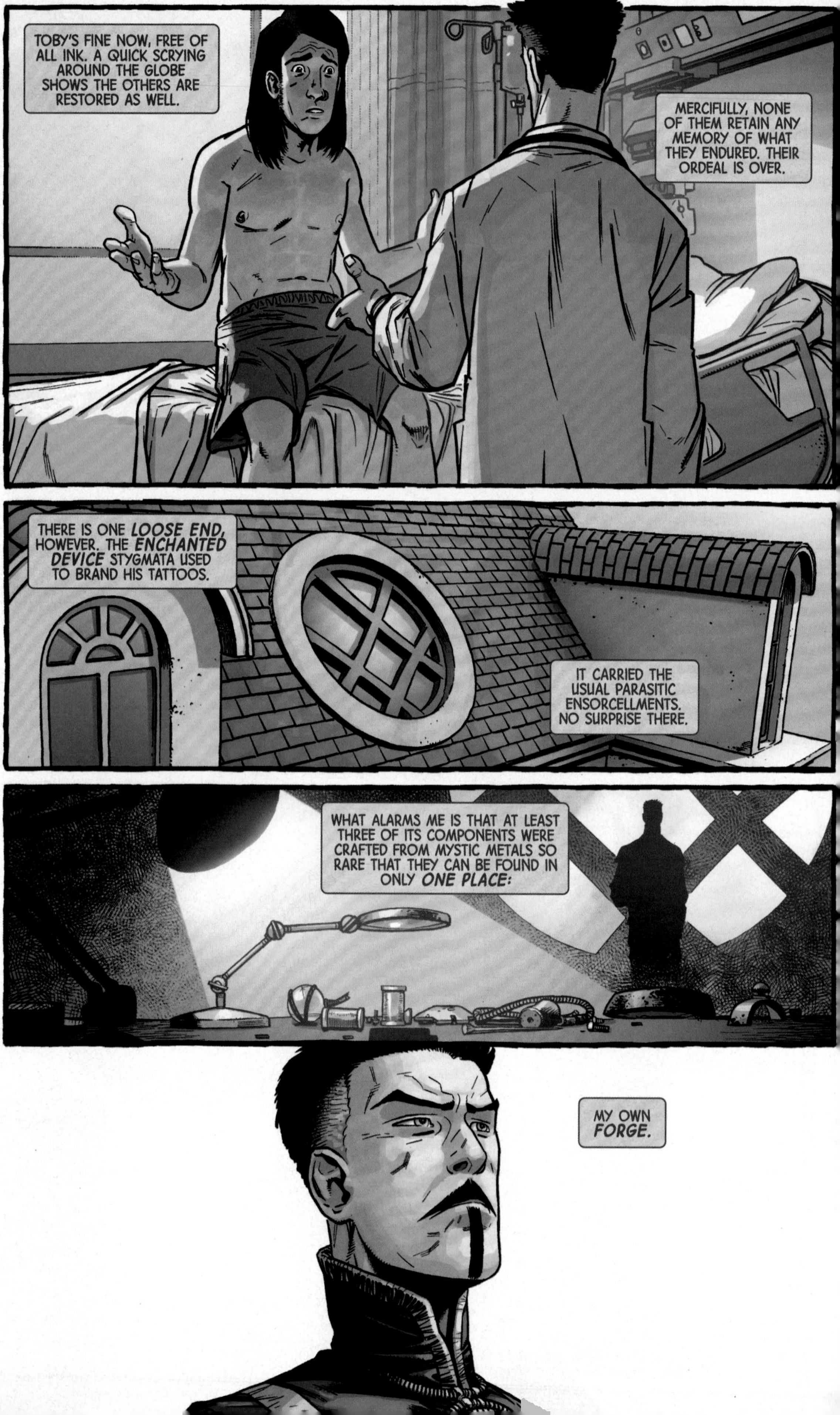
TOBY'S FINE NOW, FREE OF ALL INK. A QUICK SCRYING AROUND THE GLOBE SHOWS THE OTHERS ARE RESTORED AS WELL.
MERCIFULLY, NONE OF THEM RETAIN ANY MEMORY OF WHAT THEY ENDURED. THEIR ORDEAL IS OVER.
THERE IS ONE *LOOSE END,* HOWEVER. THE *ENCHANTED DEVICE* STYGMATA USED TO BRAND HIS TATTOOS.
IT CARRIED THE USUAL PARASITIC ENSORCELLMENTS. NO SURPRISE THERE.
WHAT ALARMS ME IS THAT AT LEAST THREE OF ITS COMPONENTS WERE CRAFTED FROM MYSTIC METALS SO RARE THAT THEY CAN BE FOUND IN ONLY *ONE PLACE:*
MY OWN *FORGE.*

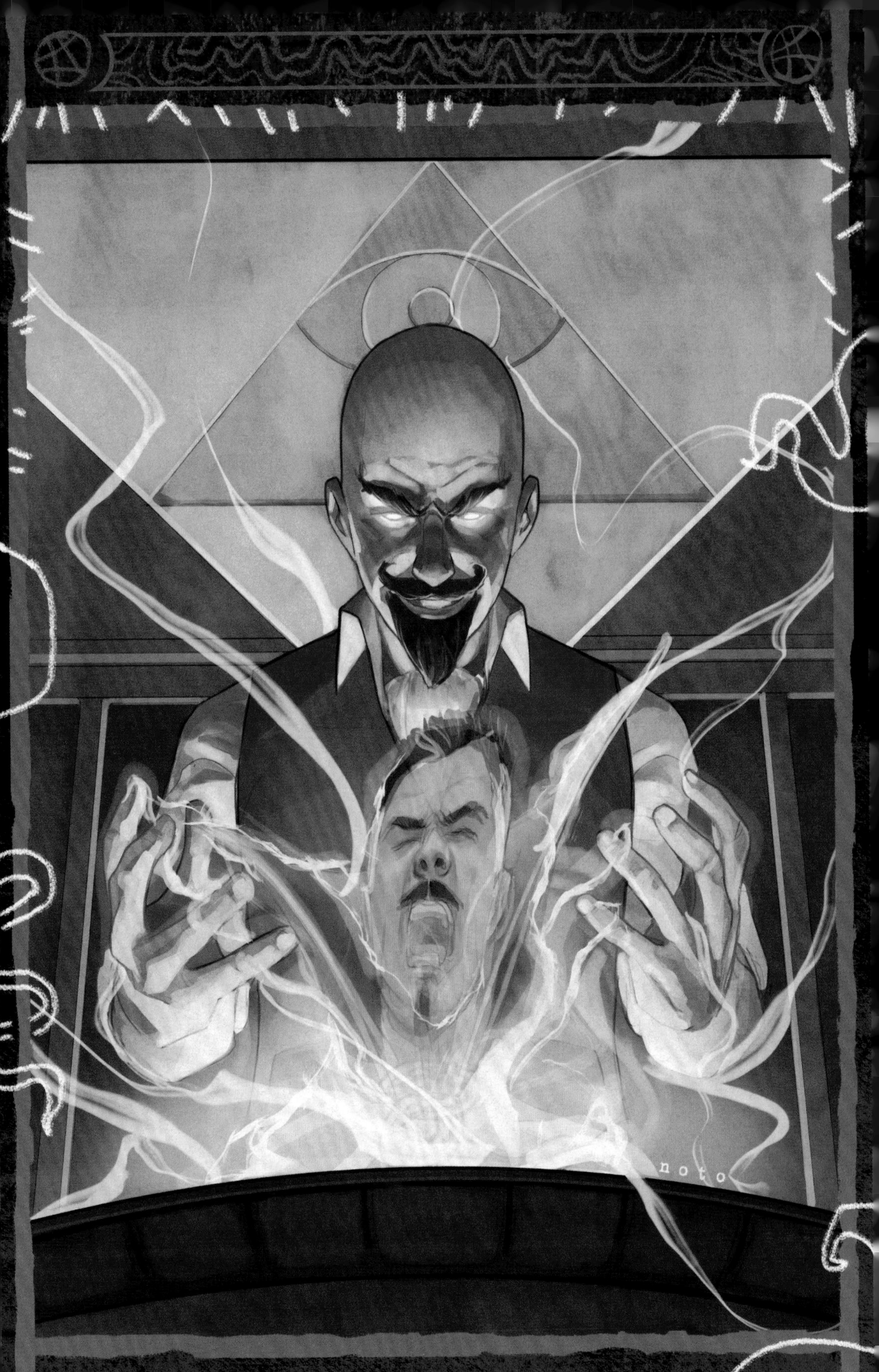
noto

4 “DRUID RESURGENT”

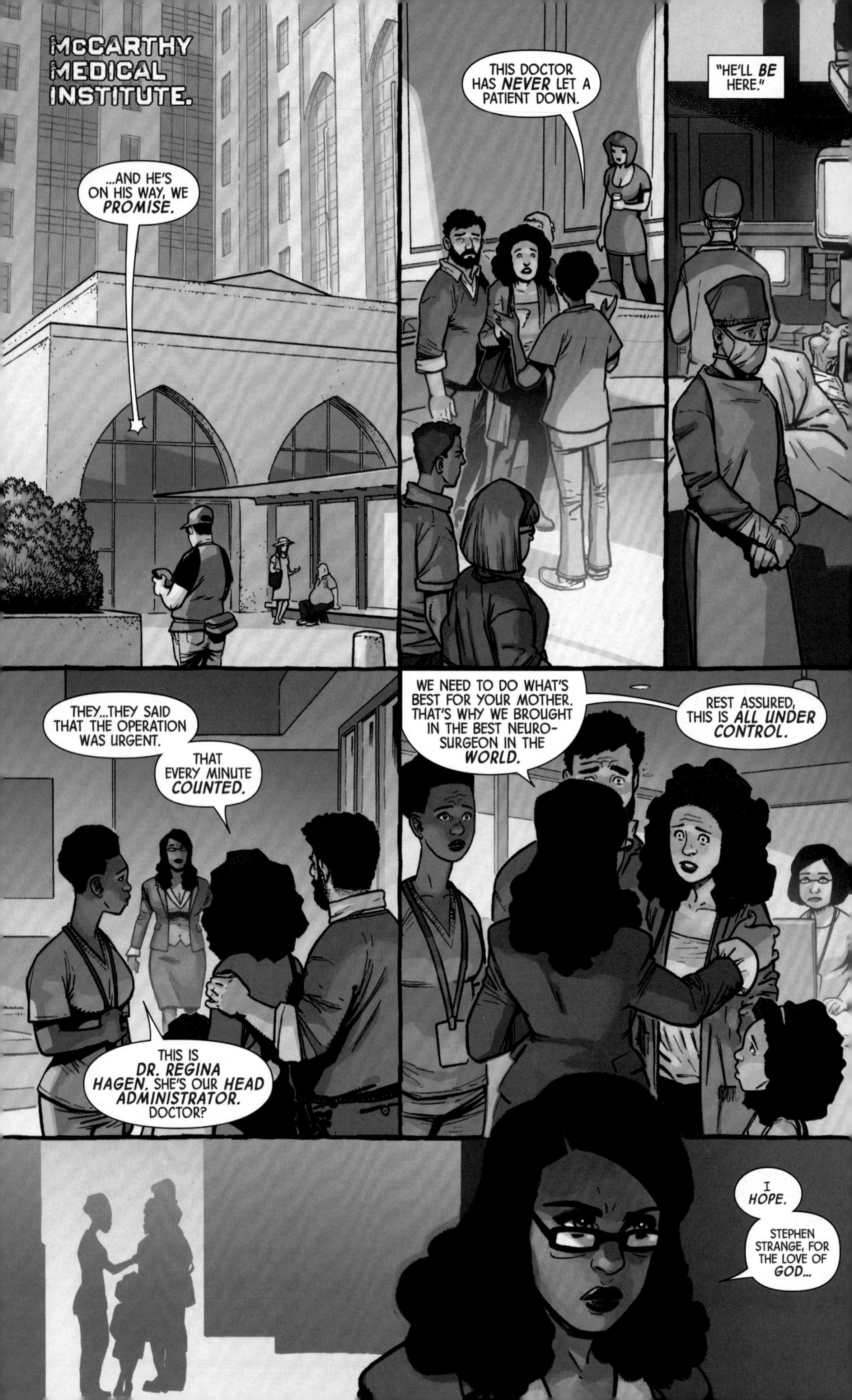
McCARTHY MEDICAL INSTITUTE.
...AND HE'S ON HIS WAY, WE PROMISE.
THIS DOCTOR HAS NEVER LET A PATIENT DOWN.
"HE'LL BE HERE."
THEY...THEY SAID THAT THE OPERATION WAS URGENT.
THAT EVERY MINUTE COUNTED.
THIS IS DR. REGINA HAGEN. SHE'S OUR HEAD ADMINISTRATOR. DOCTOR?
WE NEED TO DO WHAT'S BEST FOR YOUR MOTHER. THAT'S WHY WE BROUGHT IN THE BEST NEURO-SURGEON IN THE WORLD.
REST ASSURED, THIS IS ALL UNDER CONTROL.
I HOPE.
STEPHEN STRANGE, FOR THE LOVE OF GOD...

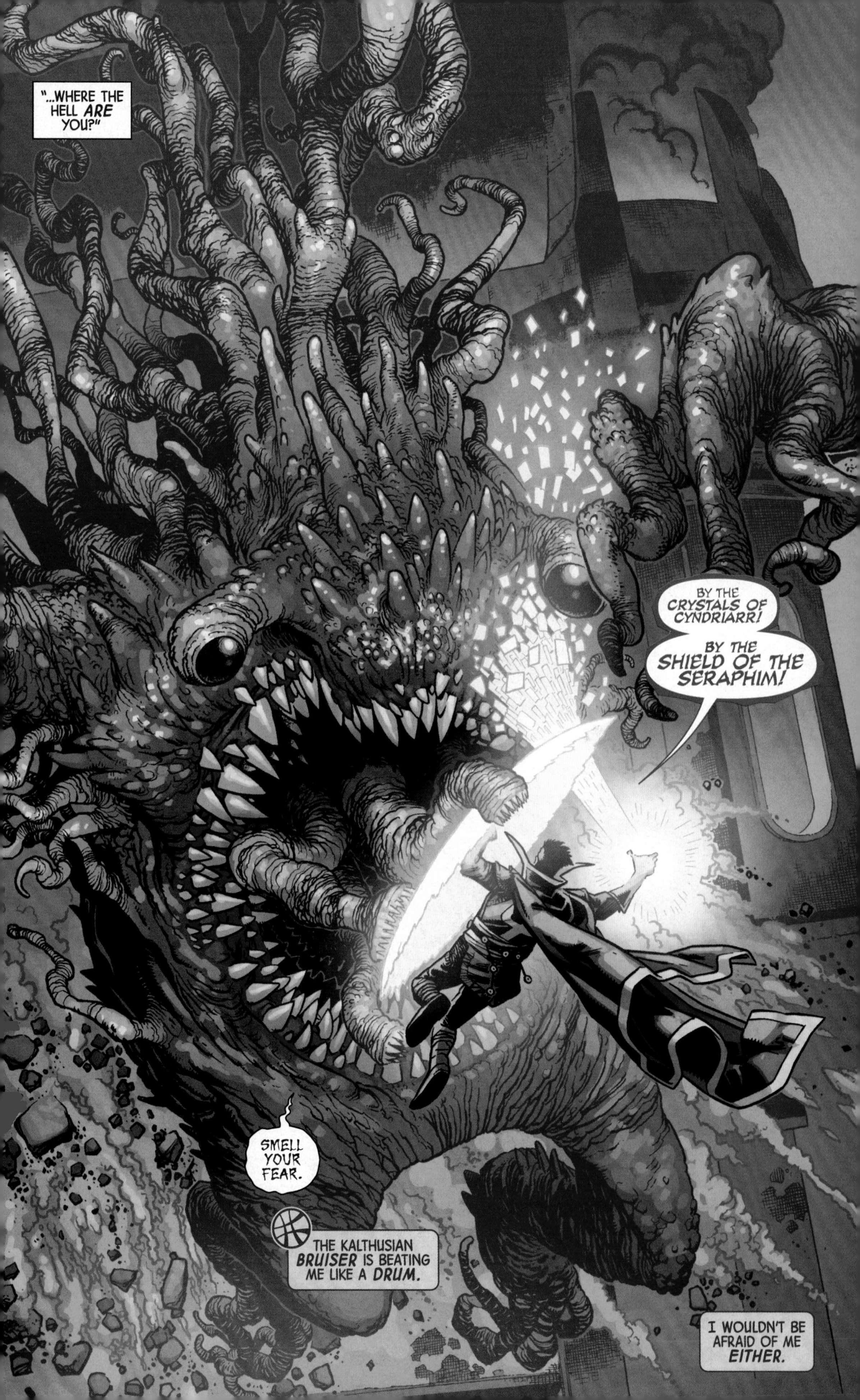
"...WHERE THE HELL ARE YOU?"
BY THE CRYSTALS OF CYNDRIARR!
BY THE SHIELD OF THE SERAPHIM!
SMELL YOUR FEAR.
THE KALTHUSIAN BRUISER IS BEATING ME LIKE A DRUM.
I WOULDN'T BE AFRAID OF ME EITHER.

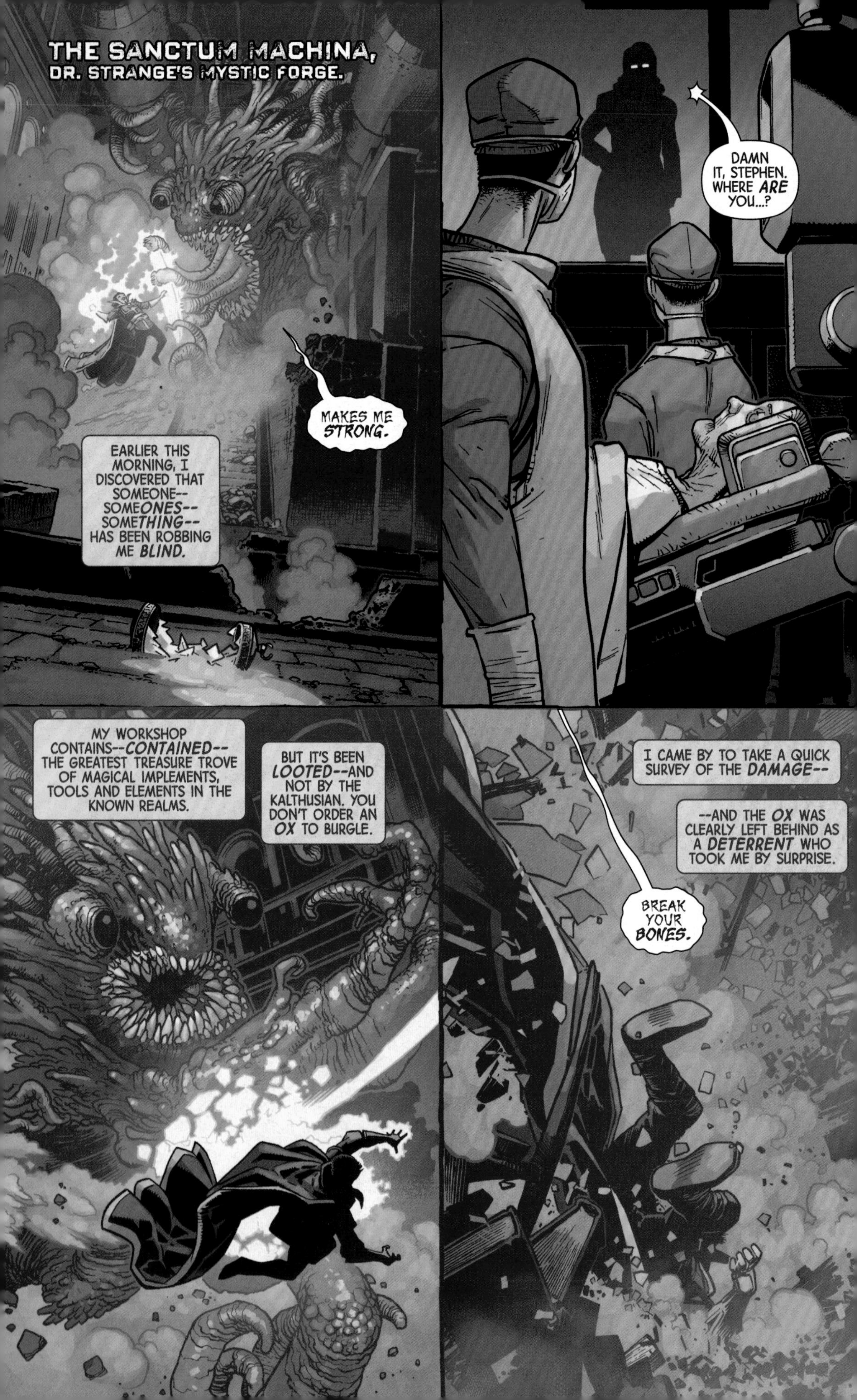
THE SANCTUM MACHINA, DR. STRANGE'S MYSTIC FORGE.
EARLIER THIS MORNING, I DISCOVERED THAT SOMEONE-- SOMEONES-- SOMETHING-- HAS BEEN ROBBING ME BLIND.
MAKES ME STRONG.
DAMN IT, STEPHEN. WHERE ARE YOU...?
MY WORKSHOP CONTAINS--CONTAINED-- THE GREATEST TREASURE TROVE OF MAGICAL IMPLEMENTS, TOOLS AND ELEMENTS IN THE KNOWN REALMS.
BUT IT'S BEEN LOOTED--AND NOT BY THE KALTHUSIAN. YOU DON'T ORDER AN OX TO BURGLE.
I CAME BY TO TAKE A QUICK SURVEY OF THE DAMAGE--
--AND THE OX WAS CLEARLY LEFT BEHIND AS A DETERRENT WHO TOOK ME BY SURPRISE.
BREAK YOUR BONES.

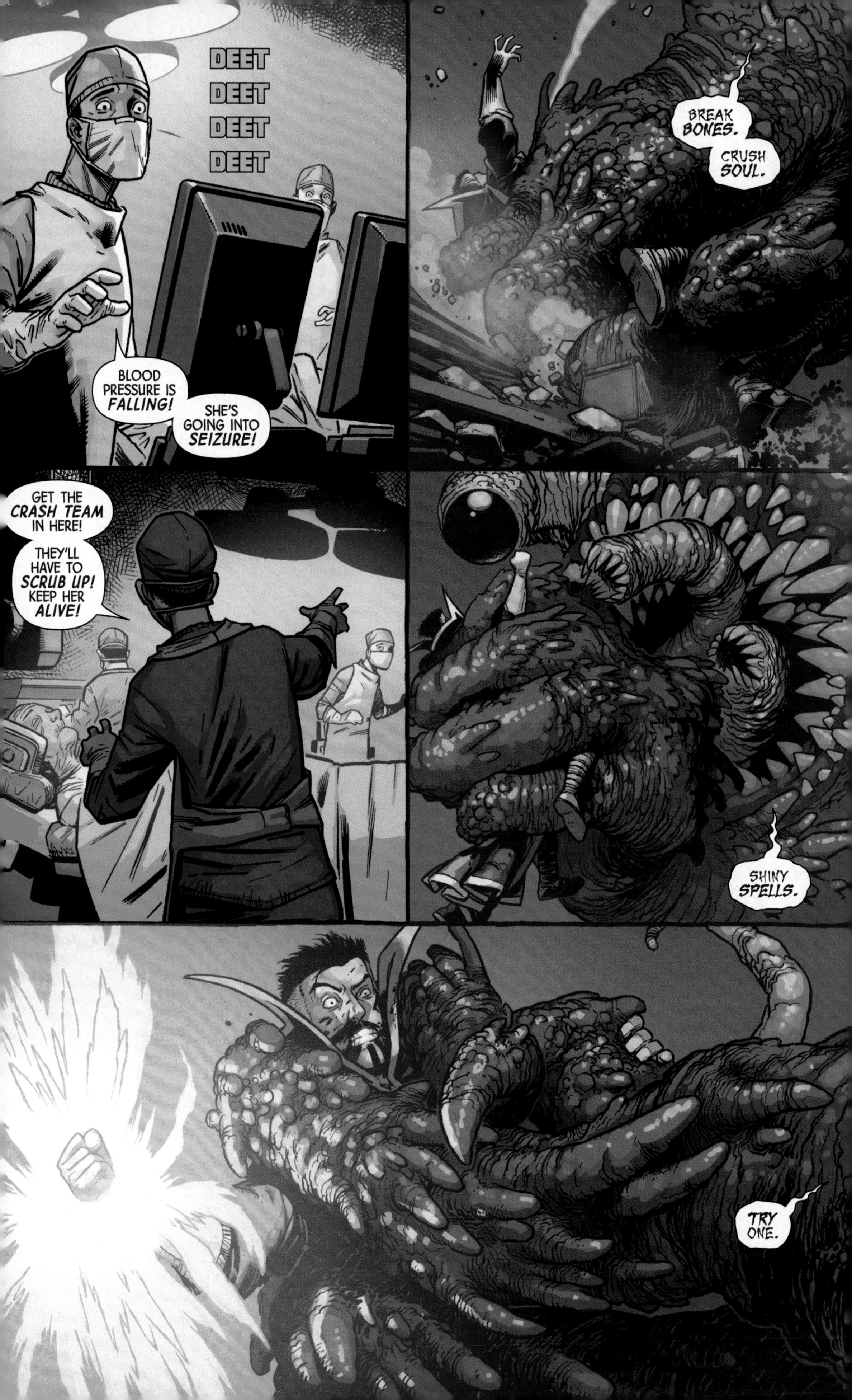
DEET
DEET
DEET
DEET
BLOOD PRESSURE IS FALLING!
SHE'S GOING INTO SEIZURE!
BREAK BONES.
CRUSH SOUL.
GET THE CRASH TEAM IN HERE!
THEY'LL HAVE TO SCRUB UP! KEEP HER ALIVE!
SHINY SPELLS.
TRY ONE.

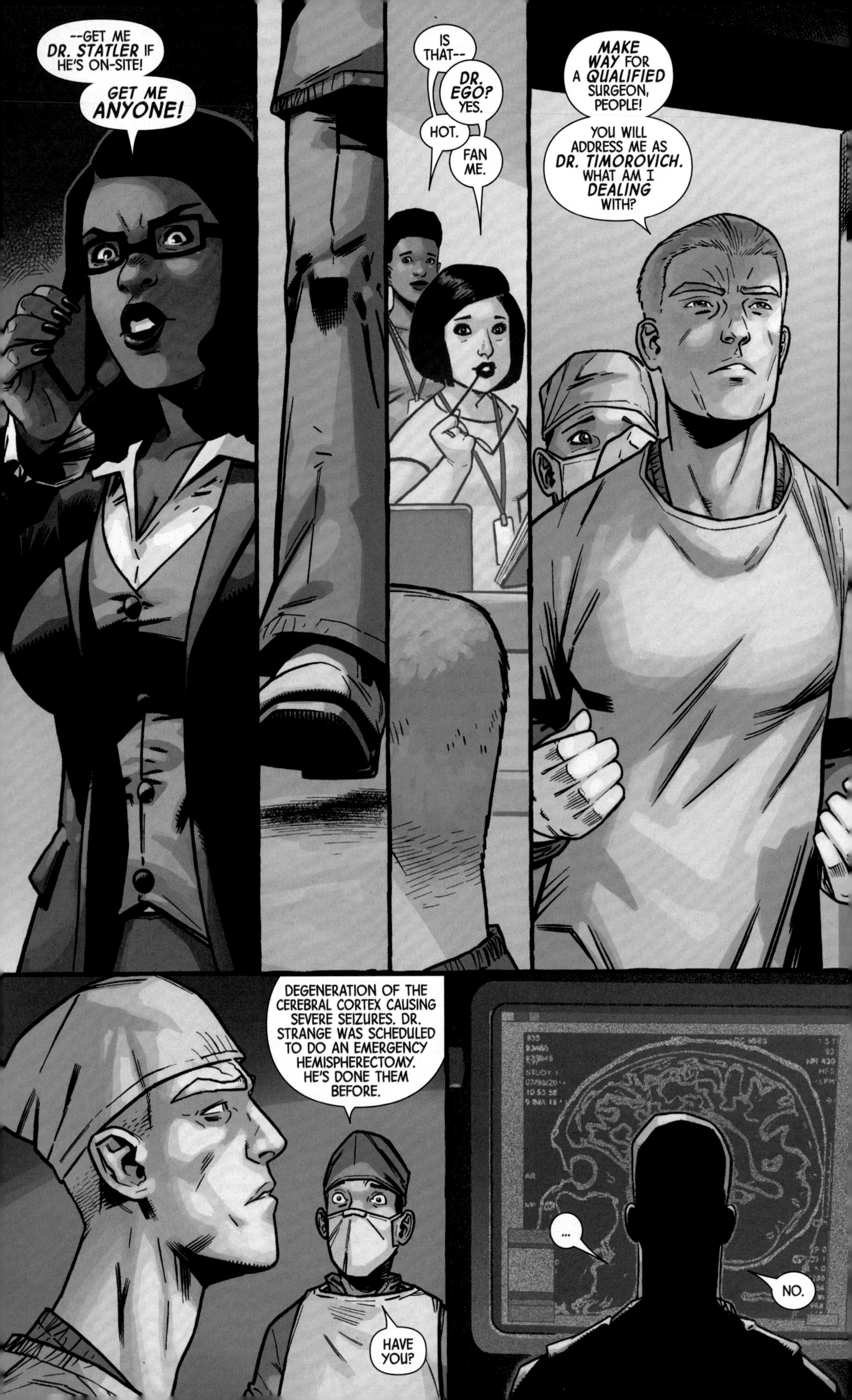
--GET ME DR. STATLER IF HE'S ON-SITE!
GET ME ANYONE!
IS THAT--
DR. EGO? YES.
HOT.
FAN ME.
MAKE WAY FOR A QUALIFIED SURGEON, PEOPLE!
YOU WILL ADDRESS ME AS DR. TIMOROVICH. WHAT AM I DEALING WITH?
DEGENERATION OF THE CEREBRAL CORTEX CAUSING SEVERE SEIZURES. DR. STRANGE WAS SCHEDULED TO DO AN EMERGENCY HEMISPHERECTOMY. HE'S DONE THEM BEFORE.
HAVE YOU?
...
NO.

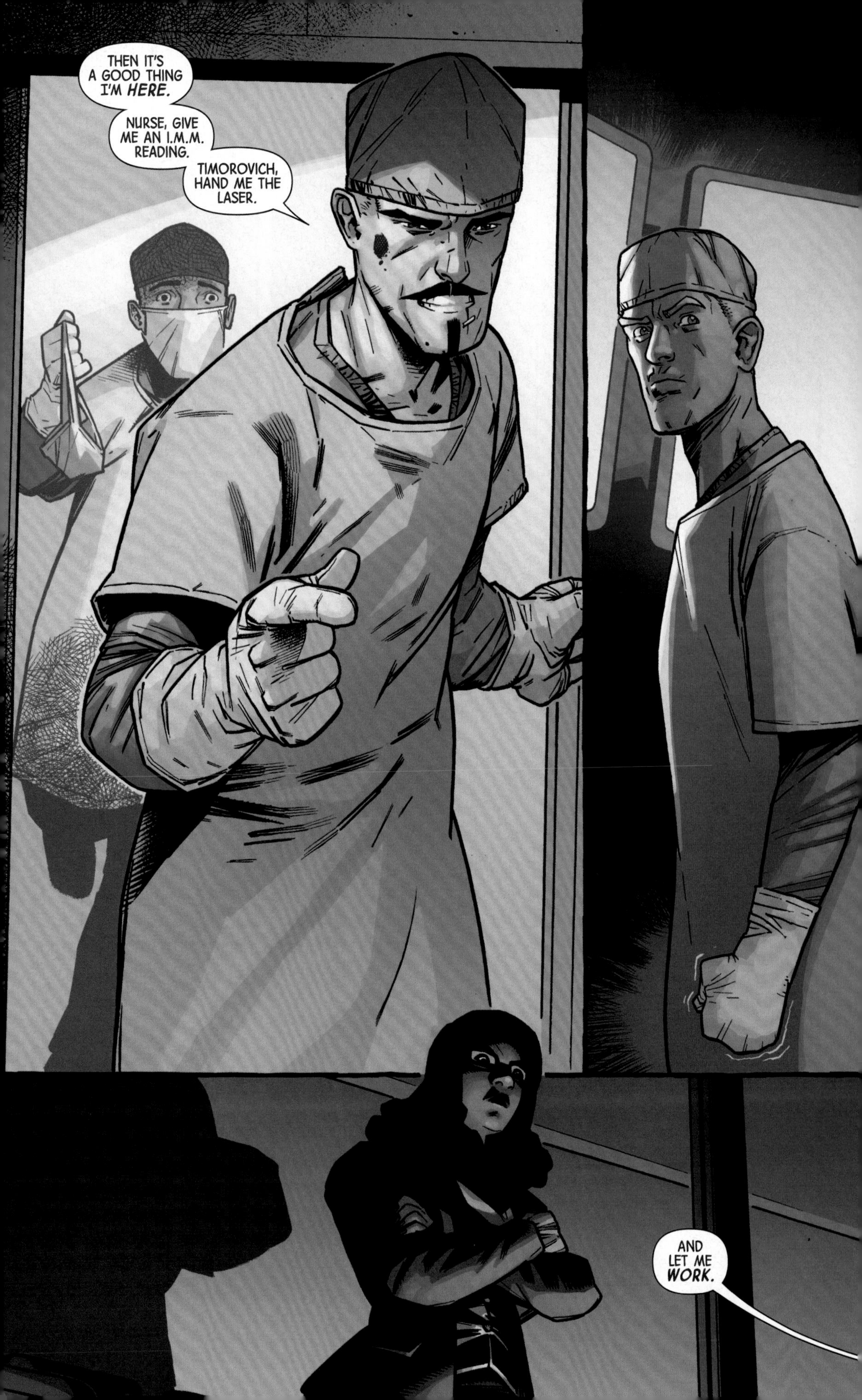
THEN IT'S A GOOD THING I'M *HERE.*
NURSE, GIVE ME AN I.M.M. READING.
TIMOROVICH, HAND ME THE LASER.
AND LET ME *WORK.*

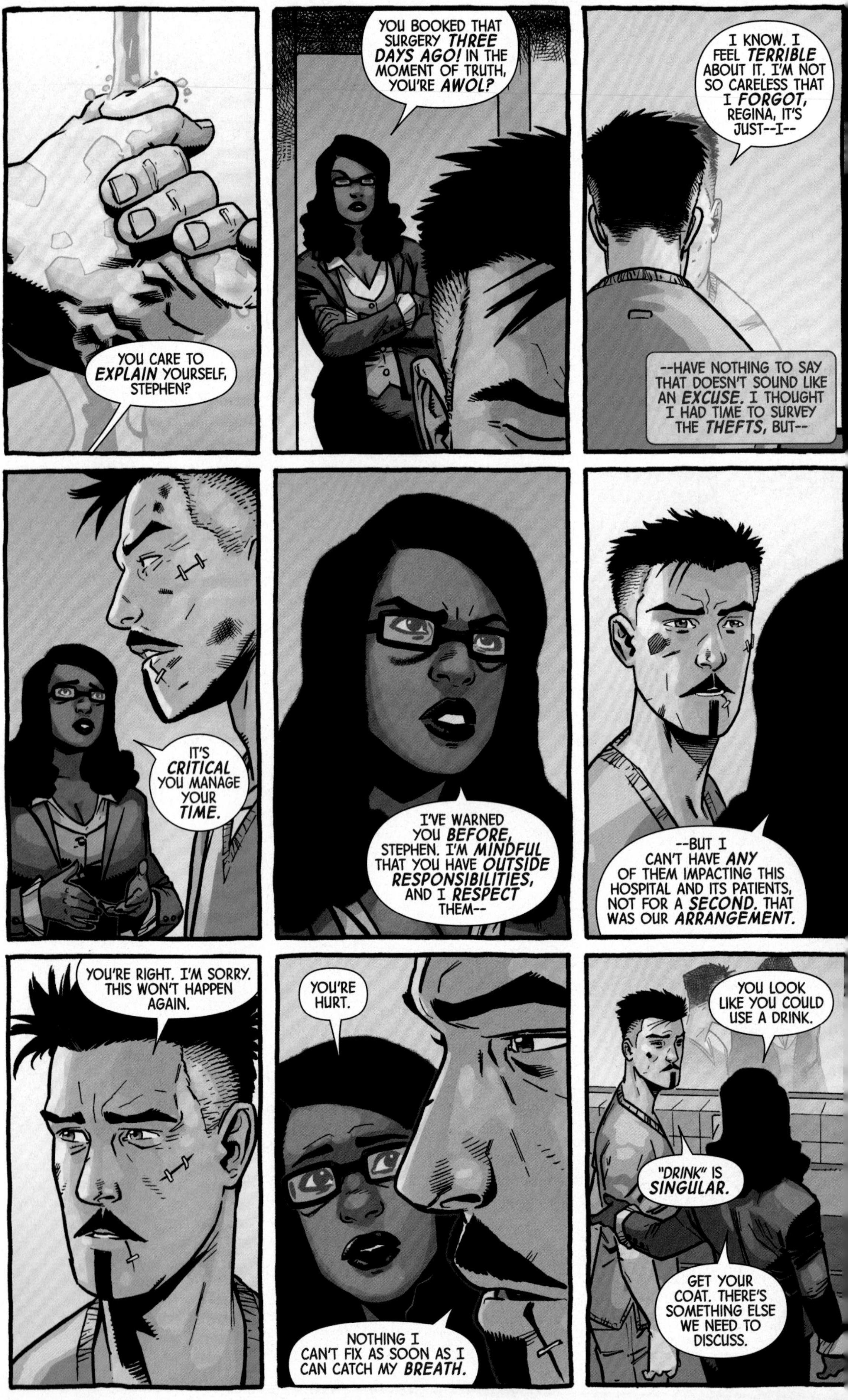
YOU CARE TO EXPLAIN YOURSELF, STEPHEN?
YOU BOOKED THAT SURGERY THREE DAYS AGO! IN THE MOMENT OF TRUTH, YOU'RE AWOL?
I KNOW. I FEEL TERRIBLE ABOUT IT. I'M NOT SO CARELESS THAT I FORGOT, REGINA, IT'S JUST--I--
--HAVE NOTHING TO SAY THAT DOESN'T SOUND LIKE AN EXCUSE. I THOUGHT I HAD TIME TO SURVEY THE THEFTS, BUT--
IT'S CRITICAL YOU MANAGE YOUR TIME.
I'VE WARNED YOU BEFORE, STEPHEN. I'M MINDFUL THAT YOU HAVE OUTSIDE RESPONSIBILITIES, AND I RESPECT THEM--
--BUT I CAN'T HAVE ANY OF THEM IMPACTING THIS HOSPITAL AND ITS PATIENTS, NOT FOR A SECOND. THAT WAS OUR ARRANGEMENT.
YOU'RE RIGHT. I'M SORRY. THIS WON'T HAPPEN AGAIN.
YOU'RE HURT.
NOTHING I CAN'T FIX AS SOON AS I CAN CATCH MY BREATH.
YOU LOOK LIKE YOU COULD USE A DRINK.
"DRINK" IS SINGULAR.
GET YOUR COAT. THERE'S SOMETHING ELSE WE NEED TO DISCUSS.

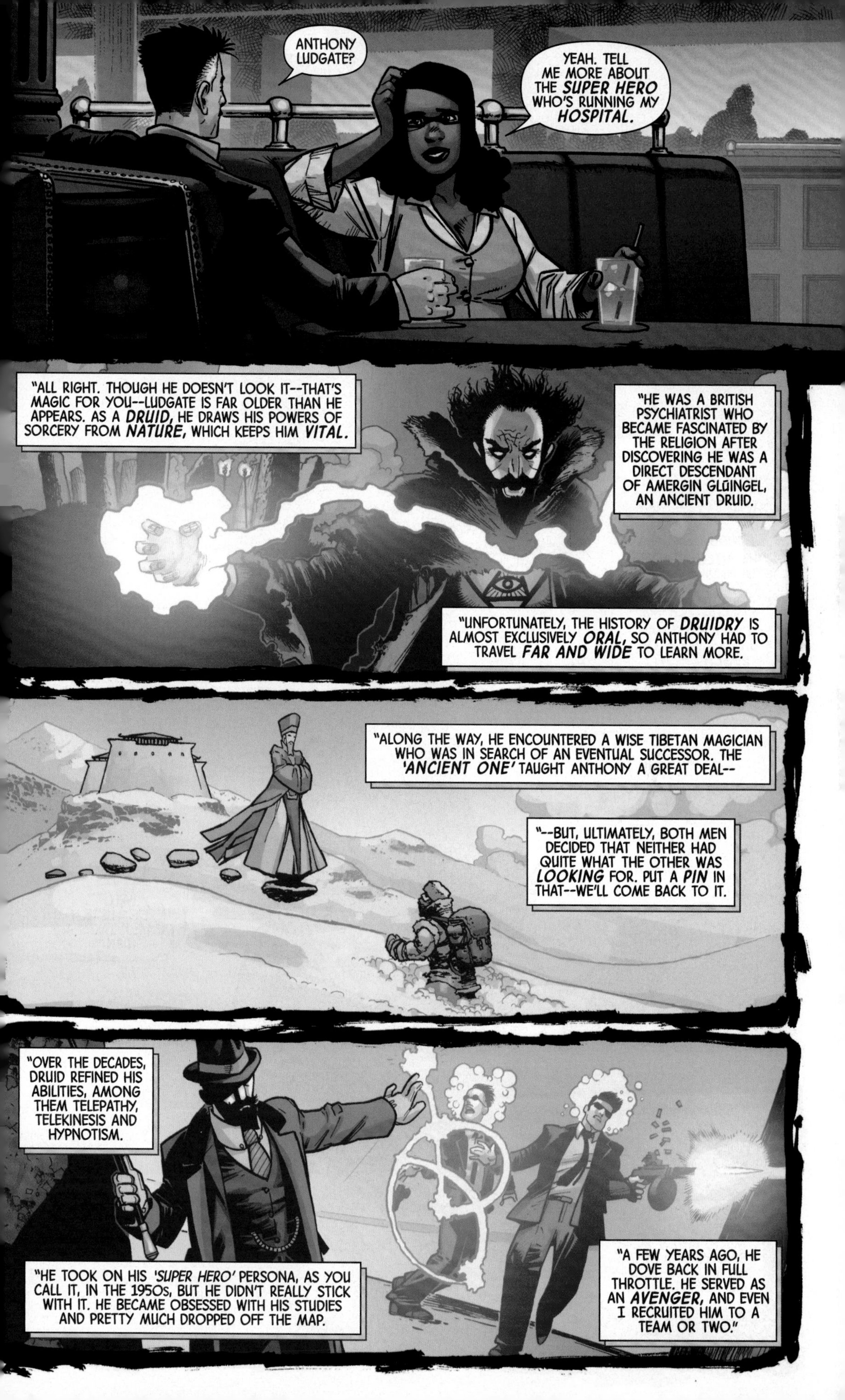
ANTHONY LUDGATE?
YEAH. TELL ME MORE ABOUT THE SUPER HERO WHO'S RUNNING MY HOSPITAL.
"ALL RIGHT. THOUGH HE DOESN'T LOOK IT--THAT'S MAGIC FOR YOU--LUDGATE IS FAR OLDER THAN HE APPEARS. AS A DRUID, HE DRAWS HIS POWERS OF SORCERY FROM NATURE, WHICH KEEPS HIM VITAL.
"HE WAS A BRITISH PSYCHIATRIST WHO BECAME FASCINATED BY THE RELIGION AFTER DISCOVERING HE WAS A DIRECT DESCENDANT OF AMERGIN GLÚINGEL, AN ANCIENT DRUID.
"UNFORTUNATELY, THE HISTORY OF DRUIDRY IS ALMOST EXCLUSIVELY ORAL, SO ANTHONY HAD TO TRAVEL FAR AND WIDE TO LEARN MORE.
"ALONG THE WAY, HE ENCOUNTERED A WISE TIBETAN MAGICIAN WHO WAS IN SEARCH OF AN EVENTUAL SUCCESSOR. THE 'ANCIENT ONE' TAUGHT ANTHONY A GREAT DEAL--
"--BUT, ULTIMATELY, BOTH MEN DECIDED THAT NEITHER HAD QUITE WHAT THE OTHER WAS LOOKING FOR. PUT A PIN IN THAT--WE'LL COME BACK TO IT.
"OVER THE DECADES, DRUID REFINED HIS ABILITIES, AMONG THEM TELEPATHY, TELEKINESIS AND HYPNOTISM.
"HE TOOK ON HIS 'SUPER HERO' PERSONA, AS YOU CALL IT, IN THE 1950s, BUT HE DIDN'T REALLY STICK WITH IT. HE BECAME OBSESSED WITH HIS STUDIES AND PRETTY MUCH DROPPED OFF THE MAP.
"A FEW YEARS AGO, HE DOVE BACK IN FULL THROTTLE. HE SERVED AS AN AVENGER, AND EVEN I RECRUITED HIM TO A TEAM OR TWO."

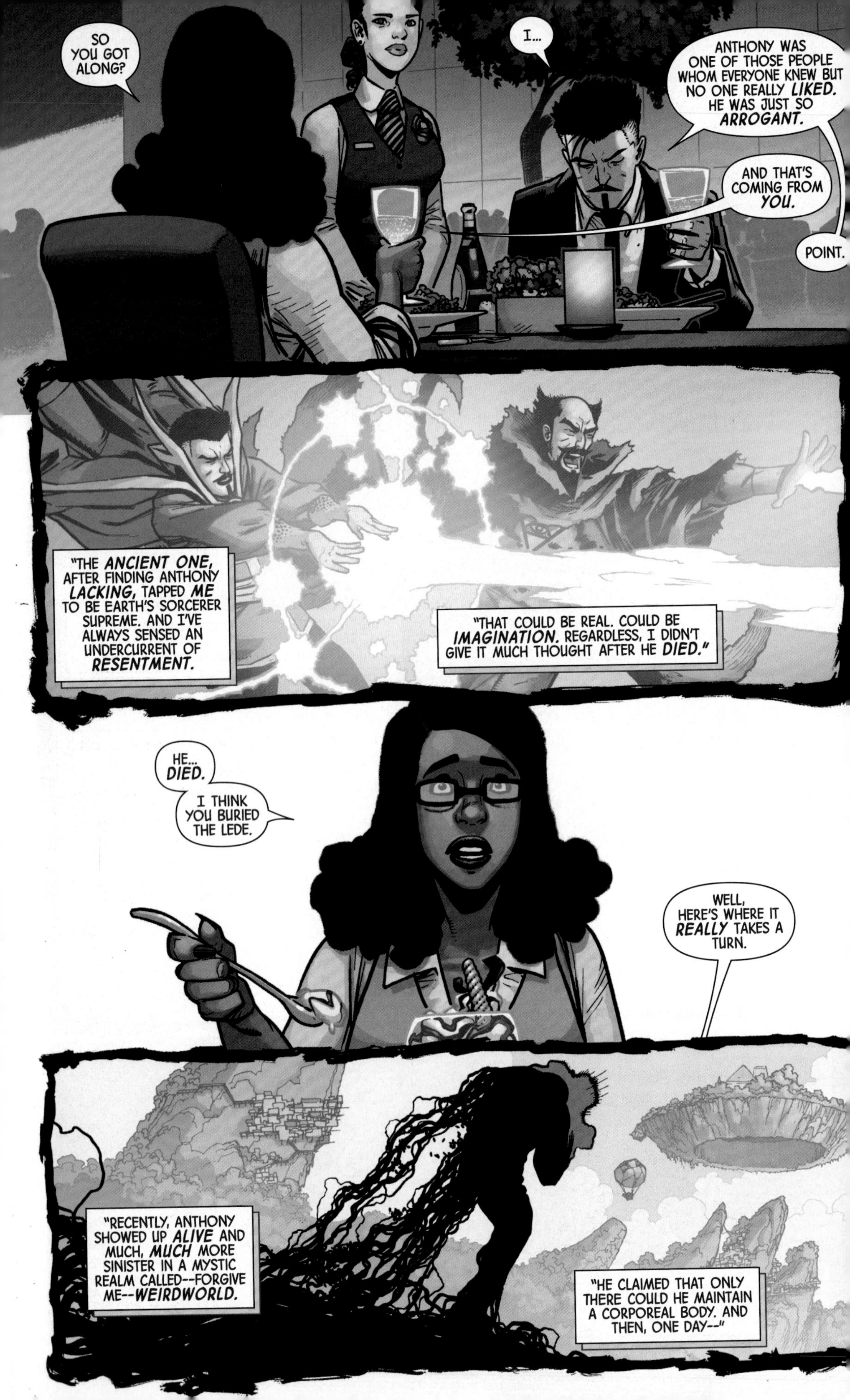
SO YOU GOT ALONG?
I...
ANTHONY WAS ONE OF THOSE PEOPLE WHOM EVERYONE KNEW BUT NO ONE REALLY LIKED. HE WAS JUST SO ARROGANT.
AND THAT'S COMING FROM YOU.
POINT.
"THE ANCIENT ONE, AFTER FINDING ANTHONY LACKING, TAPPED ME TO BE EARTH'S SORCERER SUPREME. AND I'VE ALWAYS SENSED AN UNDERCURRENT OF RESENTMENT.
"THAT COULD BE REAL. COULD BE IMAGINATION. REGARDLESS, I DIDN'T GIVE IT MUCH THOUGHT AFTER HE DIED."
HE... DIED.
I THINK YOU BURIED THE LEDE.
WELL, HERE'S WHERE IT REALLY TAKES A TURN.
"RECENTLY, ANTHONY SHOWED UP ALIVE AND MUCH, MUCH MORE SINISTER IN A MYSTIC REALM CALLED--FORGIVE ME--WEIRDWORLD.
"HE CLAIMED THAT ONLY THERE COULD HE MAINTAIN A CORPOREAL BODY. AND THEN, ONE DAY--"

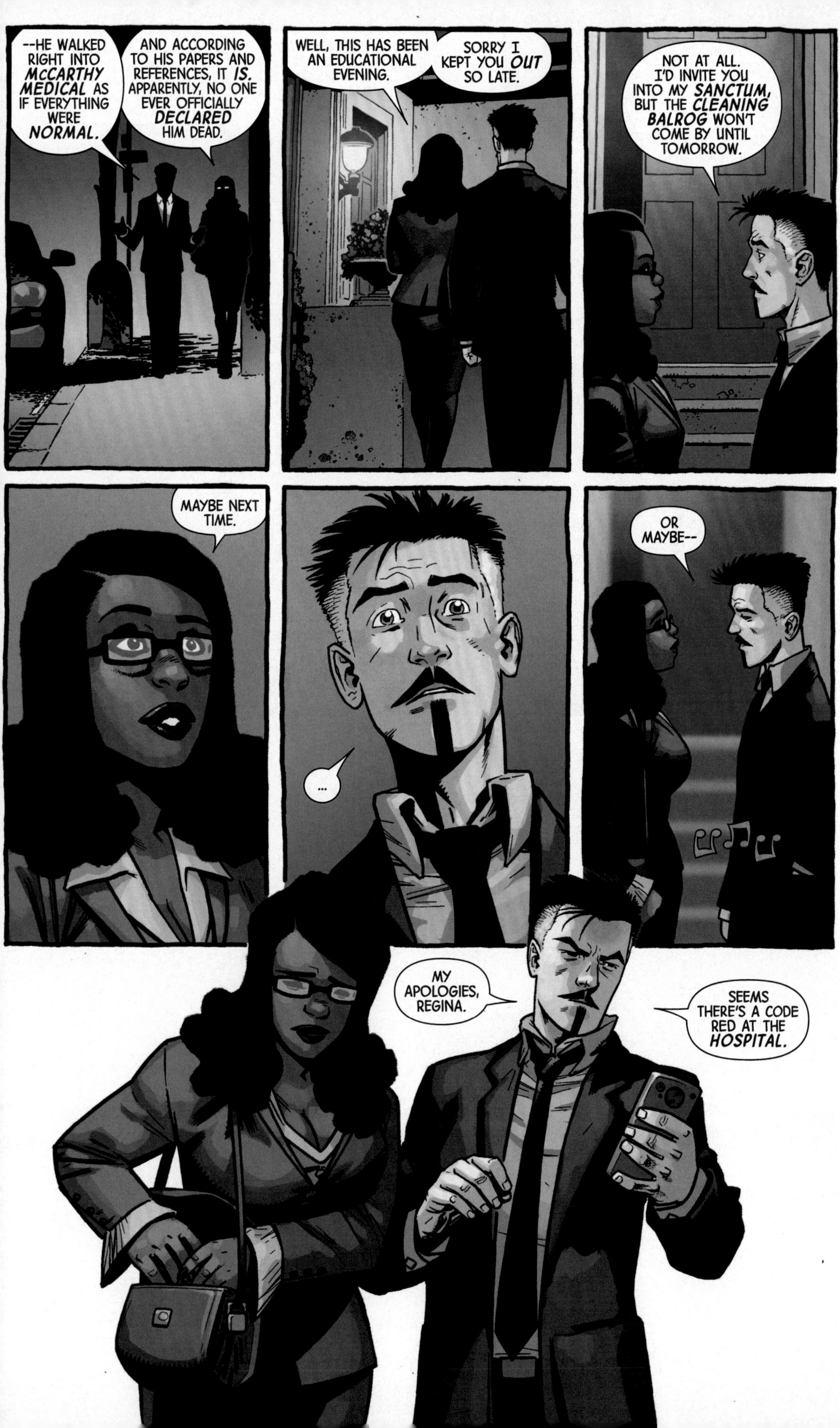
--HE WALKED RIGHT INTO McCARTHY MEDICAL AS IF EVERYTHING WERE NORMAL.
AND ACCORDING TO HIS PAPERS AND REFERENCES, IT IS. APPARENTLY, NO ONE EVER OFFICIALLY DECLARED HIM DEAD.
WELL, THIS HAS BEEN AN EDUCATIONAL EVENING.
SORRY I KEPT YOU OUT SO LATE.
NOT AT ALL. I'D INVITE YOU INTO MY SANCTUM, BUT THE CLEANING BALROG WON'T COME BY UNTIL TOMORROW.
MAYBE NEXT TIME.
...
OR MAYBE--
MY APOLOGIES, REGINA.
SEEMS THERE'S A CODE RED AT THE HOSPITAL.

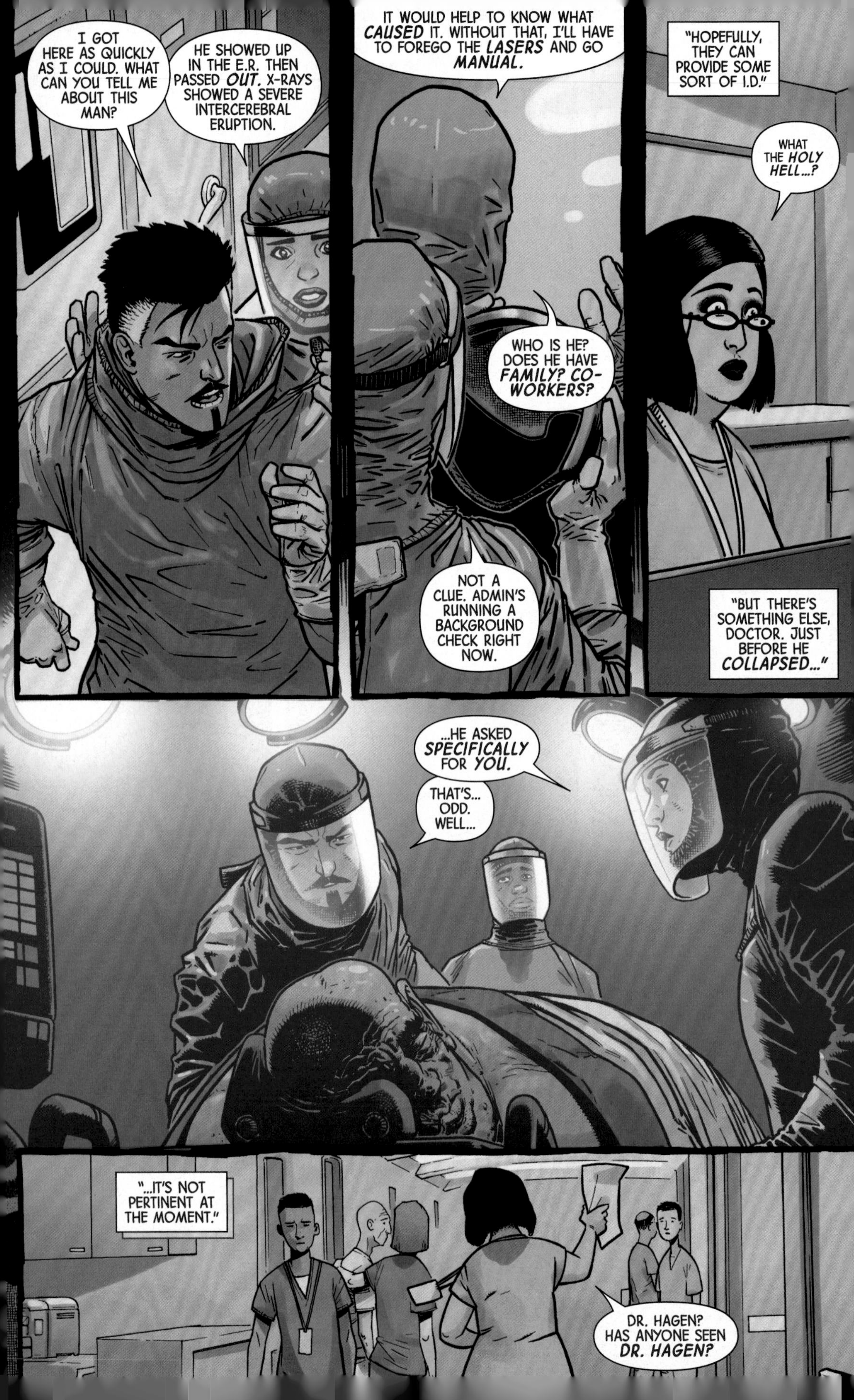
I GOT HERE AS QUICKLY AS I COULD. WHAT CAN YOU TELL ME ABOUT THIS MAN?
HE SHOWED UP IN THE E.R. THEN PASSED OUT. X-RAYS SHOWED A SEVERE INTERCEREBRAL ERUPTION.
IT WOULD HELP TO KNOW WHAT CAUSED IT. WITHOUT THAT, I'LL HAVE TO FOREGO THE LASERS AND GO MANUAL.
WHO IS HE? DOES HE HAVE FAMILY? CO-WORKERS?
NOT A CLUE. ADMIN'S RUNNING A BACKGROUND CHECK RIGHT NOW.
"HOPEFULLY, THEY CAN PROVIDE SOME SORT OF I.D."
WHAT THE HOLY HELL...?
"BUT THERE'S SOMETHING ELSE, DOCTOR. JUST BEFORE HE COLLAPSED..."
...HE ASKED SPECIFICALLY FOR YOU.
THAT'S... ODD. WELL...
"...IT'S NOT PERTINENT AT THE MOMENT."
DR. HAGEN? HAS ANYONE SEEN DR. HAGEN?

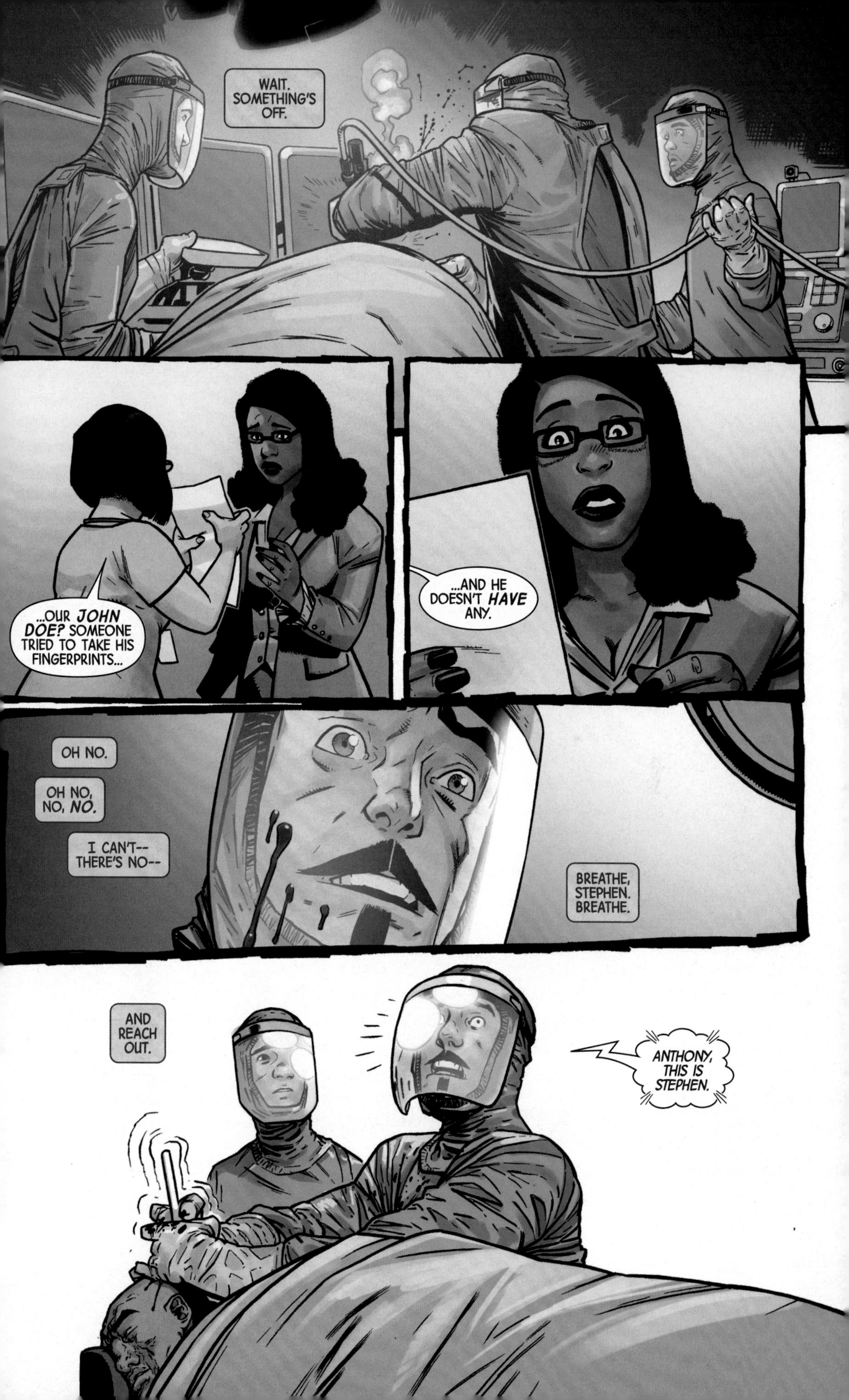
WAIT. SOMETHING'S OFF.
...OUR JOHN DOE? SOMEONE TRIED TO TAKE HIS FINGERPRINTS...
...AND HE DOESN'T HAVE ANY.
OH NO.
OH NO, NO, NO.
I CAN'T-- THERE'S NO--
BREATHE, STEPHEN. BREATHE.
AND REACH OUT.
ANTHONY, THIS IS STEPHEN.

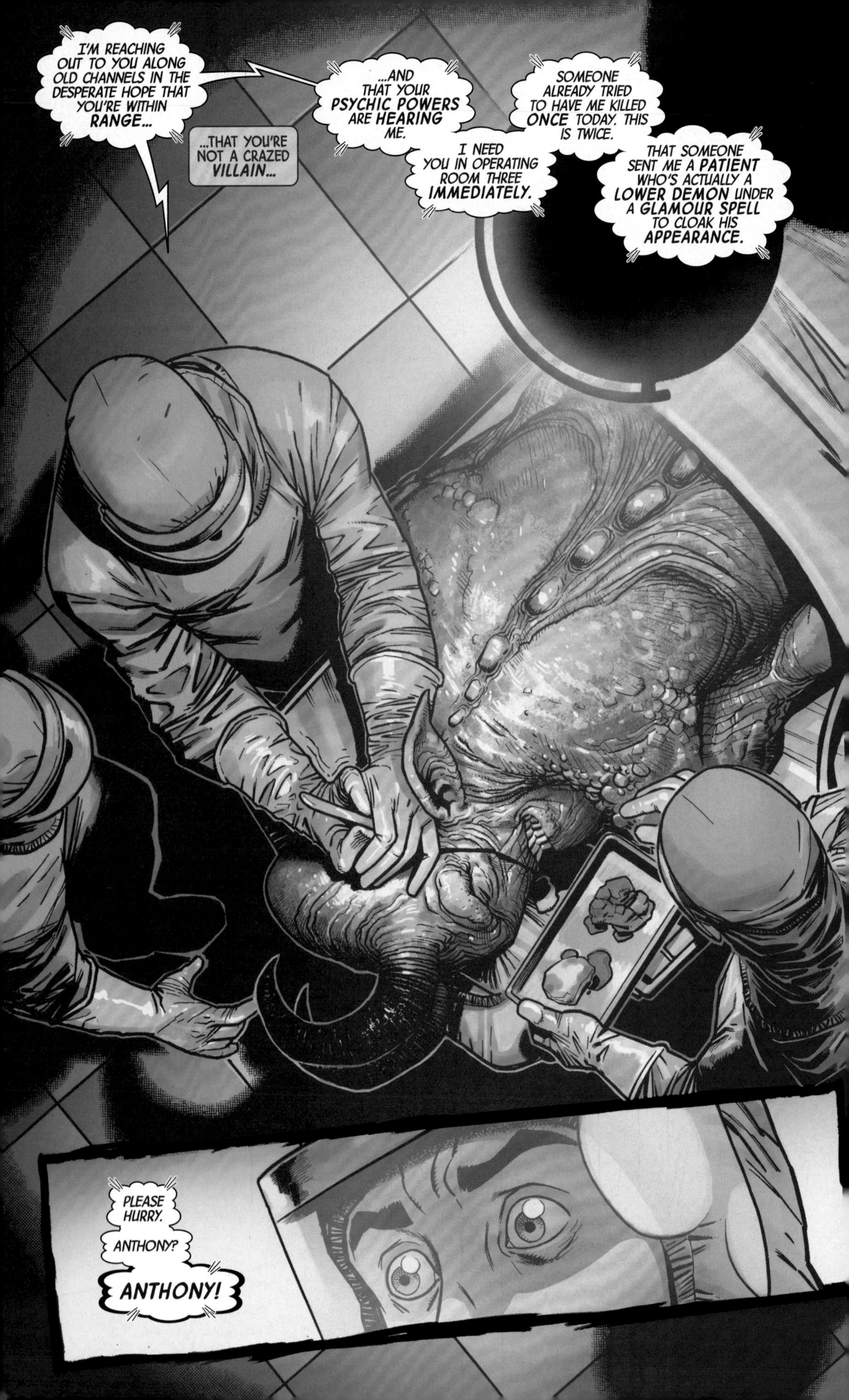
I'M REACHING OUT TO YOU ALONG OLD CHANNELS IN THE DESPERATE HOPE THAT YOU'RE WITHIN RANGE...
...THAT YOU'RE NOT A CRAZED VILLAIN...
...AND THAT YOUR PSYCHIC POWERS ARE HEARING ME.
I NEED YOU IN OPERATING ROOM THREE IMMEDIATELY.
SOMEONE ALREADY TRIED TO HAVE ME KILLED ONCE TODAY. THIS IS TWICE.
THAT SOMEONE SENT ME A PATIENT WHO'S ACTUALLY A LOWER DEMON UNDER A GLAMOUR SPELL TO CLOAK HIS APPEARANCE.
PLEASE HURRY.
ANTHONY?
ANTHONY!

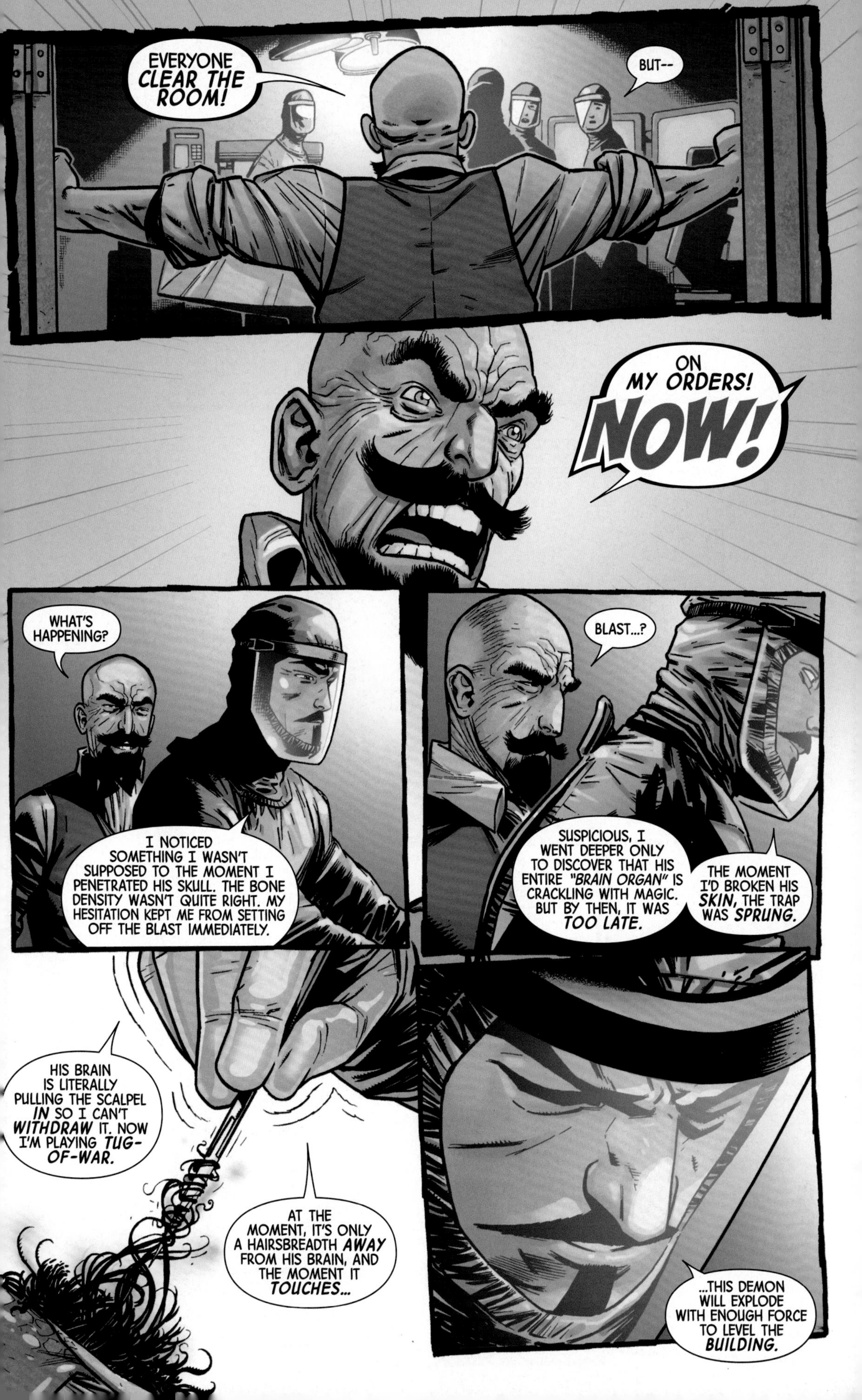

EVERYONE CLEAR THE ROOM!
BUT--
ON MY ORDERS! NOW!
WHAT'S HAPPENING?
I NOTICED SOMETHING I WASN'T SUPPOSED TO THE MOMENT I PENETRATED HIS SKULL. THE BONE DENSITY WASN'T QUITE RIGHT. MY HESITATION KEPT ME FROM SETTING OFF THE BLAST IMMEDIATELY.
BLAST...?
SUSPICIOUS, I WENT DEEPER ONLY TO DISCOVER THAT HIS ENTIRE "BRAIN ORGAN" IS CRACKLING WITH MAGIC. BUT BY THEN, IT WAS TOO LATE.
THE MOMENT I'D BROKEN HIS SKIN, THE TRAP WAS SPRUNG.
HIS BRAIN IS LITERALLY PULLING THE SCALPEL IN SO I CAN'T WITHDRAW IT. NOW I'M PLAYING TUG-OF-WAR.
AT THE MOMENT, IT'S ONLY A HAIRSBREADTH AWAY FROM HIS BRAIN, AND THE MOMENT IT TOUCHES...
...THIS DEMON WILL EXPLODE WITH ENOUGH FORCE TO LEVEL THE BUILDING.

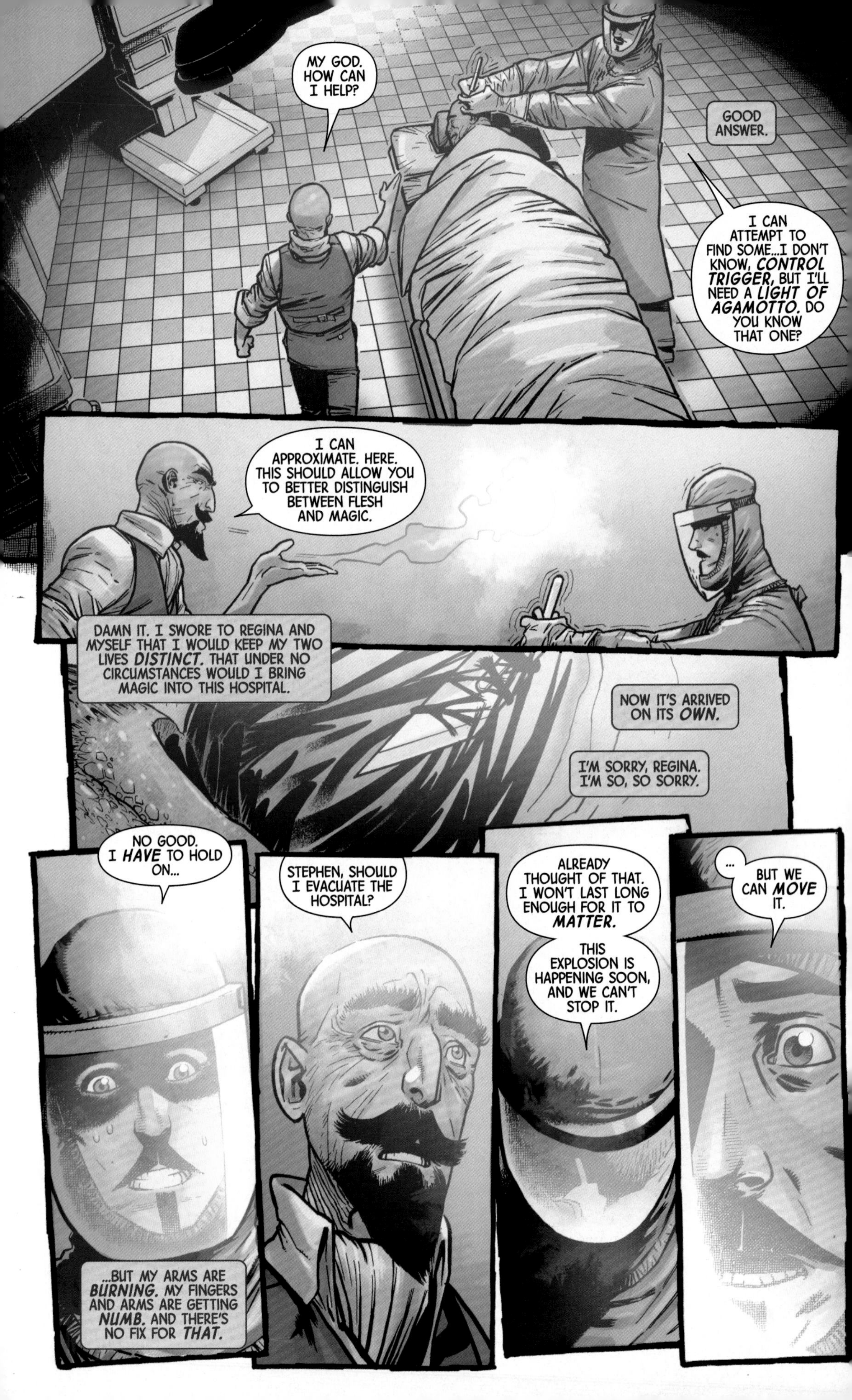
MY GOD. HOW CAN I HELP?
GOOD ANSWER.
I CAN ATTEMPT TO FIND SOME...I DON'T KNOW, CONTROL TRIGGER, BUT I'LL NEED A LIGHT OF AGAMOTTO. DO YOU KNOW THAT ONE?
I CAN APPROXIMATE. HERE. THIS SHOULD ALLOW YOU TO BETTER DISTINGUISH BETWEEN FLESH AND MAGIC.
DAMN IT. I SWORE TO REGINA AND MYSELF THAT I WOULD KEEP MY TWO LIVES DISTINCT. THAT UNDER NO CIRCUMSTANCES WOULD I BRING MAGIC INTO THIS HOSPITAL.
NOW IT'S ARRIVED ON ITS OWN.
I'M SORRY, REGINA. I'M SO, SO SORRY.
NO GOOD. I HAVE TO HOLD ON...
...BUT MY ARMS ARE BURNING. MY FINGERS AND ARMS ARE GETTING NUMB. AND THERE'S NO FIX FOR THAT.
STEPHEN, SHOULD I EVACUATE THE HOSPITAL?
ALREADY THOUGHT OF THAT. I WON'T LAST LONG ENOUGH FOR IT TO MATTER.
THIS EXPLOSION IS HAPPENING SOON, AND WE CAN'T STOP IT.
... BUT WE CAN MOVE IT.

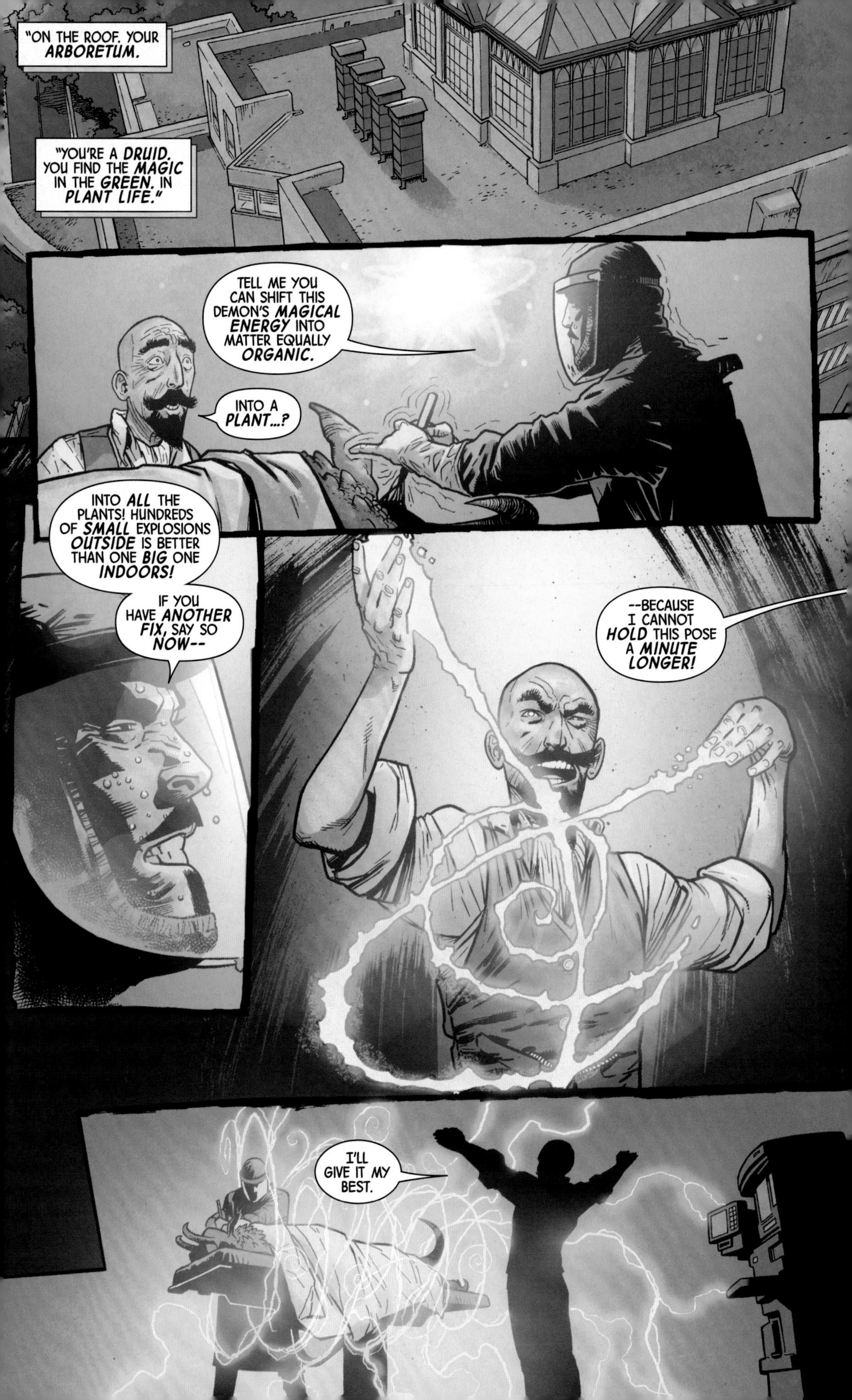
"ON THE ROOF. YOUR ARBORETUM.
"YOU'RE A DRUID. YOU FIND THE MAGIC IN THE GREEN. IN PLANT LIFE."
TELL ME YOU CAN SHIFT THIS DEMON'S MAGICAL ENERGY INTO MATTER EQUALLY ORGANIC.
INTO A PLANT...?
INTO ALL THE PLANTS! HUNDREDS OF SMALL EXPLOSIONS OUTSIDE IS BETTER THAN ONE BIG ONE INDOORS!
IF YOU HAVE ANOTHER FIX, SAY SO NOW--
--BECAUSE I CANNOT HOLD THIS POSE A MINUTE LONGER!
I'LL GIVE IT MY BEST.

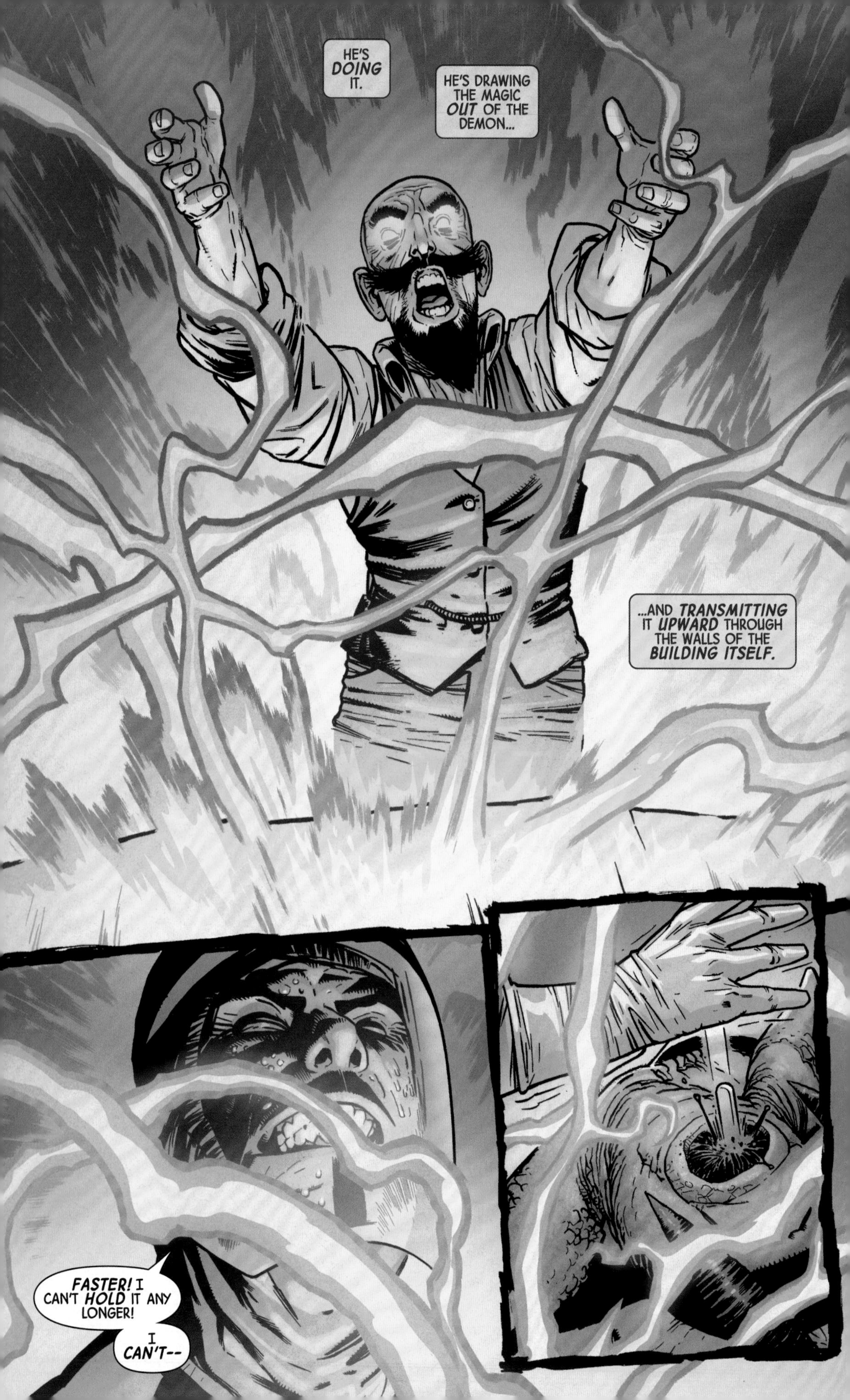

HE'S DOING IT.
HE'S DRAWING THE MAGIC OUT OF THE DEMON...
...AND TRANSMITTING IT UPWARD THROUGH THE WALLS OF THE BUILDING ITSELF.
FASTER! I CAN'T HOLD IT ANY LONGER!
I CAN'T--

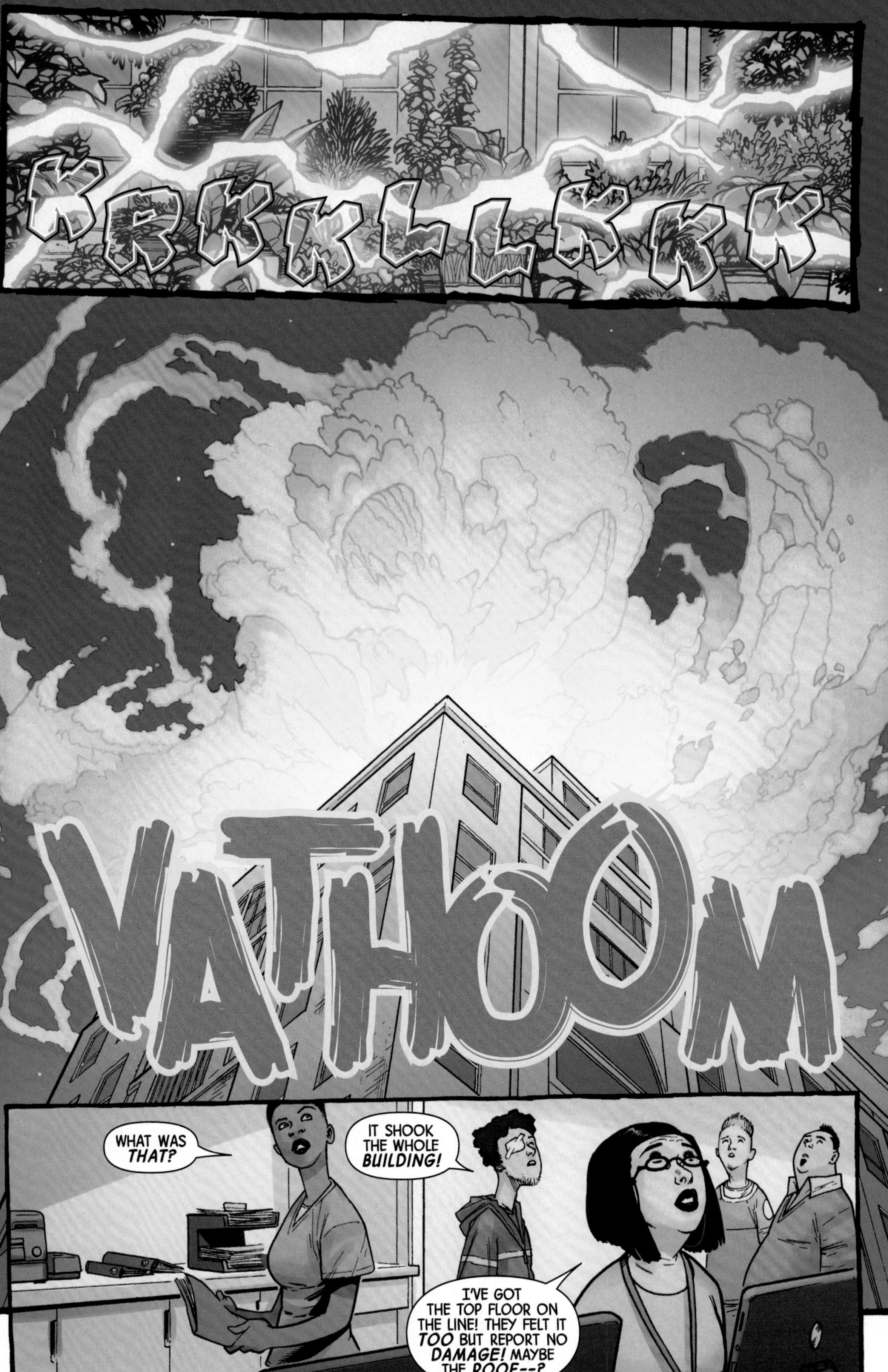
KRKKLLKKK
VATHOOM
WHAT WAS THAT?
IT SHOOK THE WHOLE BUILDING!
I'VE GOT THE TOP FLOOR ON THE LINE! THEY FELT IT TOO BUT REPORT NO DAMAGE! MAYBE THE ROOF--?

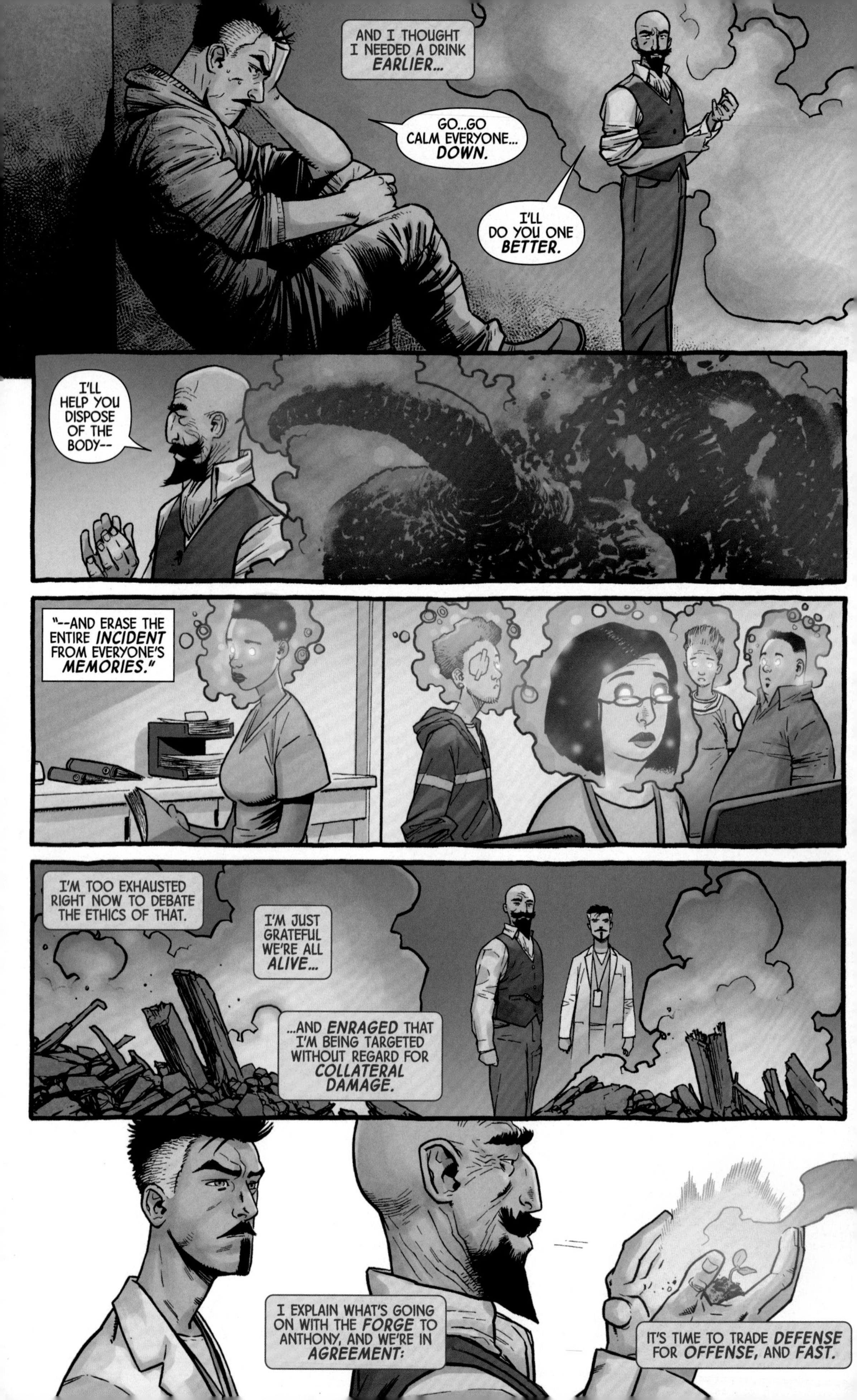
AND I THOUGHT I NEEDED A DRINK EARLIER...
GO...GO CALM EVERYONE... DOWN.
I'LL DO YOU ONE BETTER.
I'LL HELP YOU DISPOSE OF THE BODY--
"--AND ERASE THE ENTIRE INCIDENT FROM EVERYONE'S MEMORIES."
I'M TOO EXHAUSTED RIGHT NOW TO DEBATE THE ETHICS OF THAT.
I'M JUST GRATEFUL WE'RE ALL ALIVE...
...AND ENRAGED THAT I'M BEING TARGETED WITHOUT REGARD FOR COLLATERAL DAMAGE.
I EXPLAIN WHAT'S GOING ON WITH THE FORGE TO ANTHONY, AND WE'RE IN AGREEMENT:
IT'S TIME TO TRADE DEFENSE FOR OFFENSE, AND FAST.

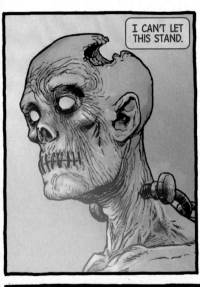

I CAN'T LET THIS STAND.

I HAVE TO FIND SOME WAY TO TAKE BACK WHAT'S BEEN STOLEN FROM ME...

...AND FIGURE OUT BY WHOM...

...BEFORE THEY FIGURE OUT HOW TO MASS-PRODUCE IT.

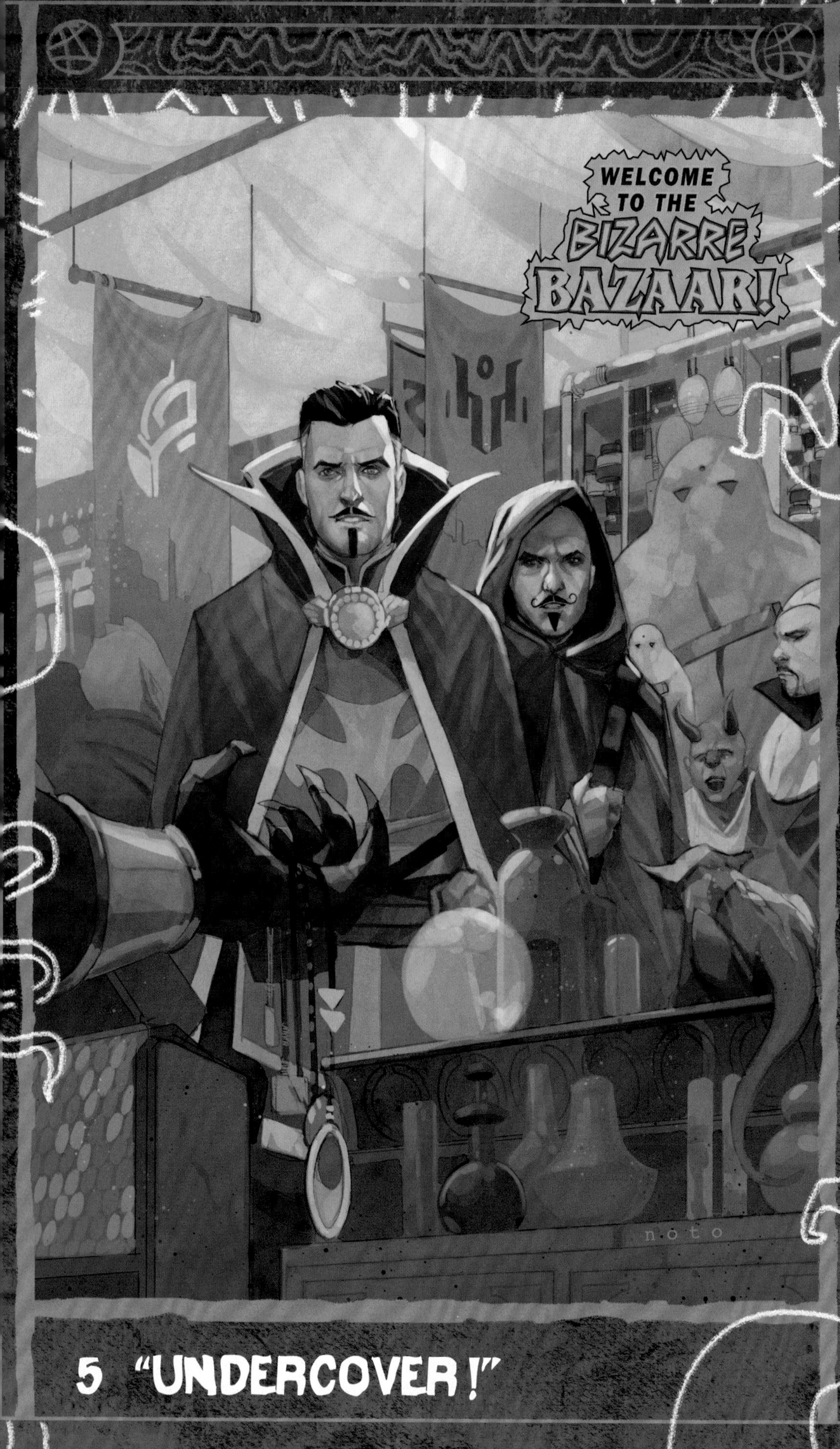
WELCOME TO THE BIZARRE BAZAAR!
noto
5 "UNDERCOVER!"

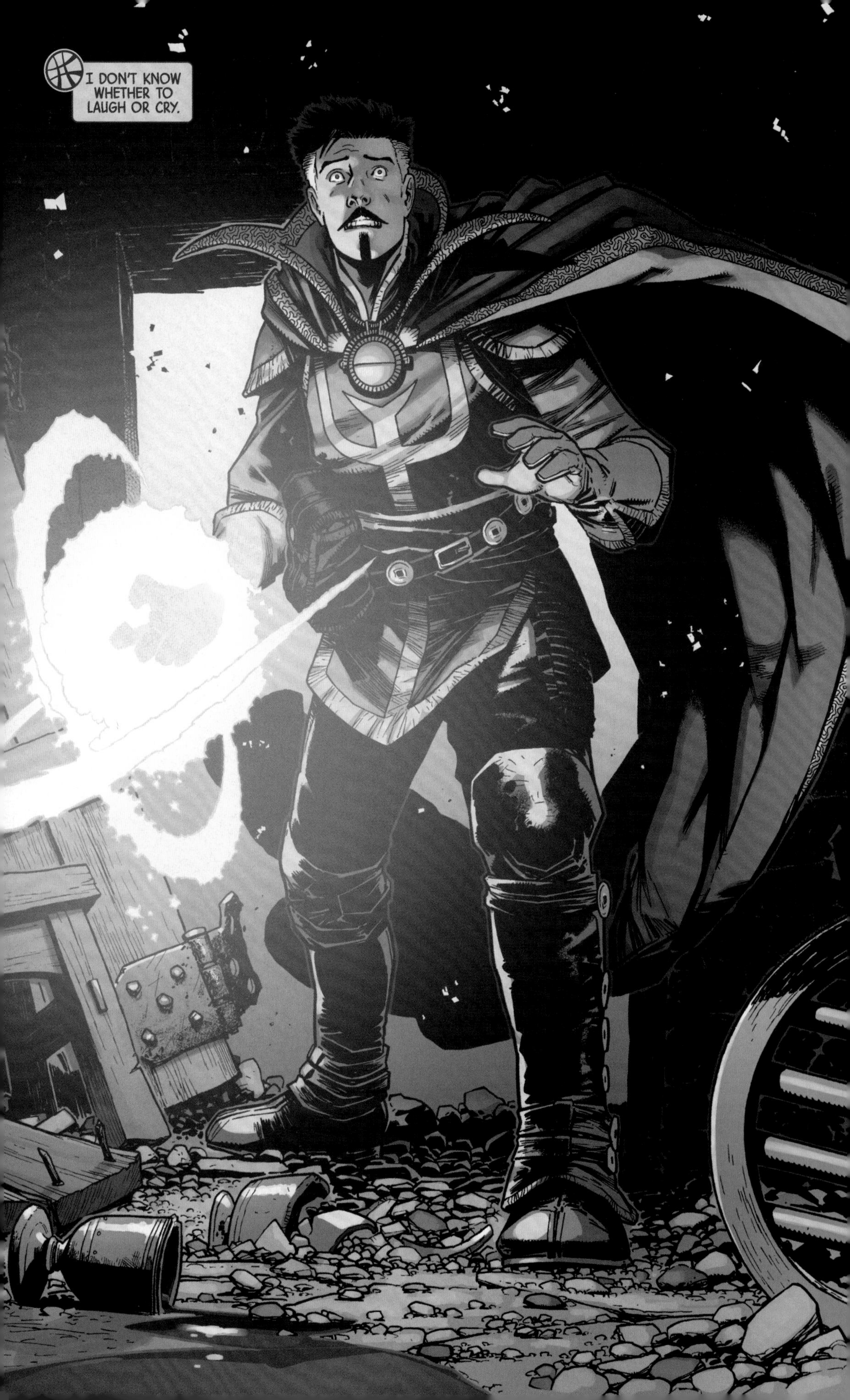
I DON'T KNOW WHETHER TO LAUGH OR CRY.

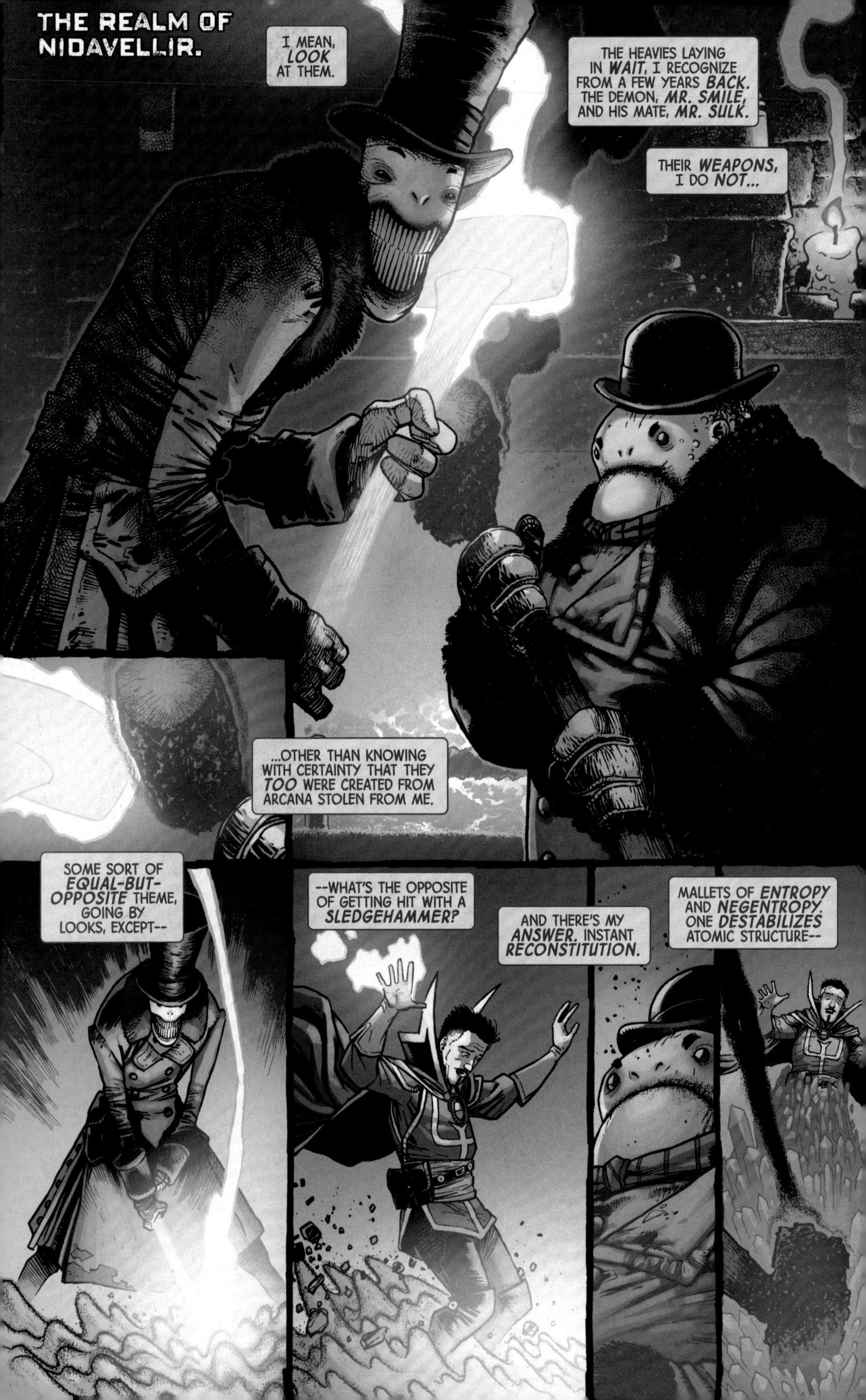
THE REALM OF NIDAVELLIR.
I MEAN, LOOK AT THEM.
THE HEAVIES LAYING IN WAIT, I RECOGNIZE FROM A FEW YEARS BACK. THE DEMON, MR. SMILE, AND HIS MATE, MR. SULK.
THEIR WEAPONS, I DO NOT...
...OTHER THAN KNOWING WITH CERTAINTY THAT THEY TOO WERE CREATED FROM ARCANA STOLEN FROM ME.
SOME SORT OF EQUAL-BUT-OPPOSITE THEME, GOING BY LOOKS, EXCEPT--
--WHAT'S THE OPPOSITE OF GETTING HIT WITH A SLEDGEHAMMER?
AND THERE'S MY ANSWER. INSTANT RECONSTITUTION.
MALLETS OF ENTROPY AND NEGENTROPY. ONE DESTABILIZES ATOMIC STRUCTURE--

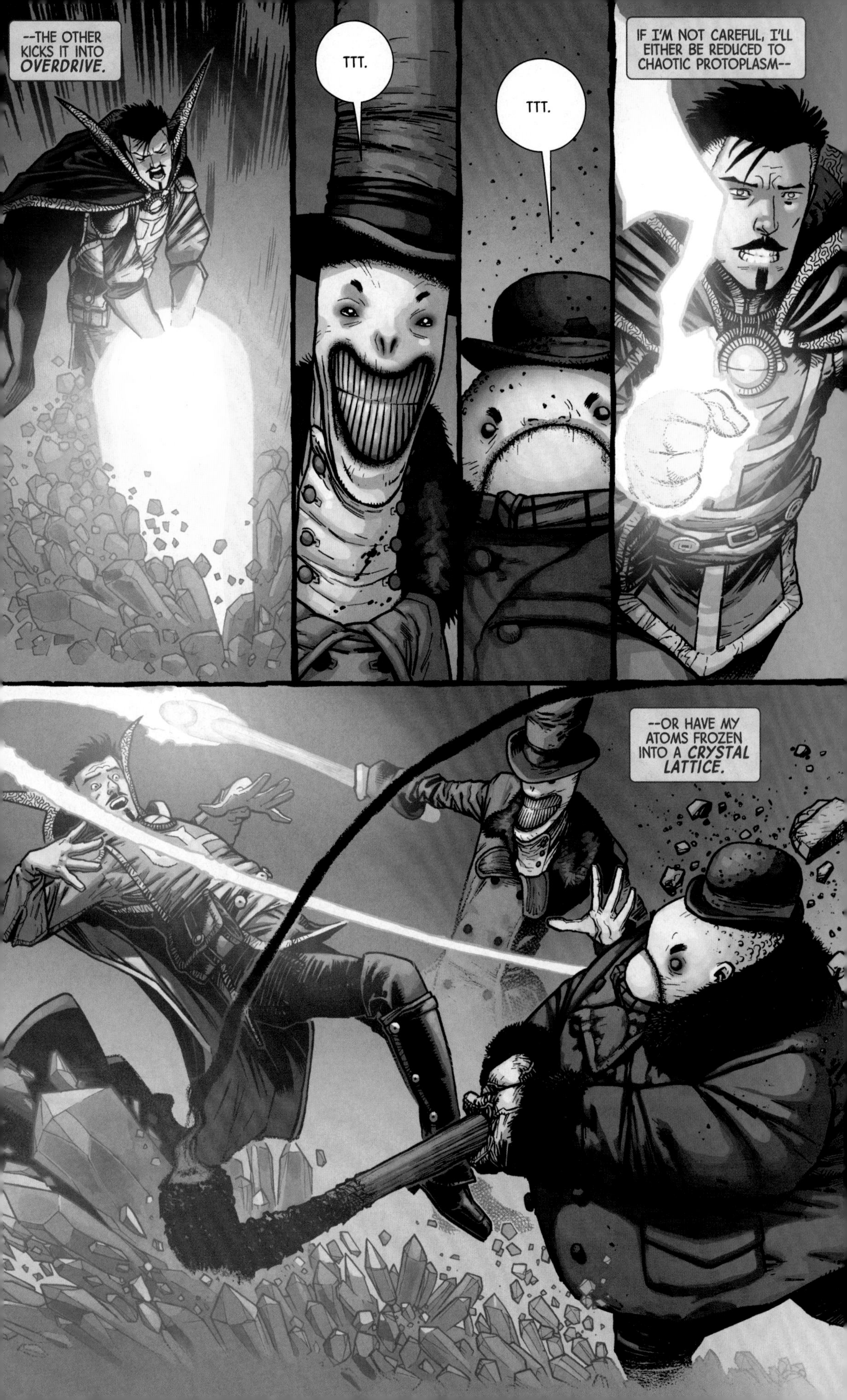
--THE OTHER KICKS IT INTO OVERDRIVE.
TTT.
TTT.
IF I'M NOT CAREFUL, I'LL EITHER BE REDUCED TO CHAOTIC PROTOPLASM--
--OR HAVE MY ATOMS FROZEN INTO A CRYSTAL LATTICE.

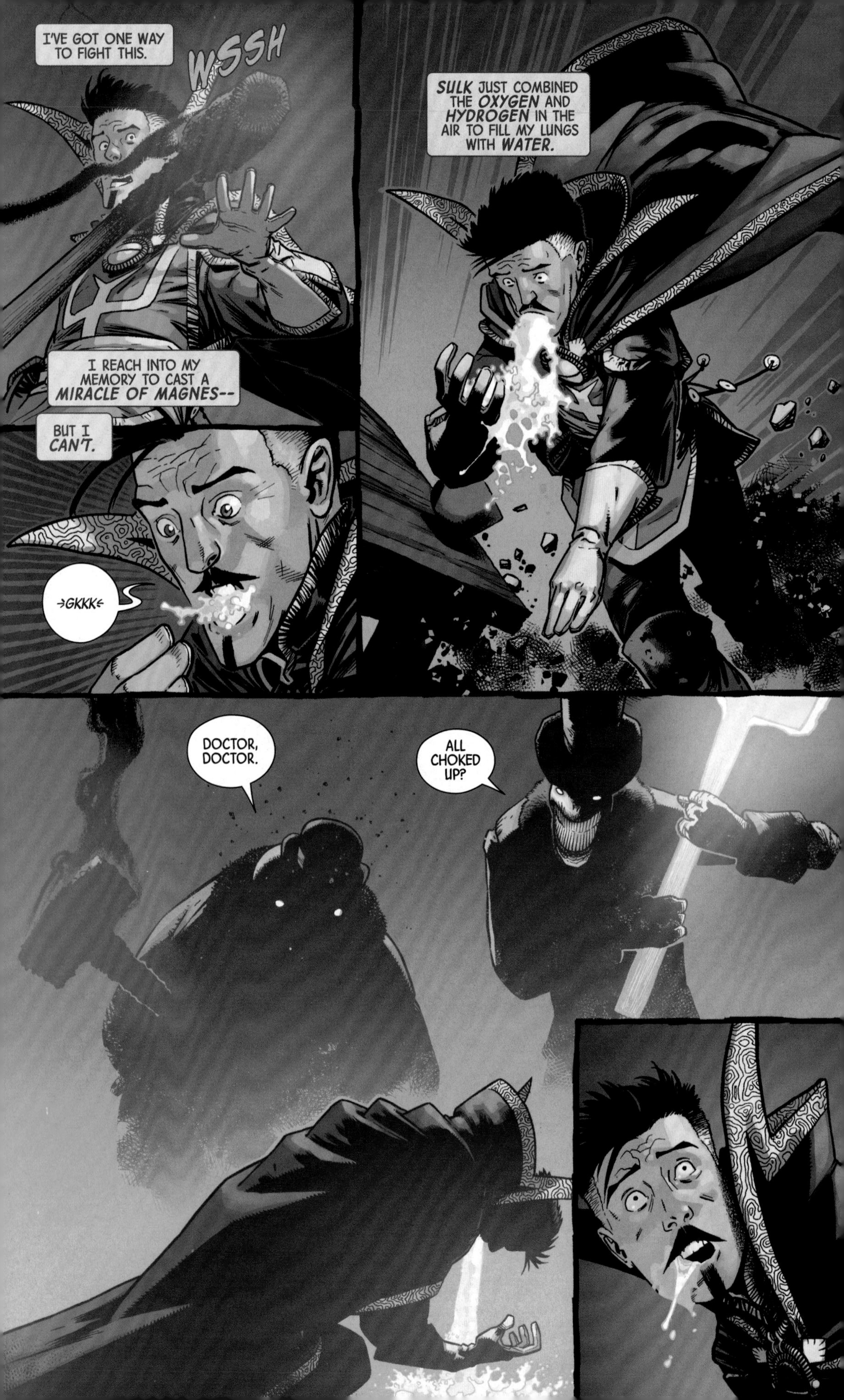
I'VE GOT ONE WAY TO FIGHT THIS.
WSSH
I REACH INTO MY MEMORY TO CAST A MIRACLE OF MAGNES--
BUT I CAN'T.
GKKK
SULK JUST COMBINED THE OXYGEN AND HYDROGEN IN THE AIR TO FILL MY LUNGS WITH WATER.
DOCTOR, DOCTOR.
ALL CHOKED UP?

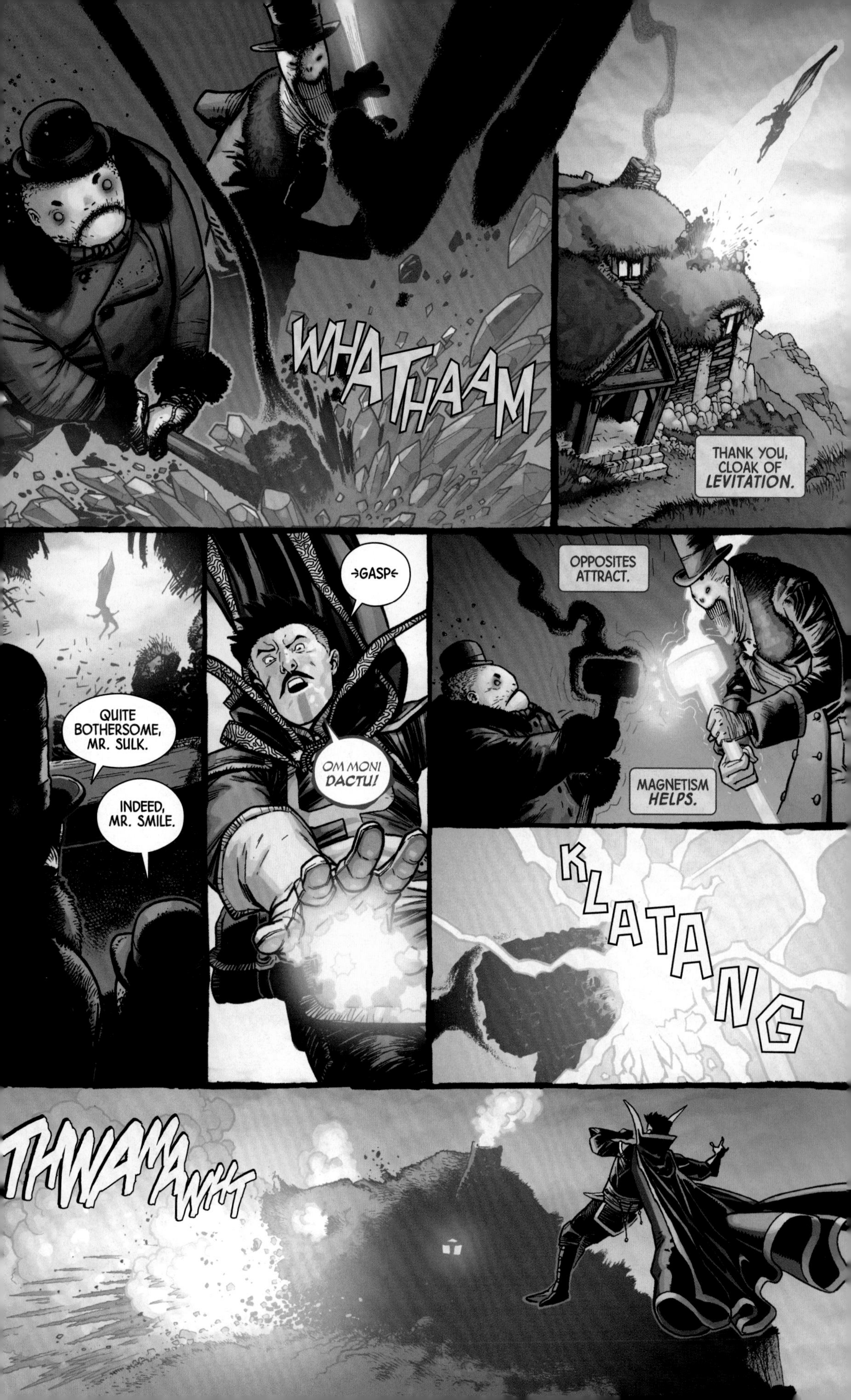
WHATHAAM
THANK YOU, CLOAK OF LEVITATION.
QUITE BOTHERSOME, MR. SULK.
INDEED, MR. SMILE.
GASP
OM MONI DACTU!
OPPOSITES ATTRACT.
MAGNETISM HELPS.
KLATANG
THWAMAWHT

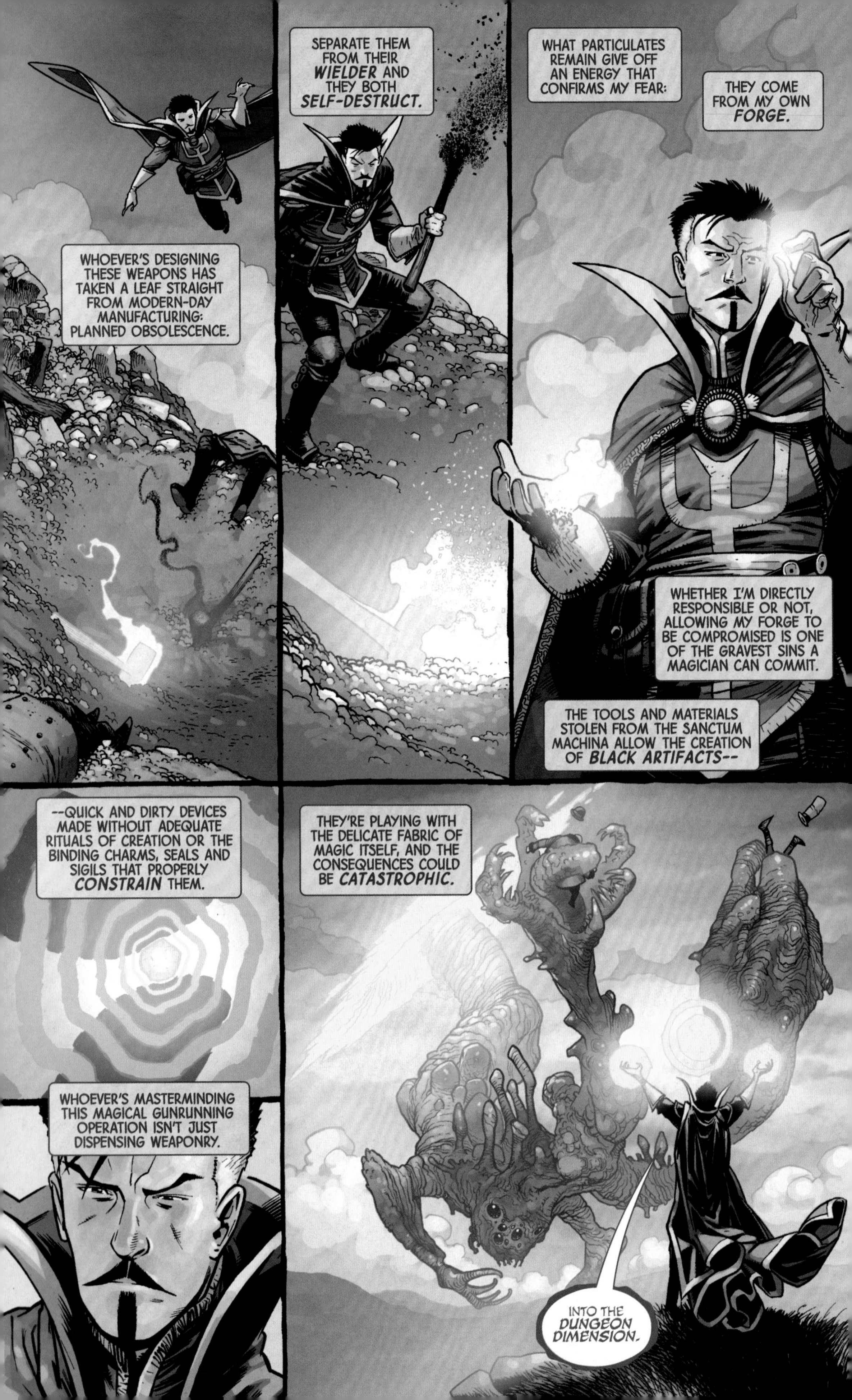
WHOEVER'S DESIGNING THESE WEAPONS HAS TAKEN A LEAF STRAIGHT FROM MODERN-DAY MANUFACTURING: PLANNED OBSOLESCENCE.
SEPARATE THEM FROM THEIR WIELDER AND THEY BOTH SELF-DESTRUCT.
WHAT PARTICULATES REMAIN GIVE OFF AN ENERGY THAT CONFIRMS MY FEAR:
THEY COME FROM MY OWN FORGE.
WHETHER I'M DIRECTLY RESPONSIBLE OR NOT, ALLOWING MY FORGE TO BE COMPROMISED IS ONE OF THE GRAVEST SINS A MAGICIAN CAN COMMIT.
THE TOOLS AND MATERIALS STOLEN FROM THE SANCTUM MACHINA ALLOW THE CREATION OF BLACK ARTIFACTS--
--QUICK AND DIRTY DEVICES MADE WITHOUT ADEQUATE RITUALS OF CREATION OR THE BINDING CHARMS, SEALS AND SIGILS THAT PROPERLY CONSTRAIN THEM.
WHOEVER'S MASTERMINDING THIS MAGICAL GUNRUNNING OPERATION ISN'T JUST DISPENSING WEAPONRY.
THEY'RE PLAYING WITH THE DELICATE FABRIC OF MAGIC ITSELF, AND THE CONSEQUENCES COULD BE CATASTROPHIC.
INTO THE DUNGEON DIMENSION.

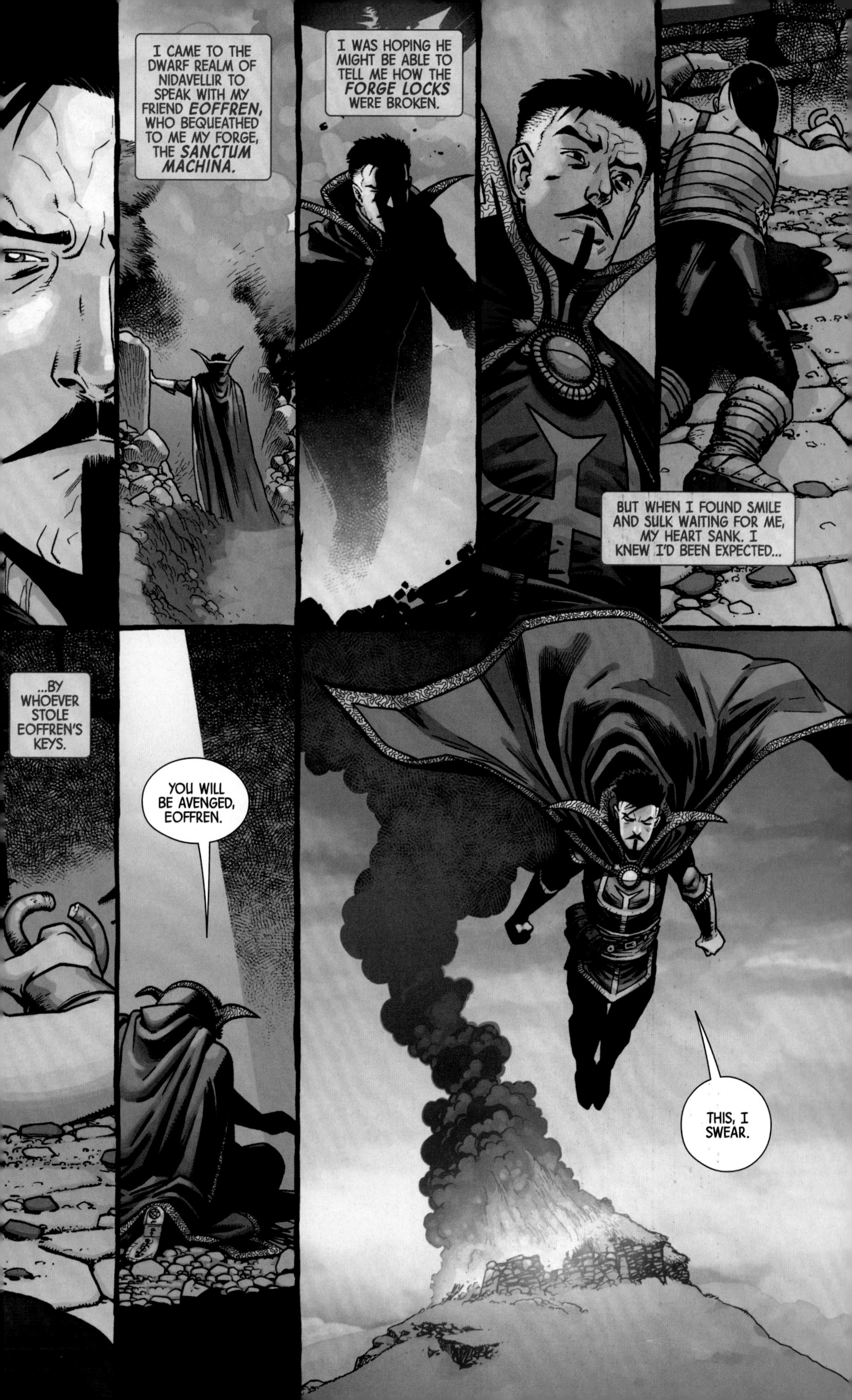
I CAME TO THE DWARF REALM OF NIDAVELLIR TO SPEAK WITH MY FRIEND EOFFREN, WHO BEQUEATHED TO ME MY FORGE, THE SANCTUM MACHINA.
I WAS HOPING HE MIGHT BE ABLE TO TELL ME HOW THE FORGE LOCKS WERE BROKEN.
BUT WHEN I FOUND SMILE AND SULK WAITING FOR ME, MY HEART SANK. I KNEW I'D BEEN EXPECTED...
...BY WHOEVER STOLE EOFFREN'S KEYS.
YOU WILL BE AVENGED, EOFFREN.
THIS, I SWEAR.

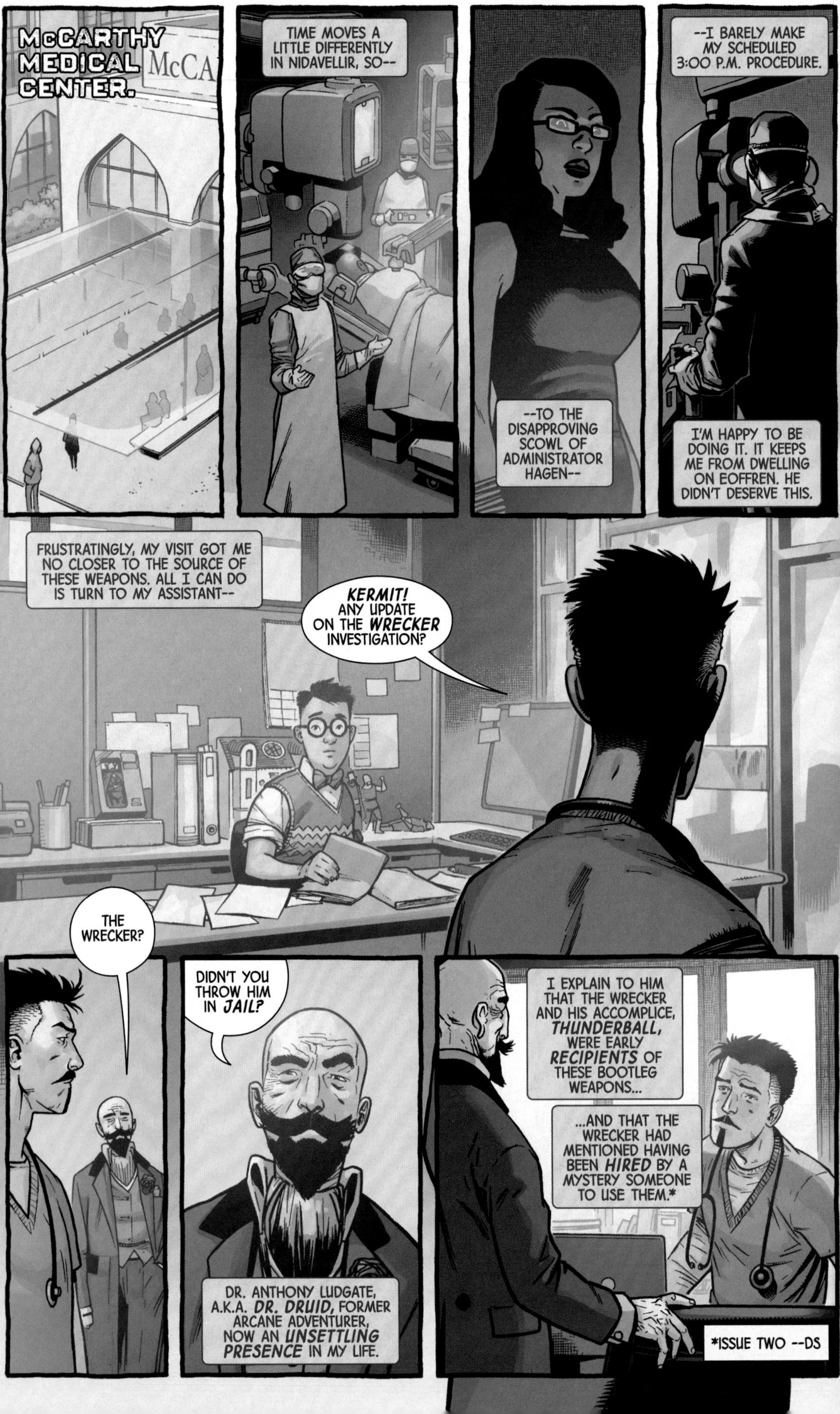
McCARTHY MEDICAL CENTER.
TIME MOVES A LITTLE DIFFERENTLY IN NIDAVELLIR, SO--
--I BARELY MAKE MY SCHEDULED 3:00 P.M. PROCEDURE.
--TO THE DISAPPROVING SCOWL OF ADMINISTRATOR HAGEN--
I'M HAPPY TO BE DOING IT. IT KEEPS ME FROM DWELLING ON EOFFREN. HE DIDN'T DESERVE THIS.
FRUSTRATINGLY, MY VISIT GOT ME NO CLOSER TO THE SOURCE OF THESE WEAPONS. ALL I CAN DO IS TURN TO MY ASSISTANT--
KERMIT! ANY UPDATE ON THE WRECKER INVESTIGATION?
THE WRECKER?
DIDN'T YOU THROW HIM IN JAIL?
DR. ANTHONY LUDGATE, A.K.A. DR. DRUID, FORMER ARCANE ADVENTURER, NOW AN UNSETTLING PRESENCE IN MY LIFE.
I EXPLAIN TO HIM THAT THE WRECKER AND HIS ACCOMPLICE, THUNDERBALL, WERE EARLY RECIPIENTS OF THESE BOOTLEG WEAPONS...
...AND THAT THE WRECKER HAD MENTIONED HAVING BEEN HIRED BY A MYSTERY SOMEONE TO USE THEM.*
*ISSUE TWO --DS

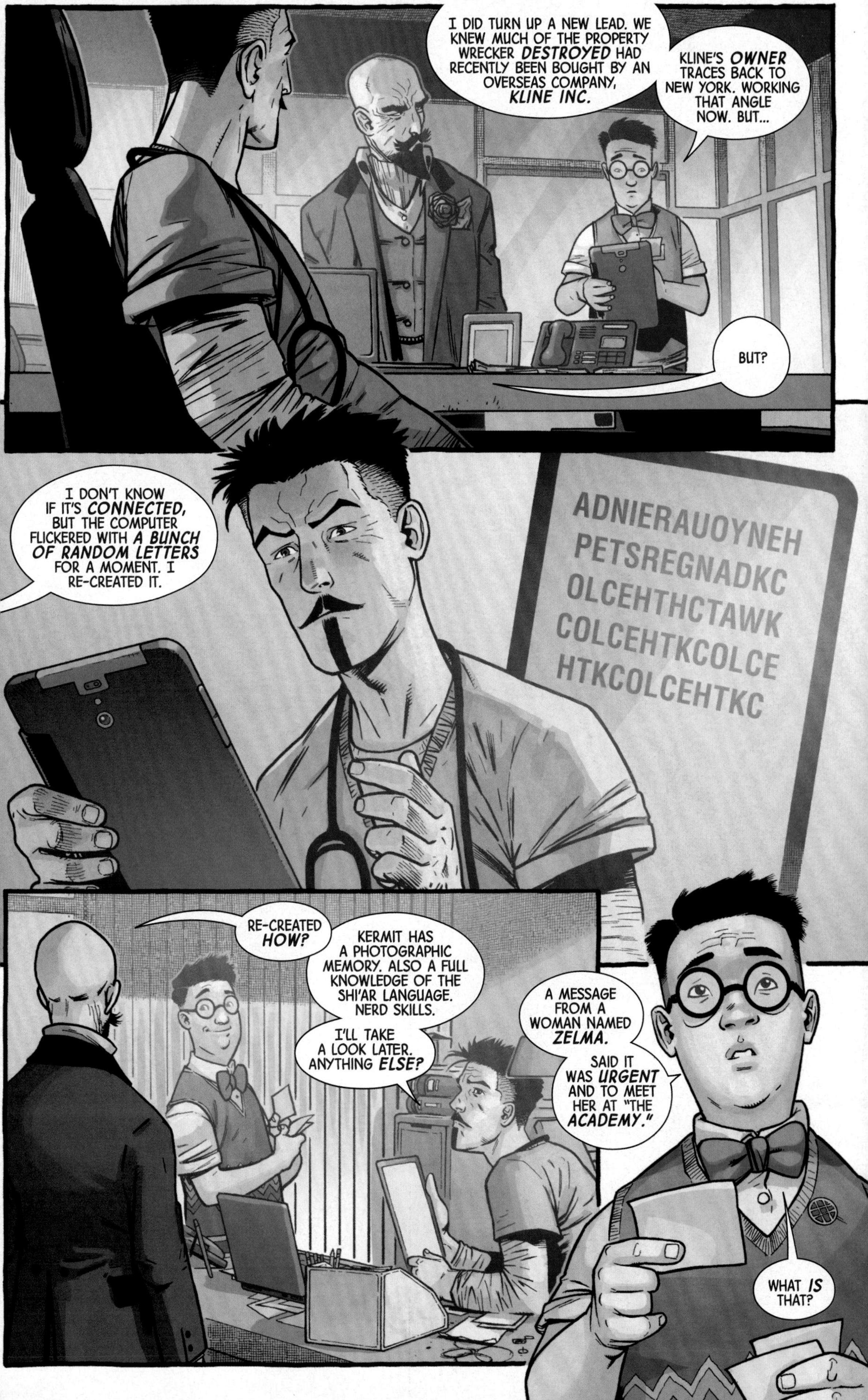
I DID TURN UP A NEW LEAD. WE KNEW MUCH OF THE PROPERTY WRECKER DESTROYED HAD RECENTLY BEEN BOUGHT BY AN OVERSEAS COMPANY, KLINE INC.
KLINE'S OWNER TRACES BACK TO NEW YORK. WORKING THAT ANGLE NOW. BUT...
BUT?
I DON'T KNOW IF IT'S CONNECTED, BUT THE COMPUTER FLICKERED WITH A BUNCH OF RANDOM LETTERS FOR A MOMENT. I RE-CREATED IT.
ADNIERAUOYNEH
PETSREGNADKC
OLCEHTHCTAWK
COLCEHTKCOLCE
HTKCOLCEHTKC
RE-CREATED HOW?
KERMIT HAS A PHOTOGRAPHIC MEMORY. ALSO A FULL KNOWLEDGE OF THE SHI'AR LANGUAGE. NERD SKILLS.
I'LL TAKE A LOOK LATER. ANYTHING ELSE?
A MESSAGE FROM A WOMAN NAMED ZELMA.
SAID IT WAS URGENT AND TO MEET HER AT "THE ACADEMY."
WHAT IS THAT?

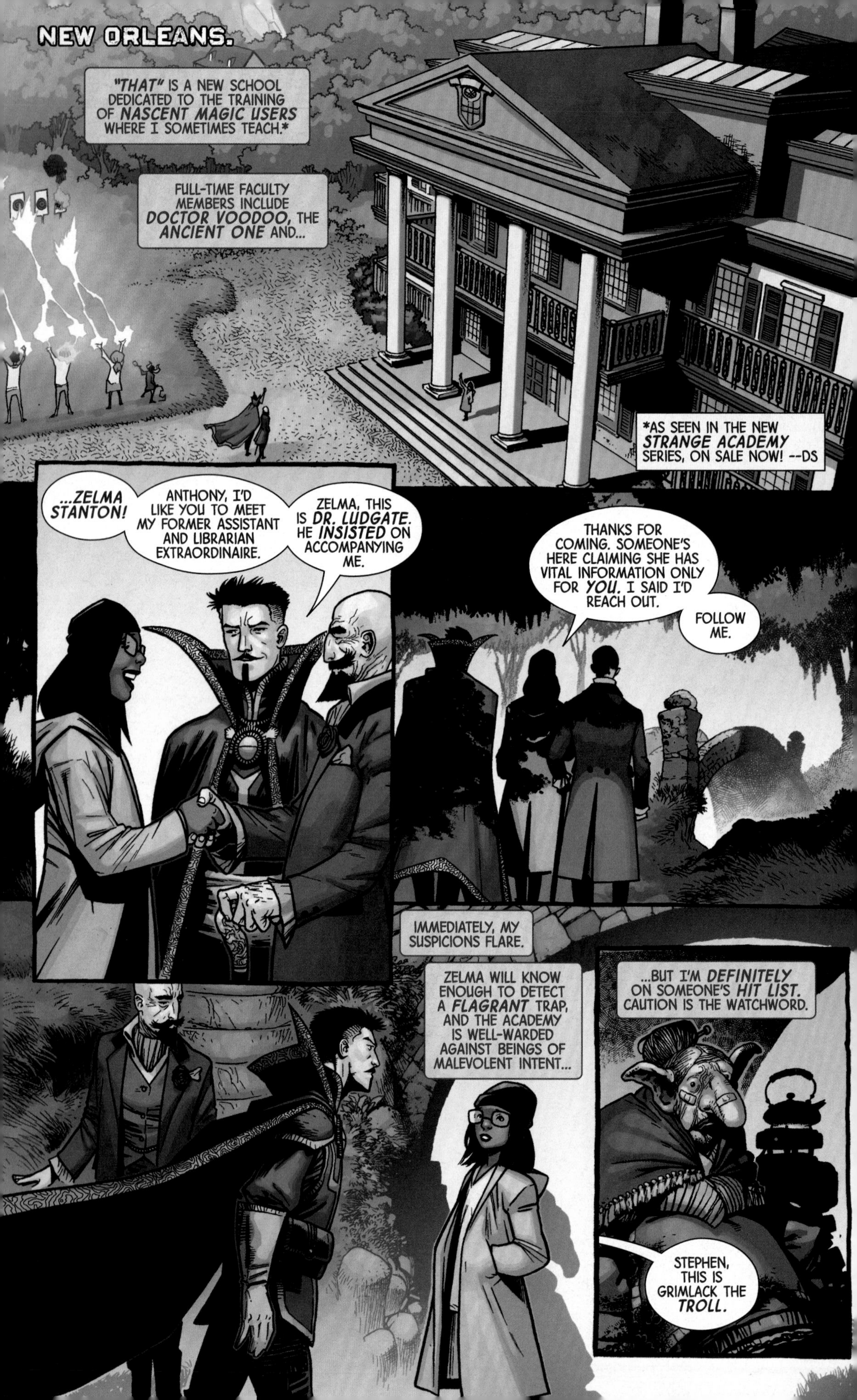
NEW ORLEANS.
"THAT" IS A NEW SCHOOL DEDICATED TO THE TRAINING OF NASCENT MAGIC USERS WHERE I SOMETIMES TEACH.*
FULL-TIME FACULTY MEMBERS INCLUDE DOCTOR VOODOO, THE ANCIENT ONE AND...
*AS SEEN IN THE NEW STRANGE ACADEMY SERIES, ON SALE NOW! --DS
...ZELMA STANTON!
ANTHONY, I'D LIKE YOU TO MEET MY FORMER ASSISTANT AND LIBRARIAN EXTRAORDINAIRE.
ZELMA, THIS IS DR. LUDGATE. HE INSISTED ON ACCOMPANYING ME.
THANKS FOR COMING. SOMEONE'S HERE CLAIMING SHE HAS VITAL INFORMATION ONLY FOR YOU. I SAID I'D REACH OUT.
FOLLOW ME.
IMMEDIATELY, MY SUSPICIONS FLARE.
ZELMA WILL KNOW ENOUGH TO DETECT A FLAGRANT TRAP, AND THE ACADEMY IS WELL-WARDED AGAINST BEINGS OF MALEVOLENT INTENT...
...BUT I'M DEFINITELY ON SOMEONE'S HIT LIST. CAUTION IS THE WATCHWORD.
STEPHEN, THIS IS GRIMLACK THE TROLL.

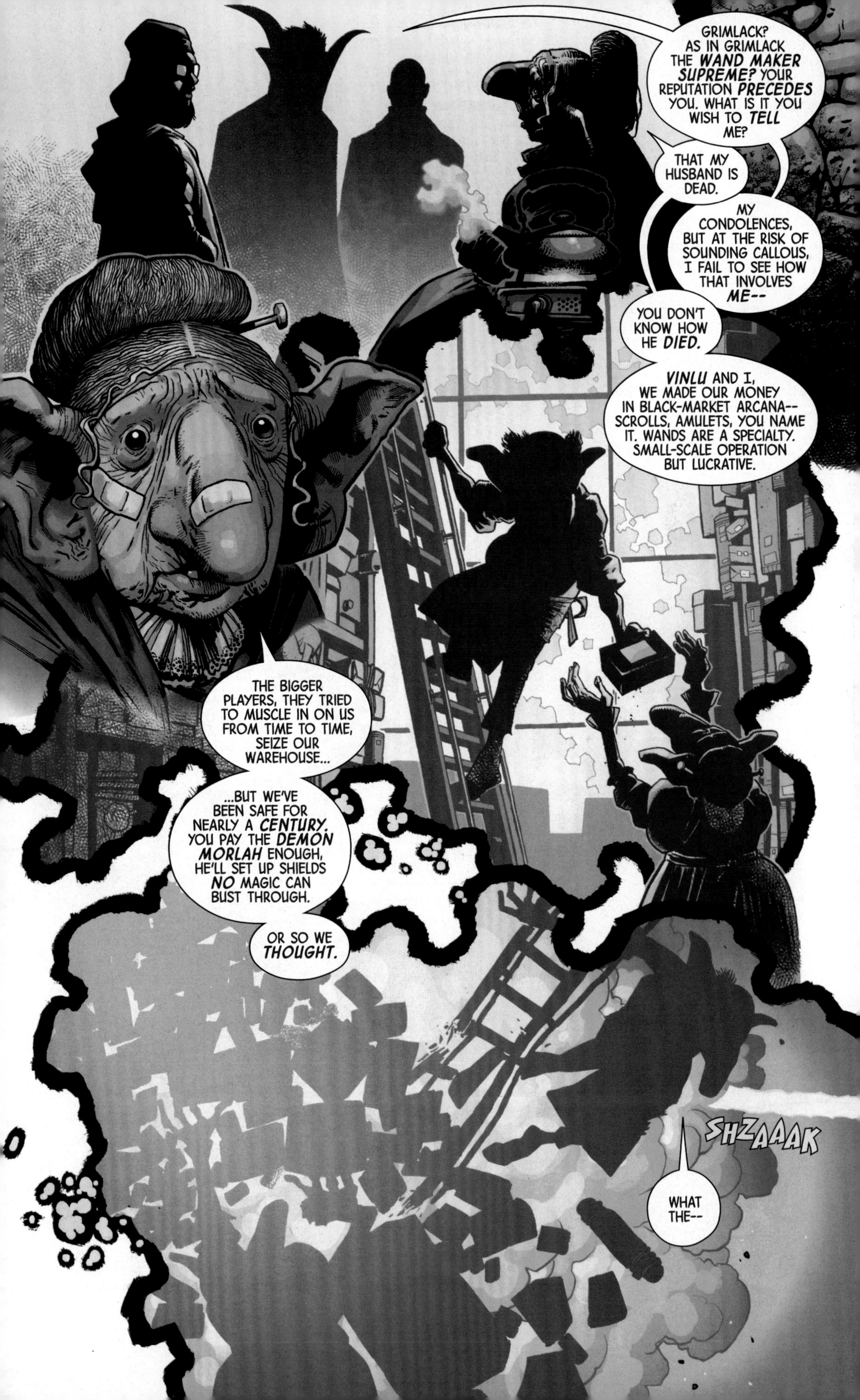
GRIMLACK? AS IN GRIMLACK THE WAND MAKER SUPREME? YOUR REPUTATION PRECEDES YOU. WHAT IS IT YOU WISH TO TELL ME?
THAT MY HUSBAND IS DEAD.
MY CONDOLENCES, BUT AT THE RISK OF SOUNDING CALLOUS, I FAIL TO SEE HOW THAT INVOLVES ME--
YOU DON'T KNOW HOW HE DIED.
VINLU AND I, WE MADE OUR MONEY IN BLACK-MARKET ARCANA-- SCROLLS, AMULETS, YOU NAME IT. WANDS ARE A SPECIALTY. SMALL-SCALE OPERATION BUT LUCRATIVE.
THE BIGGER PLAYERS, THEY TRIED TO MUSCLE IN ON US FROM TIME TO TIME, SEIZE OUR WAREHOUSE...
...BUT WE'VE BEEN SAFE FOR NEARLY A CENTURY. YOU PAY THE DEMON MORLAH ENOUGH, HE'LL SET UP SHIELDS NO MAGIC CAN BUST THROUGH.
OR SO WE THOUGHT.
SHZAAAK
WHAT THE--

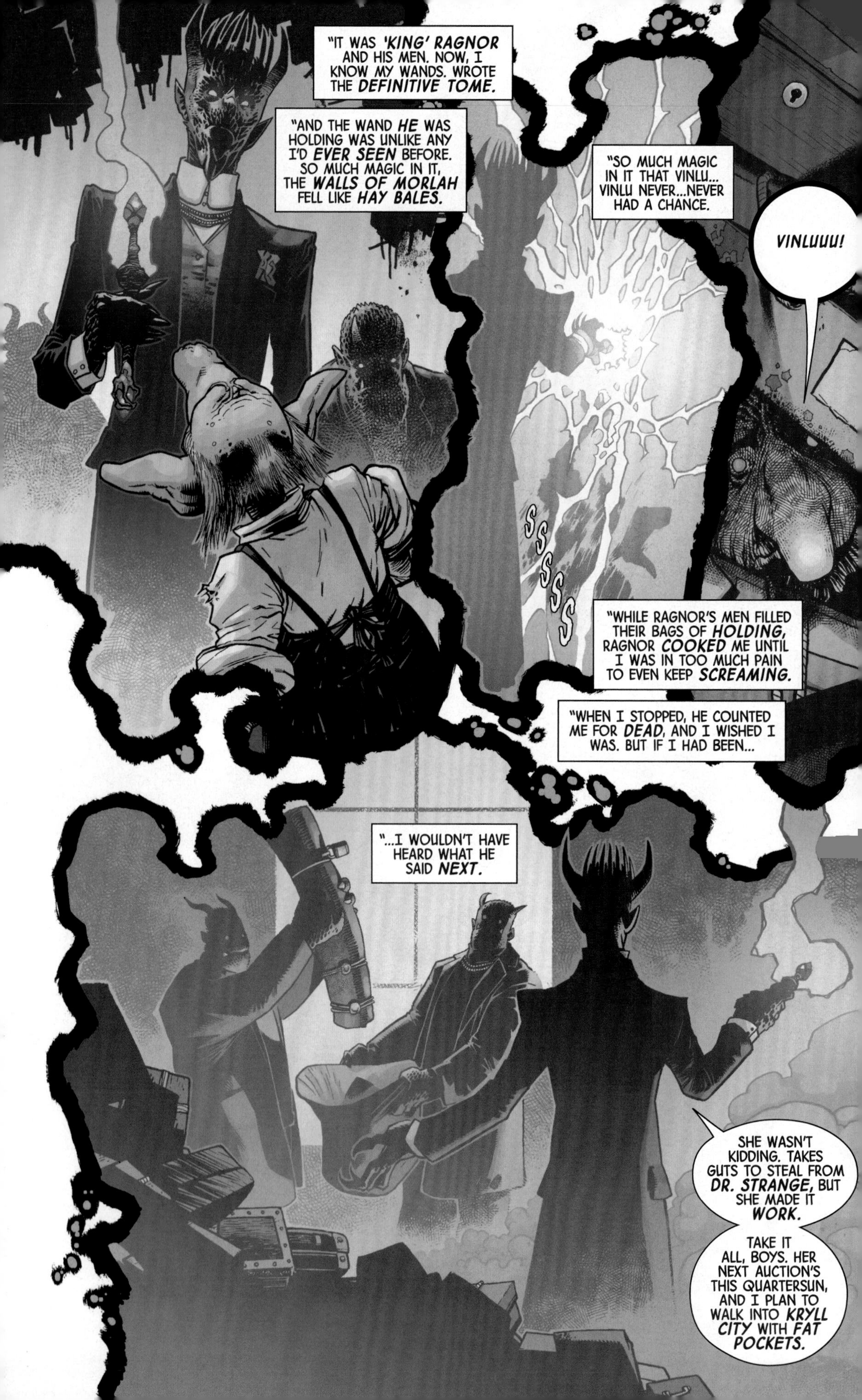
"IT WAS 'KING' RAGNOR AND HIS MEN. NOW, I KNOW MY WANDS. WROTE THE DEFINITIVE TOME.
"AND THE WAND HE WAS HOLDING WAS UNLIKE ANY I'D EVER SEEN BEFORE. SO MUCH MAGIC IN IT, THE WALLS OF MORLAH FELL LIKE HAY BALES.
"SO MUCH MAGIC IN IT THAT VINLU... VINLU NEVER...NEVER HAD A CHANCE.
VINLUUU!
SSSSS
"WHILE RAGNOR'S MEN FILLED THEIR BAGS OF HOLDING, RAGNOR COOKED ME UNTIL I WAS IN TOO MUCH PAIN TO EVEN KEEP SCREAMING.
"WHEN I STOPPED, HE COUNTED ME FOR DEAD, AND I WISHED I WAS. BUT IF I HAD BEEN...
"...I WOULDN'T HAVE HEARD WHAT HE SAID NEXT.
SHE WASN'T KIDDING. TAKES GUTS TO STEAL FROM DR. STRANGE, BUT SHE MADE IT WORK.
TAKE IT ALL, BOYS. HER NEXT AUCTION'S THIS QUARTERSUN, AND I PLAN TO WALK INTO KRYLL CITY WITH FAT POCKETS.

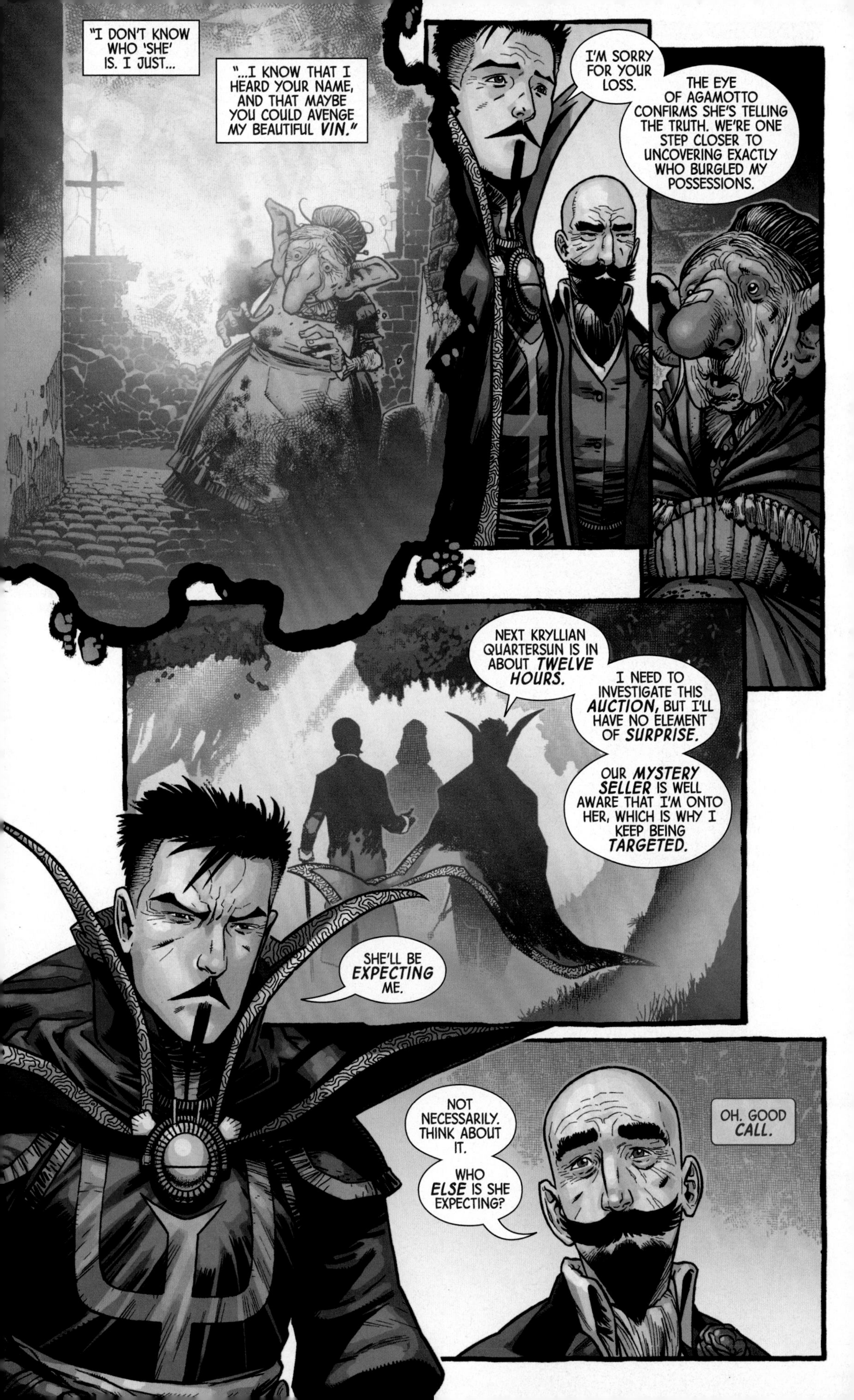
"I DON'T KNOW WHO 'SHE' IS. I JUST...
"...I KNOW THAT I HEARD YOUR NAME, AND THAT MAYBE YOU COULD AVENGE MY BEAUTIFUL VIN."
I'M SORRY FOR YOUR LOSS.
THE EYE OF AGAMOTTO CONFIRMS SHE'S TELLING THE TRUTH. WE'RE ONE STEP CLOSER TO UNCOVERING EXACTLY WHO BURGLED MY POSSESSIONS.
NEXT KRYLLIAN QUARTERSUN IS IN ABOUT TWELVE HOURS.
I NEED TO INVESTIGATE THIS AUCTION, BUT I'LL HAVE NO ELEMENT OF SURPRISE.
OUR MYSTERY SELLER IS WELL AWARE THAT I'M ONTO HER, WHICH IS WHY I KEEP BEING TARGETED.
SHE'LL BE EXPECTING ME.
NOT NECESSARILY. THINK ABOUT IT.
WHO ELSE IS SHE EXPECTING?
OH. GOOD CALL.

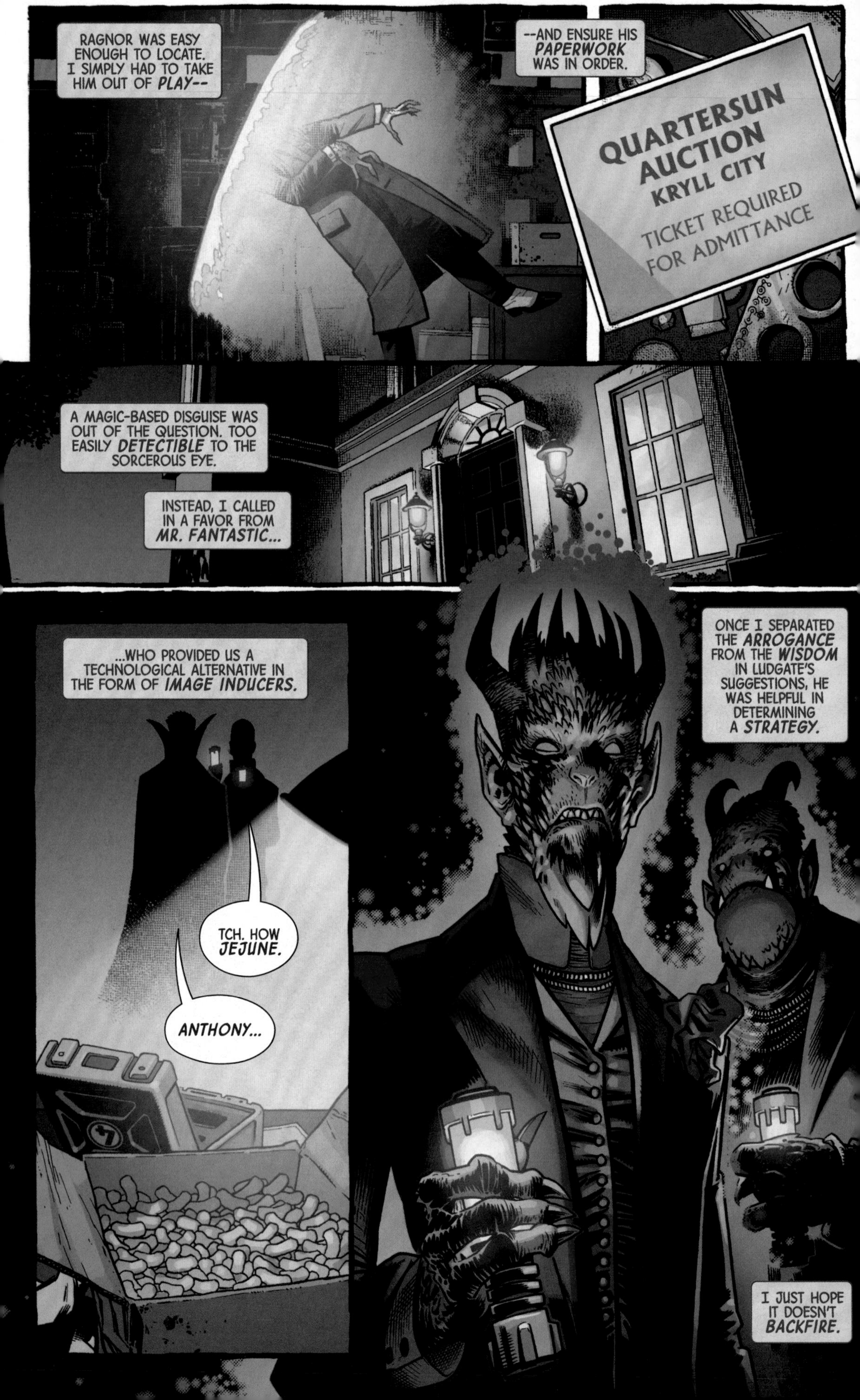
RAGNOR WAS EASY ENOUGH TO LOCATE. I SIMPLY HAD TO TAKE HIM OUT OF PLAY--
--AND ENSURE HIS PAPERWORK WAS IN ORDER.
QUARTERSUN AUCTION
KRYLL CITY
TICKET REQUIRED FOR ADMITTANCE
A MAGIC-BASED DISGUISE WAS OUT OF THE QUESTION. TOO EASILY DETECTIBLE TO THE SORCEROUS EYE.
INSTEAD, I CALLED IN A FAVOR FROM MR. FANTASTIC...
...WHO PROVIDED US A TECHNOLOGICAL ALTERNATIVE IN THE FORM OF IMAGE INDUCERS.
TCH. HOW JEJUNE.
ANTHONY...
ONCE I SEPARATED THE ARROGANCE FROM THE WISDOM IN LUDGATE'S SUGGESTIONS, HE WAS HELPFUL IN DETERMINING A STRATEGY.
I JUST HOPE IT DOESN'T BACKFIRE.

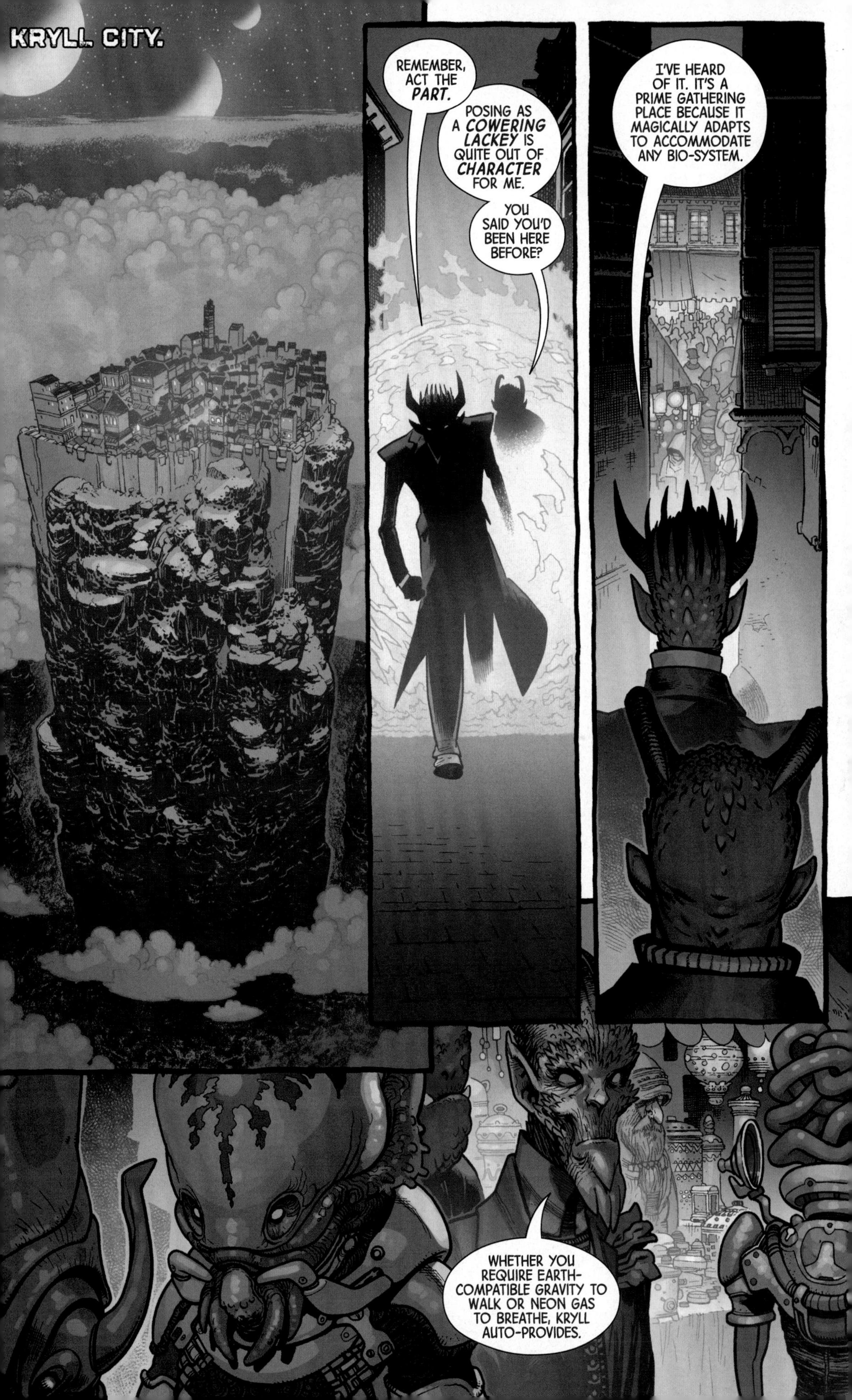
KRYLL CITY.
REMEMBER, ACT THE PART.
POSING AS A COWERING LACKEY IS QUITE OUT OF CHARACTER FOR ME.
YOU SAID YOU'D BEEN HERE BEFORE?
I'VE HEARD OF IT. IT'S A PRIME GATHERING PLACE BECAUSE IT MAGICALLY ADAPTS TO ACCOMMODATE ANY BIO-SYSTEM.
WHETHER YOU REQUIRE EARTH-COMPATIBLE GRAVITY TO WALK OR NEON GAS TO BREATHE, KRYLL AUTO-PROVIDES.

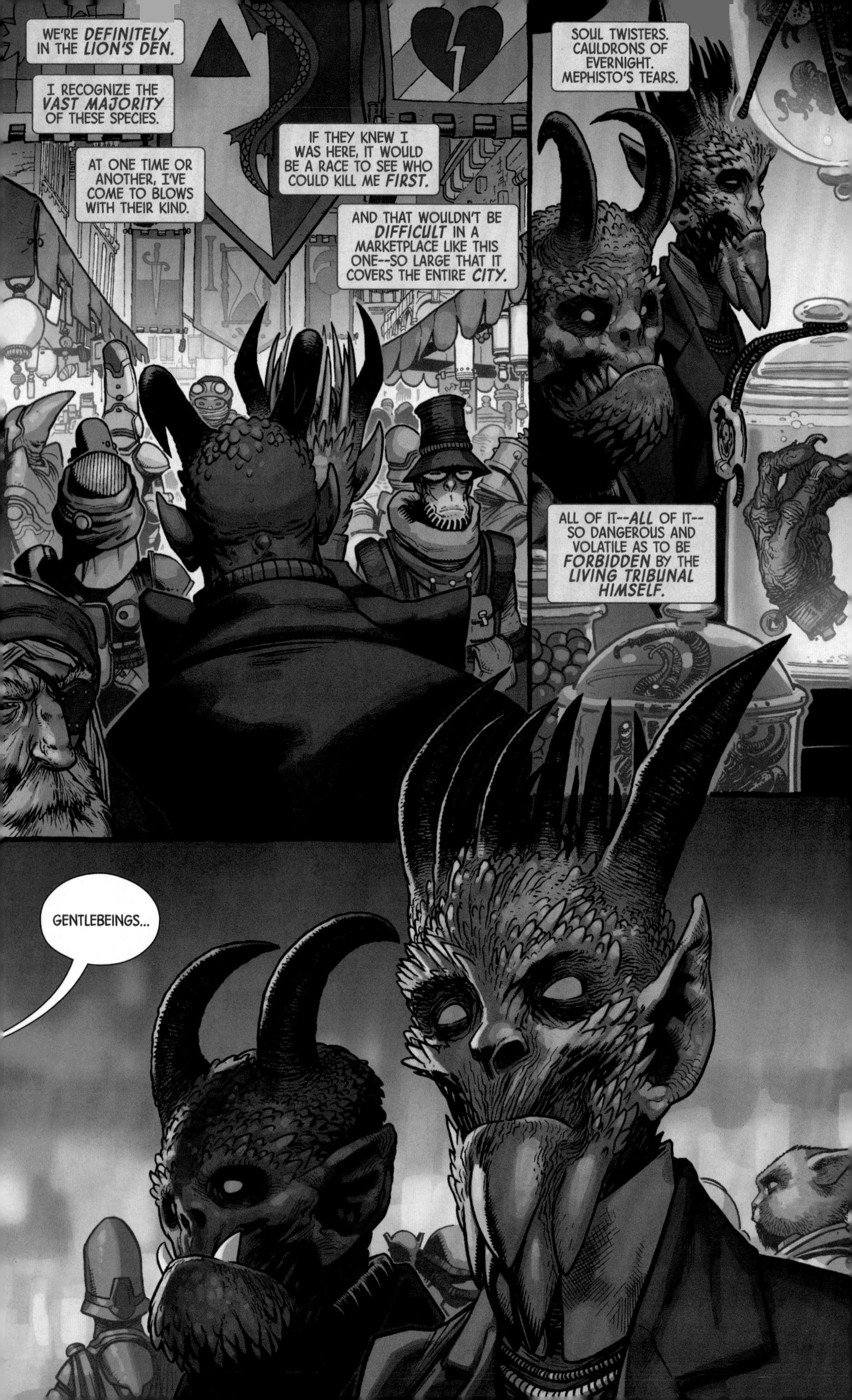
WE'RE DEFINITELY IN THE LION'S DEN.
I RECOGNIZE THE VAST MAJORITY OF THESE SPECIES.
AT ONE TIME OR ANOTHER, I'VE COME TO BLOWS WITH THEIR KIND.
IF THEY KNEW I WAS HERE, IT WOULD BE A RACE TO SEE WHO COULD KILL ME FIRST.
AND THAT WOULDN'T BE DIFFICULT IN A MARKETPLACE LIKE THIS ONE--SO LARGE THAT IT COVERS THE ENTIRE CITY.
SOUL TWISTERS. CAULDRONS OF EVERNIGHT. MEPHISTO'S TEARS.
ALL OF IT--ALL OF IT--SO DANGEROUS AND VOLATILE AS TO BE FORBIDDEN BY THE LIVING TRIBUNAL HIMSELF.
GENTLEBEINGS...

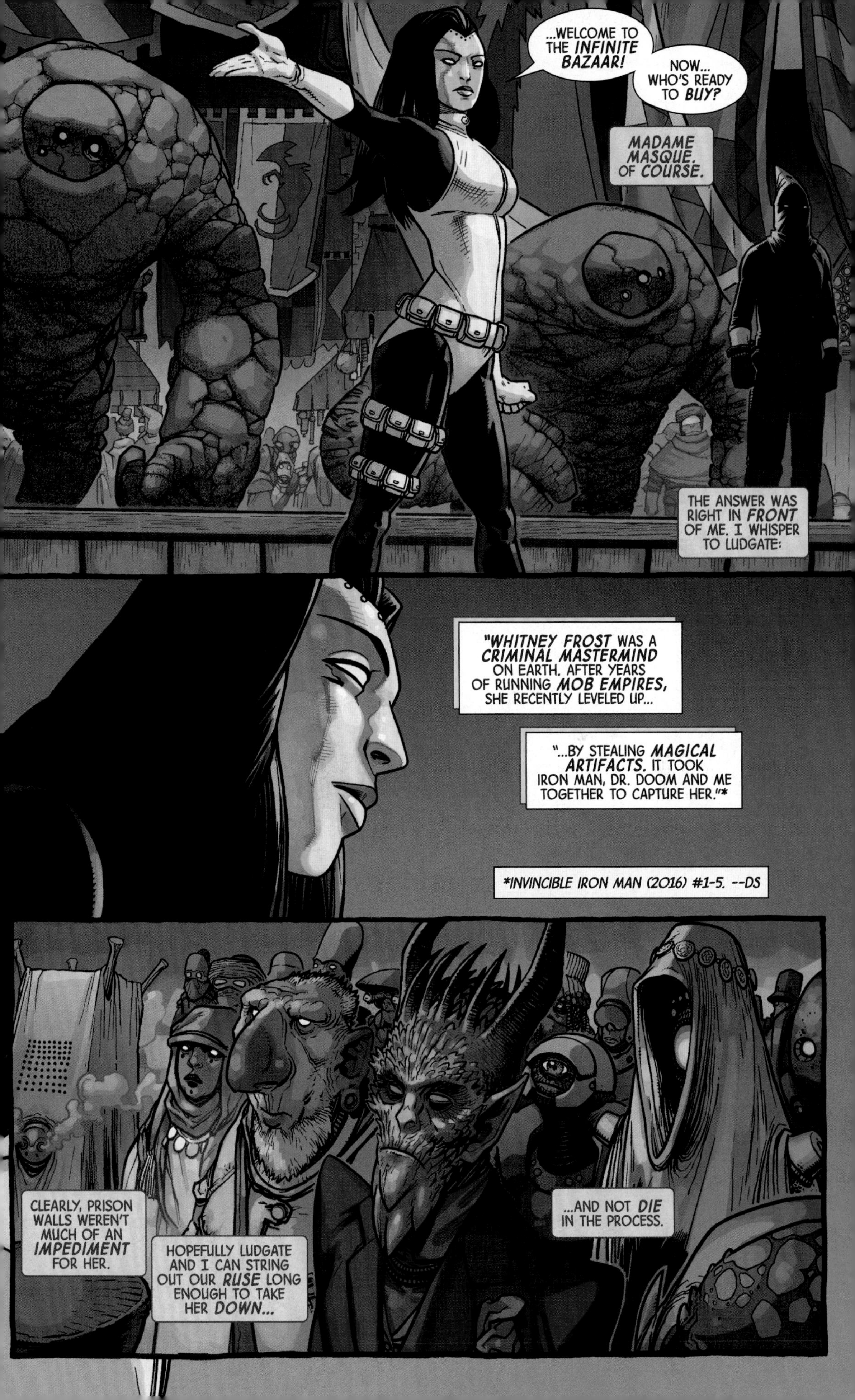
...WELCOME TO THE INFINITE BAZAAR!
NOW... WHO'S READY TO BUY?
MADAME MASQUE. OF COURSE.
THE ANSWER WAS RIGHT IN FRONT OF ME. I WHISPER TO LUDGATE:
"WHITNEY FROST WAS A CRIMINAL MASTERMIND ON EARTH. AFTER YEARS OF RUNNING MOB EMPIRES, SHE RECENTLY LEVELED UP...
"...BY STEALING MAGICAL ARTIFACTS. IT TOOK IRON MAN, DR. DOOM AND ME TOGETHER TO CAPTURE HER."*
*INVINCIBLE IRON MAN (2016) #1-5. --DS
CLEARLY, PRISON WALLS WEREN'T MUCH OF AN IMPEDIMENT FOR HER.
HOPEFULLY LUDGATE AND I CAN STRING OUT OUR RUSE LONG ENOUGH TO TAKE HER DOWN...
...AND NOT DIE IN THE PROCESS.

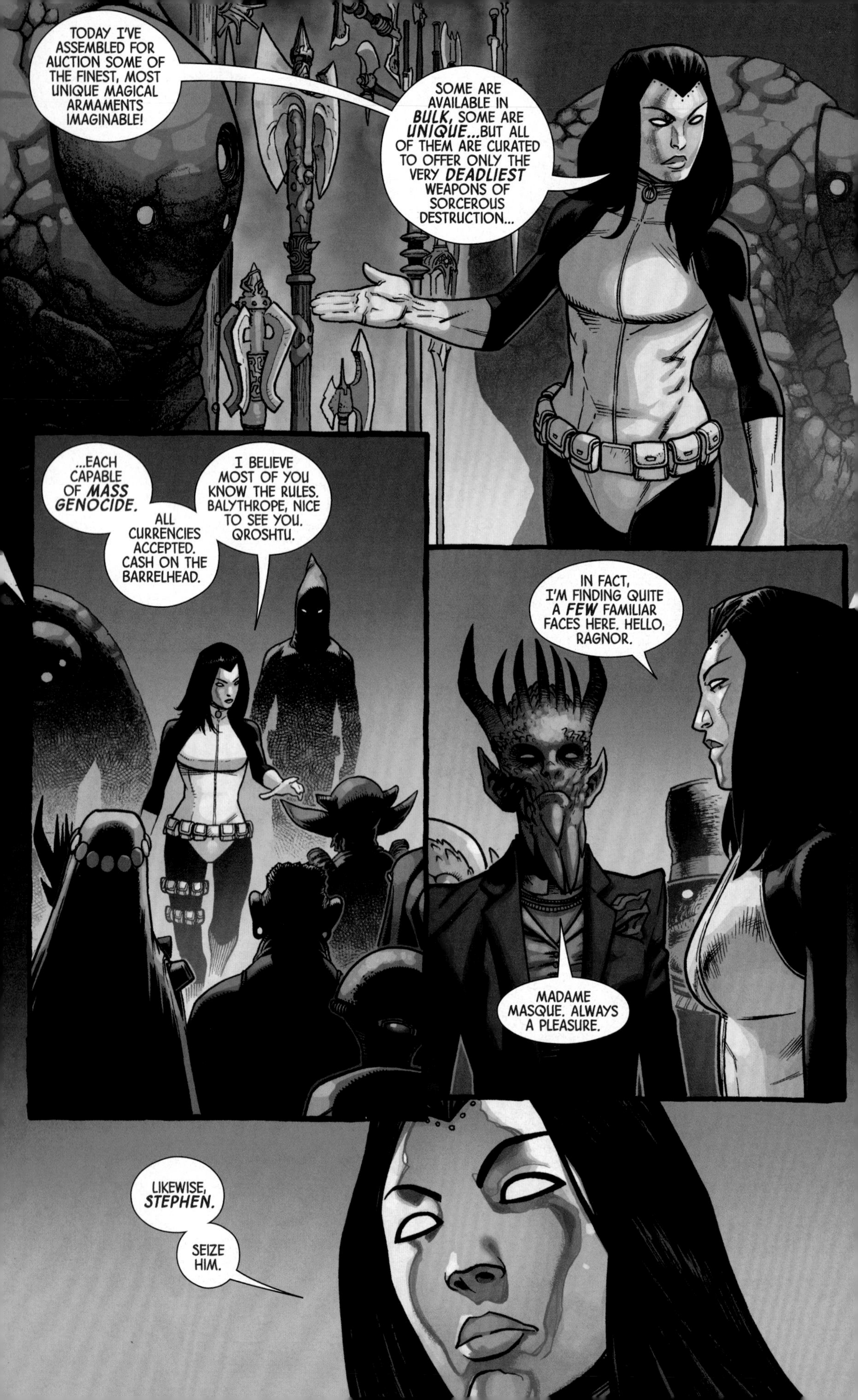
TODAY I'VE ASSEMBLED FOR AUCTION SOME OF THE FINEST, MOST UNIQUE MAGICAL ARMAMENTS IMAGINABLE!
SOME ARE AVAILABLE IN **BULK**, SOME ARE **UNIQUE**...BUT ALL OF THEM ARE CURATED TO OFFER ONLY THE VERY **DEADLIEST** WEAPONS OF SORCEROUS DESTRUCTION...
...EACH CAPABLE OF **MASS GENOCIDE.**
ALL CURRENCIES ACCEPTED. CASH ON THE BARRELHEAD.
I BELIEVE MOST OF YOU KNOW THE RULES. BALYTHROPE, NICE TO SEE YOU. QROSHTU.
IN FACT, I'M FINDING QUITE A **FEW** FAMILIAR FACES HERE. HELLO, RAGNOR.
MADAME MASQUE. ALWAYS A PLEASURE.
LIKEWISE, **STEPHEN.**
SEIZE HIM.

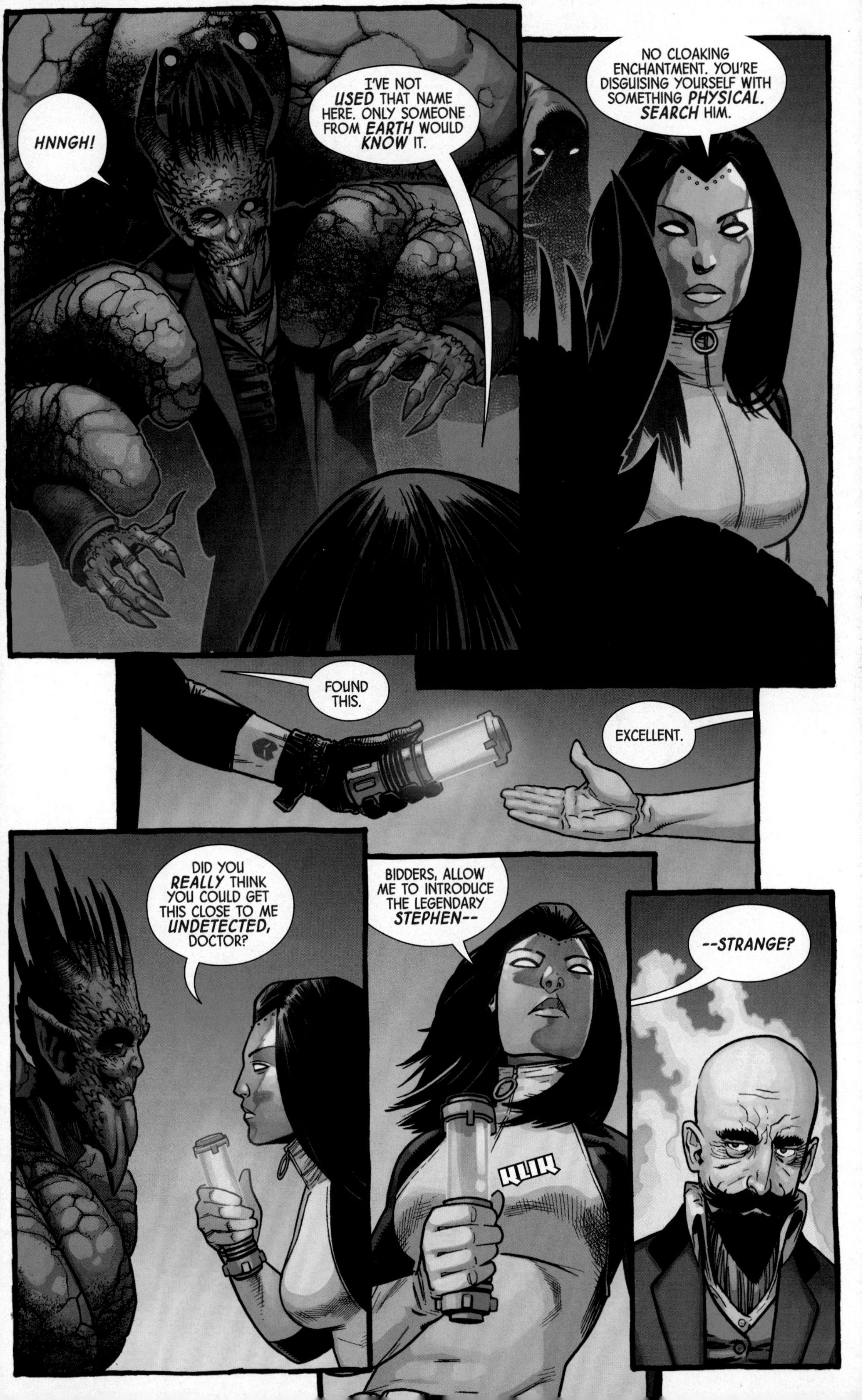
HNNGH!
I'VE NOT USED THAT NAME HERE. ONLY SOMEONE FROM EARTH WOULD KNOW IT.
NO CLOAKING ENCHANTMENT. YOU'RE DISGUISING YOURSELF WITH SOMETHING PHYSICAL. SEARCH HIM.
FOUND THIS.
EXCELLENT.
DID YOU REALLY THINK YOU COULD GET THIS CLOSE TO ME UNDETECTED, DOCTOR?
BIDDERS, ALLOW ME TO INTRODUCE THE LEGENDARY STEPHEN--
KLIK
--STRANGE?

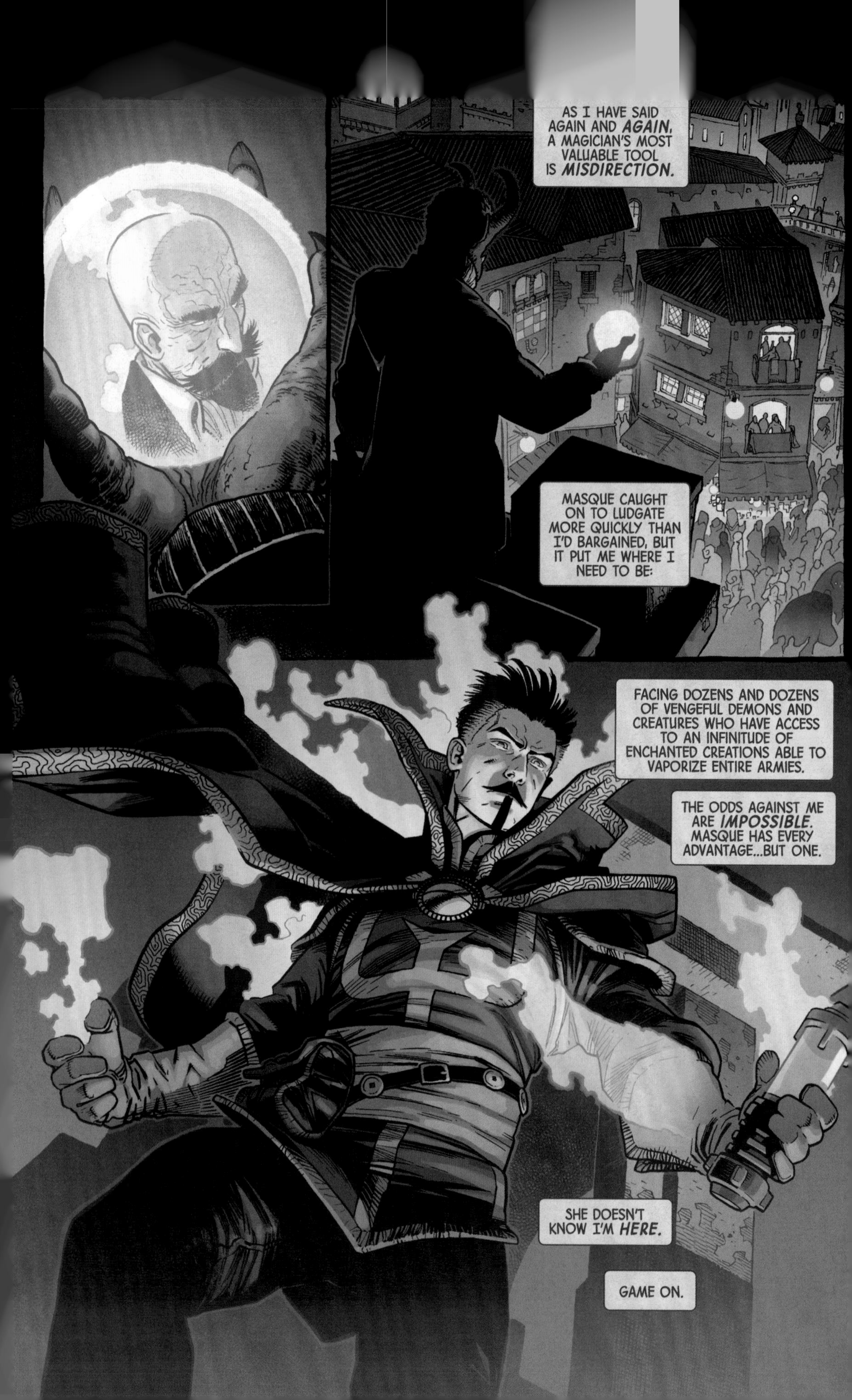
AS I HAVE SAID AGAIN AND AGAIN, A MAGICIAN'S MOST VALUABLE TOOL IS MISDIRECTION.
MASQUE CAUGHT ON TO LUDGATE MORE QUICKLY THAN I'D BARGAINED, BUT IT PUT ME WHERE I NEED TO BE:
FACING DOZENS AND DOZENS OF VENGEFUL DEMONS AND CREATURES WHO HAVE ACCESS TO AN INFINITUDE OF ENCHANTED CREATIONS ABLE TO VAPORIZE ENTIRE ARMIES.
THE ODDS AGAINST ME ARE IMPOSSIBLE. MASQUE HAS EVERY ADVANTAGE...BUT ONE.
SHE DOESN'T KNOW I'M HERE.
GAME ON.

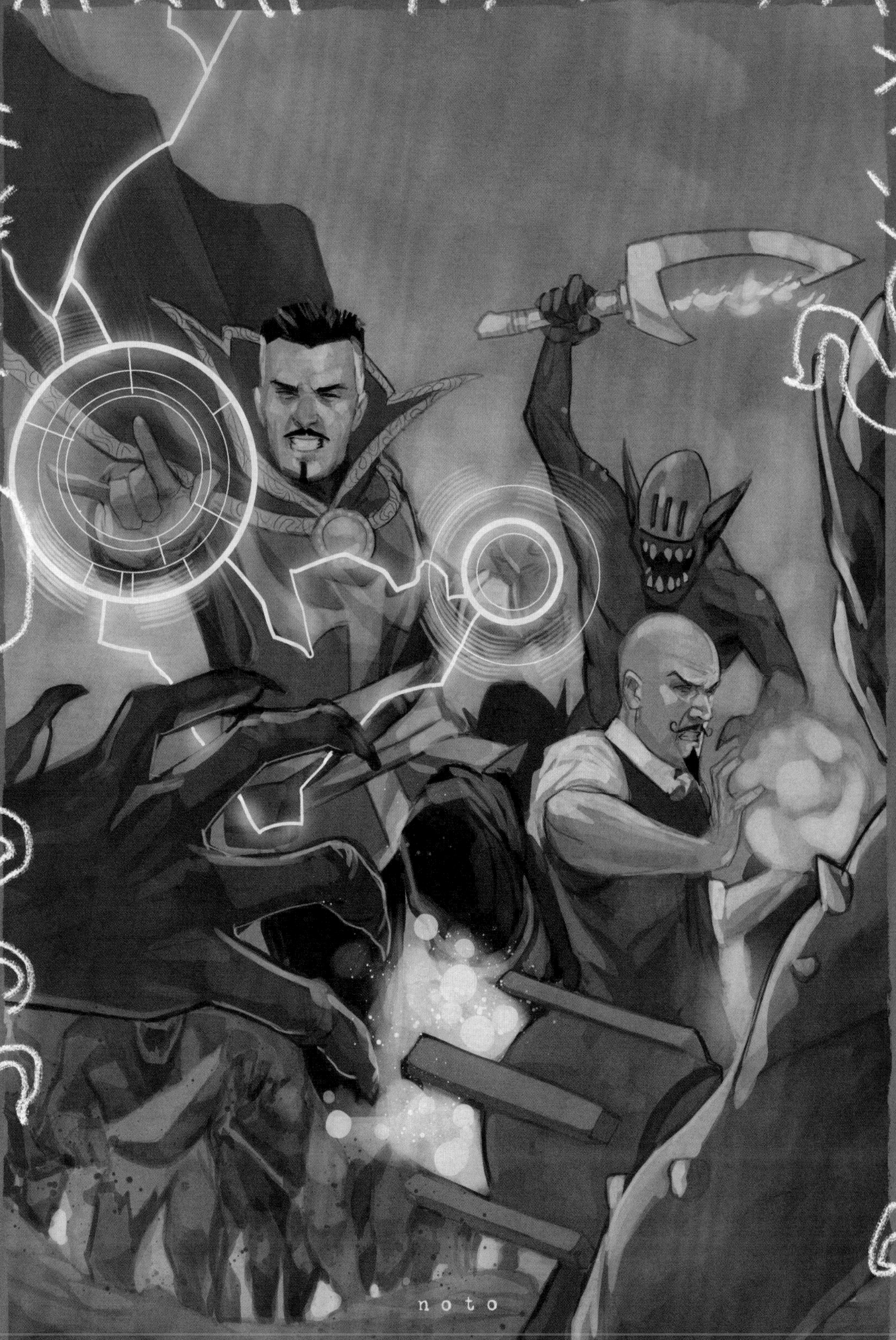
noto

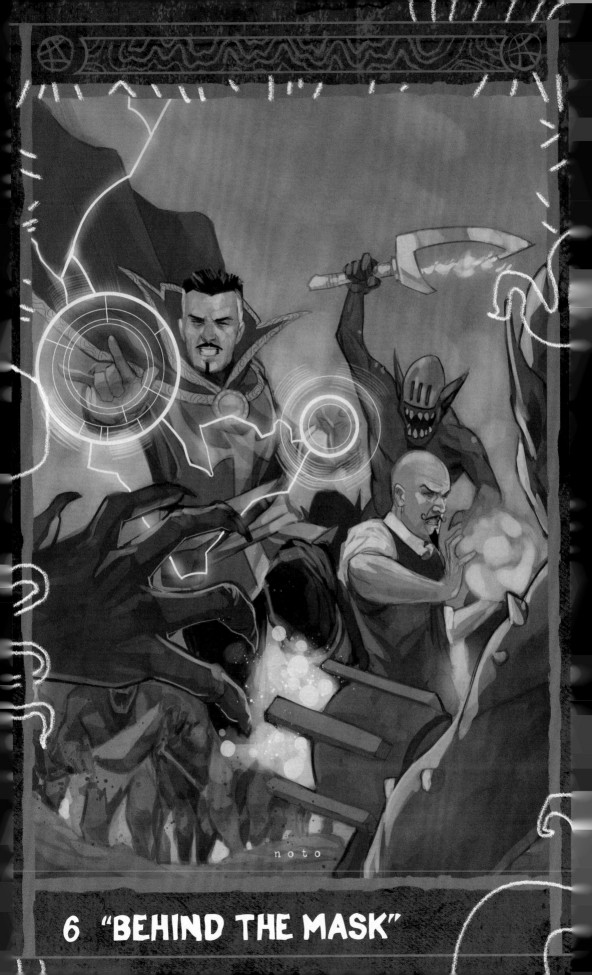

6 "BEHIND THE MASK"

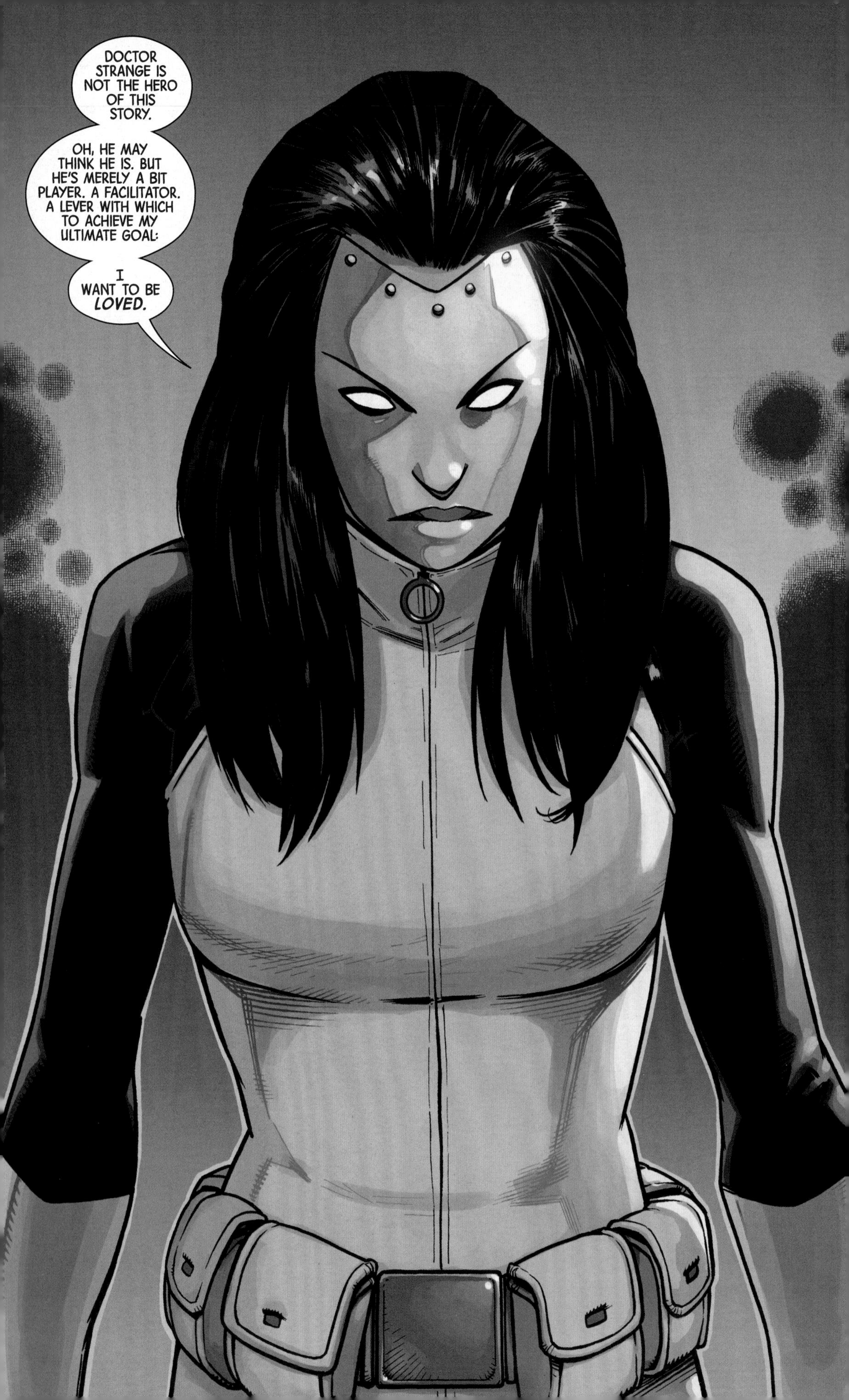
DOCTOR STRANGE IS NOT THE HERO OF THIS STORY.
OH, HE MAY THINK HE IS. BUT HE'S MERELY A BIT PLAYER. A FACILITATOR. A LEVER WITH WHICH TO ACHIEVE MY ULTIMATE GOAL:
I WANT TO BE *LOVED.*

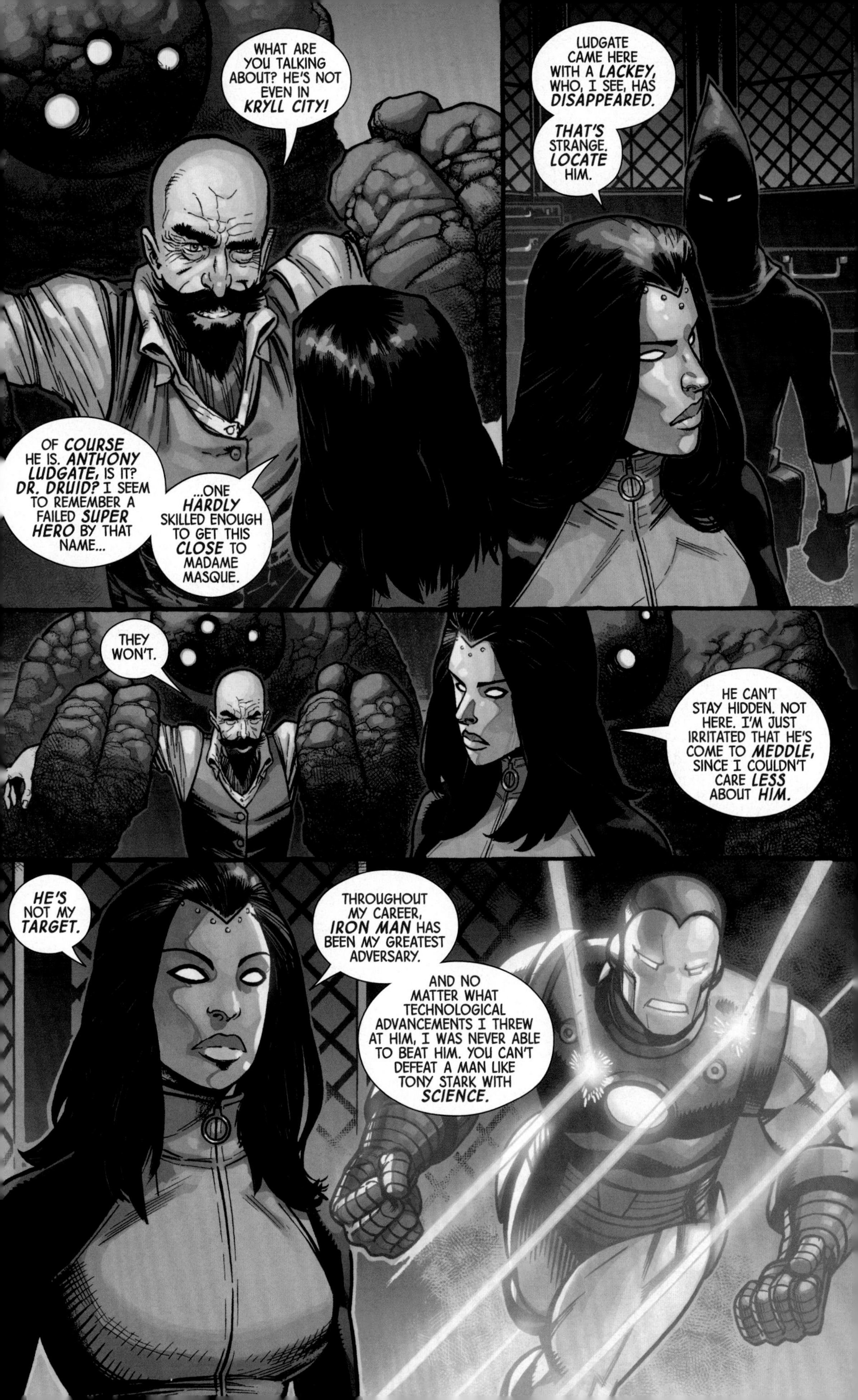

WHAT ARE YOU TALKING ABOUT? HE'S NOT EVEN IN KRYLL CITY!
OF COURSE HE IS. ANTHONY LUDGATE, IS IT? DR. DRUID? I SEEM TO REMEMBER A FAILED SUPER HERO BY THAT NAME...
...ONE HARDLY SKILLED ENOUGH TO GET THIS CLOSE TO MADAME MASQUE.
LUDGATE CAME HERE WITH A LACKEY, WHO, I SEE, HAS DISAPPEARED.
THAT'S STRANGE. LOCATE HIM.
THEY WON'T.
HE CAN'T STAY HIDDEN. NOT HERE. I'M JUST IRRITATED THAT HE'S COME TO MEDDLE, SINCE I COULDN'T CARE LESS ABOUT HIM.
HE'S NOT MY TARGET.
THROUGHOUT MY CAREER, IRON MAN HAS BEEN MY GREATEST ADVERSARY.
AND NO MATTER WHAT TECHNOLOGICAL ADVANCEMENTS I THREW AT HIM, I WAS NEVER ABLE TO BEAT HIM. YOU CAN'T DEFEAT A MAN LIKE TONY STARK WITH SCIENCE.

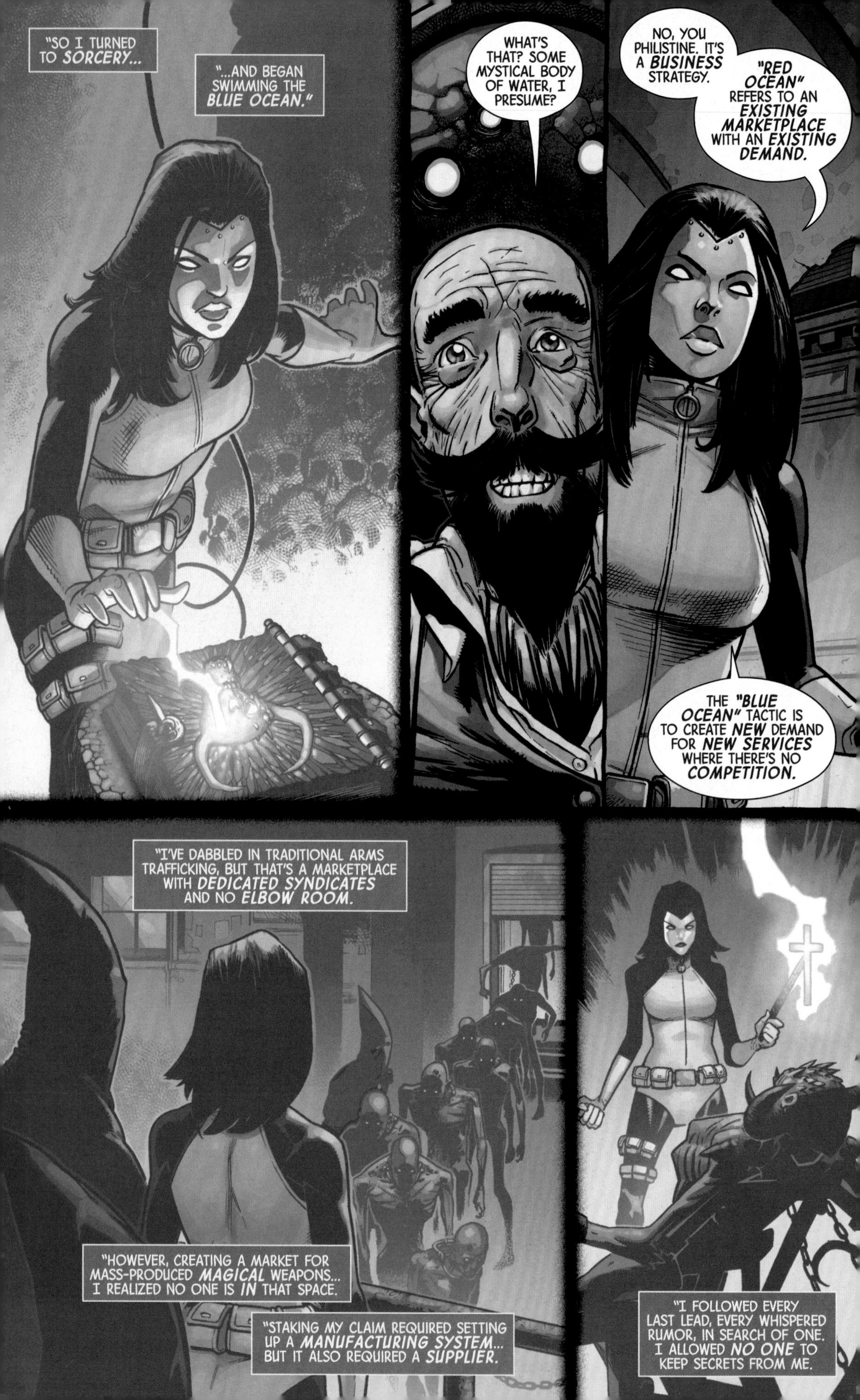
"SO I TURNED TO SORCERY...
"...AND BEGAN SWIMMING THE BLUE OCEAN."
WHAT'S THAT? SOME MYSTICAL BODY OF WATER, I PRESUME?
NO, YOU PHILISTINE. IT'S A BUSINESS STRATEGY.
"RED OCEAN" REFERS TO AN EXISTING MARKETPLACE WITH AN EXISTING DEMAND.
THE "BLUE OCEAN" TACTIC IS TO CREATE NEW DEMAND FOR NEW SERVICES WHERE THERE'S NO COMPETITION.
"I'VE DABBLED IN TRADITIONAL ARMS TRAFFICKING, BUT THAT'S A MARKETPLACE WITH DEDICATED SYNDICATES AND NO ELBOW ROOM.
"HOWEVER, CREATING A MARKET FOR MASS-PRODUCED MAGICAL WEAPONS... I REALIZED NO ONE IS IN THAT SPACE.
"STAKING MY CLAIM REQUIRED SETTING UP A MANUFACTURING SYSTEM... BUT IT ALSO REQUIRED A SUPPLIER.
"I FOLLOWED EVERY LAST LEAD, EVERY WHISPERED RUMOR, IN SEARCH OF ONE. I ALLOWED NO ONE TO KEEP SECRETS FROM ME.

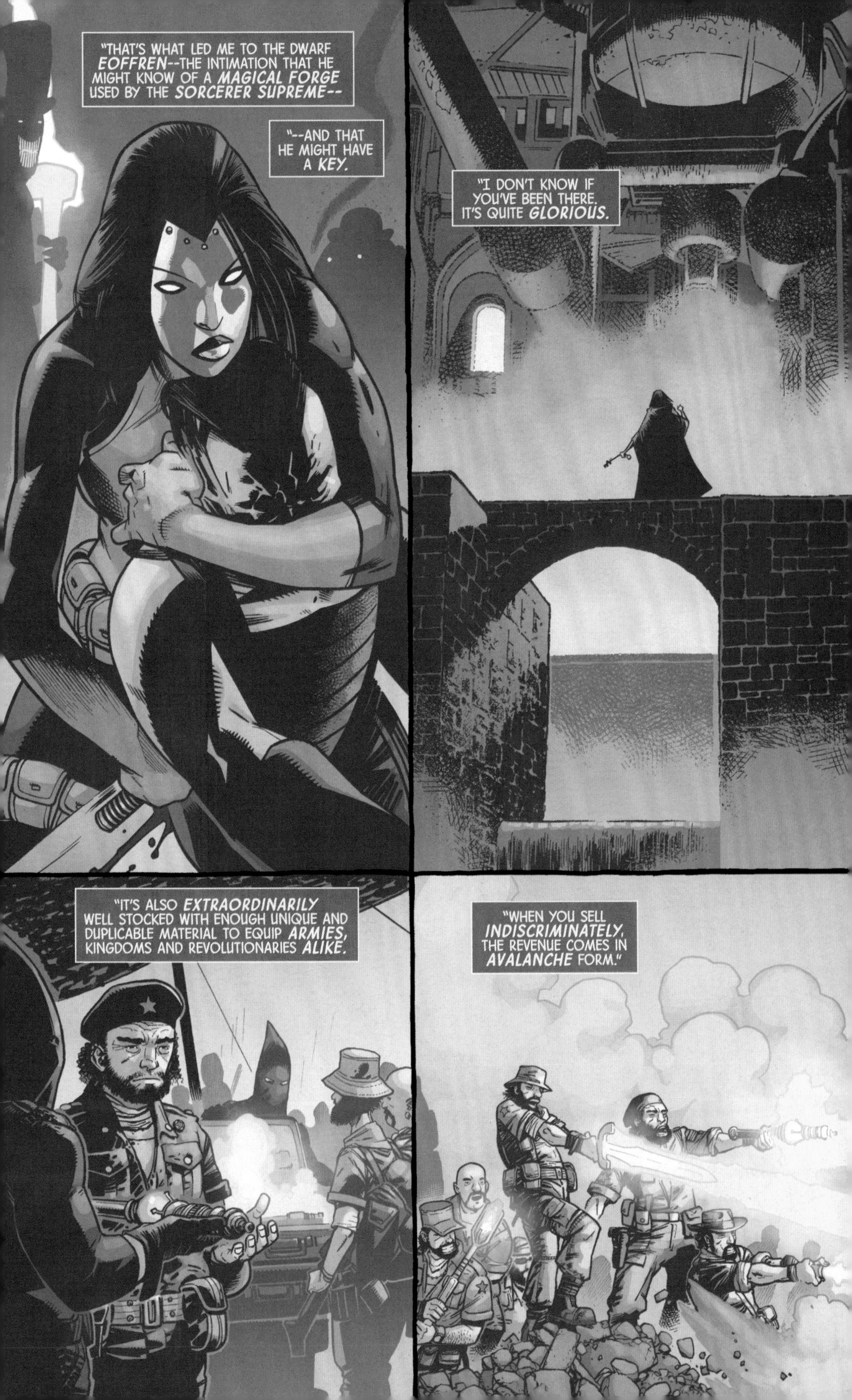
"THAT'S WHAT LED ME TO THE DWARF EOFFREN--THE INTIMATION THAT HE MIGHT KNOW OF A MAGICAL FORGE USED BY THE SORCERER SUPREME--
"--AND THAT HE MIGHT HAVE A KEY.
"I DON'T KNOW IF YOU'VE BEEN THERE. IT'S QUITE GLORIOUS.
"IT'S ALSO EXTRAORDINARILY WELL STOCKED WITH ENOUGH UNIQUE AND DUPLICABLE MATERIAL TO EQUIP ARMIES, KINGDOMS AND REVOLUTIONARIES ALIKE.
"WHEN YOU SELL INDISCRIMINATELY, THE REVENUE COMES IN AVALANCHE FORM."

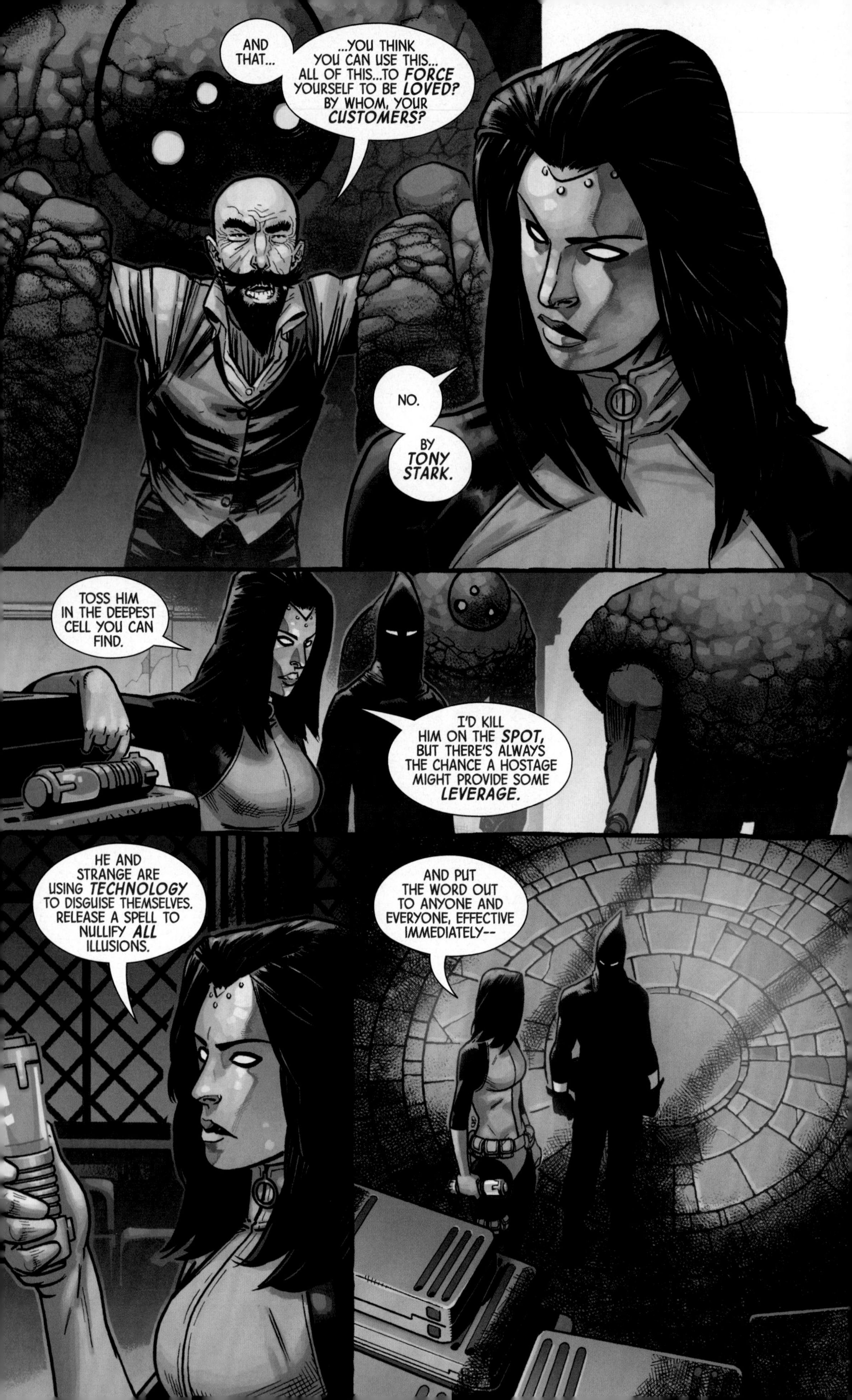
AND THAT...
...YOU THINK YOU CAN USE THIS... ALL OF THIS...TO FORCE YOURSELF TO BE LOVED? BY WHOM, YOUR CUSTOMERS?
NO.
BY TONY STARK.
TOSS HIM IN THE DEEPEST CELL YOU CAN FIND.
I'D KILL HIM ON THE SPOT, BUT THERE'S ALWAYS THE CHANCE A HOSTAGE MIGHT PROVIDE SOME LEVERAGE.
HE AND STRANGE ARE USING TECHNOLOGY TO DISGUISE THEMSELVES. RELEASE A SPELL TO NULLIFY ALL ILLUSIONS.
AND PUT THE WORD OUT TO ANYONE AND EVERYONE, EFFECTIVE IMMEDIATELY--

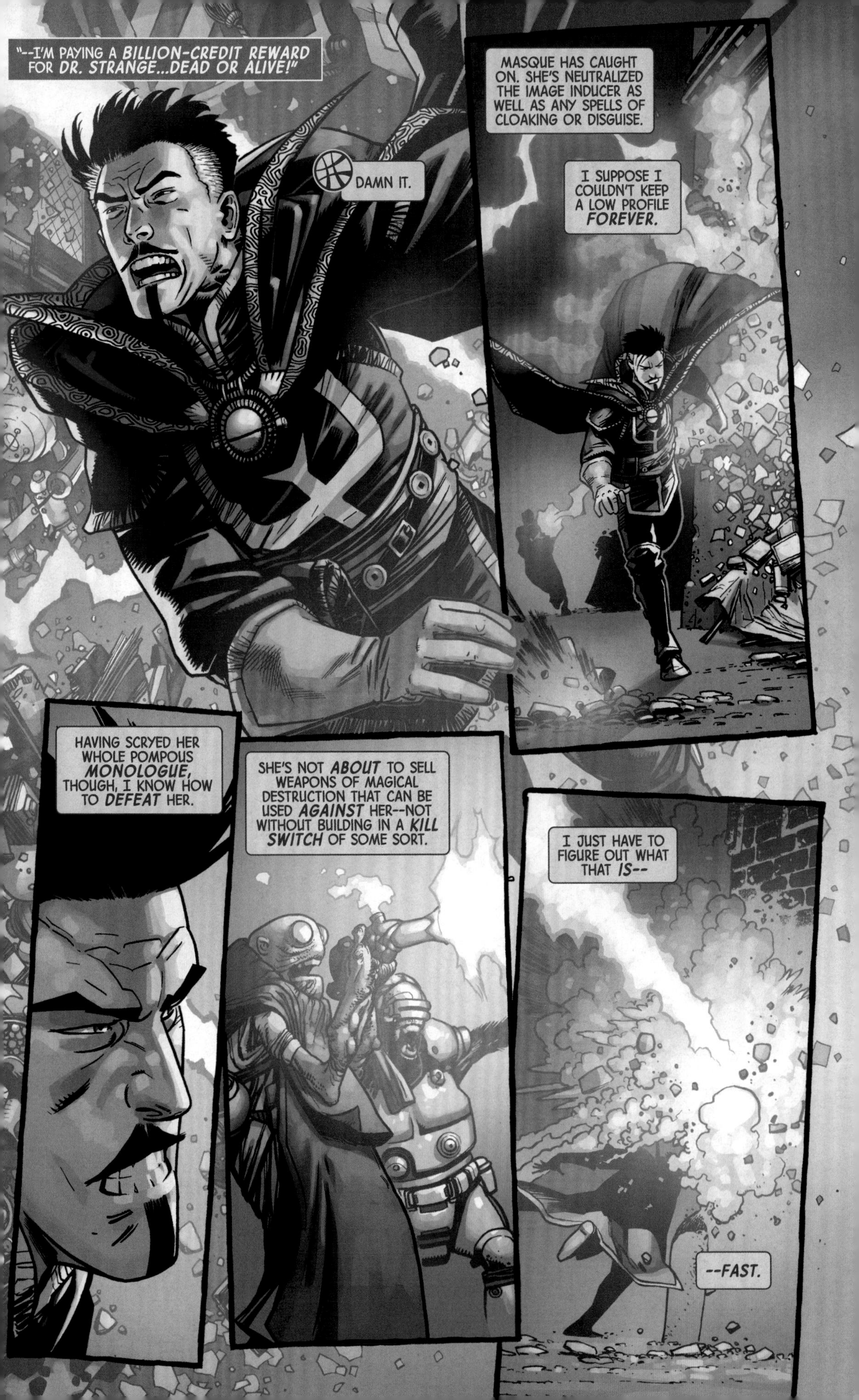
"--I'M PAYING A BILLION-CREDIT REWARD FOR DR. STRANGE...DEAD OR ALIVE!"
DAMN IT.
MASQUE HAS CAUGHT ON. SHE'S NEUTRALIZED THE IMAGE INDUCER AS WELL AS ANY SPELLS OF CLOAKING OR DISGUISE.
I SUPPOSE I COULDN'T KEEP A LOW PROFILE FOREVER.
HAVING SCRYED HER WHOLE POMPOUS MONOLOGUE, THOUGH, I KNOW HOW TO DEFEAT HER.
SHE'S NOT ABOUT TO SELL WEAPONS OF MAGICAL DESTRUCTION THAT CAN BE USED AGAINST HER--NOT WITHOUT BUILDING IN A KILL SWITCH OF SOME SORT.
I JUST HAVE TO FIGURE OUT WHAT THAT IS--
--FAST.

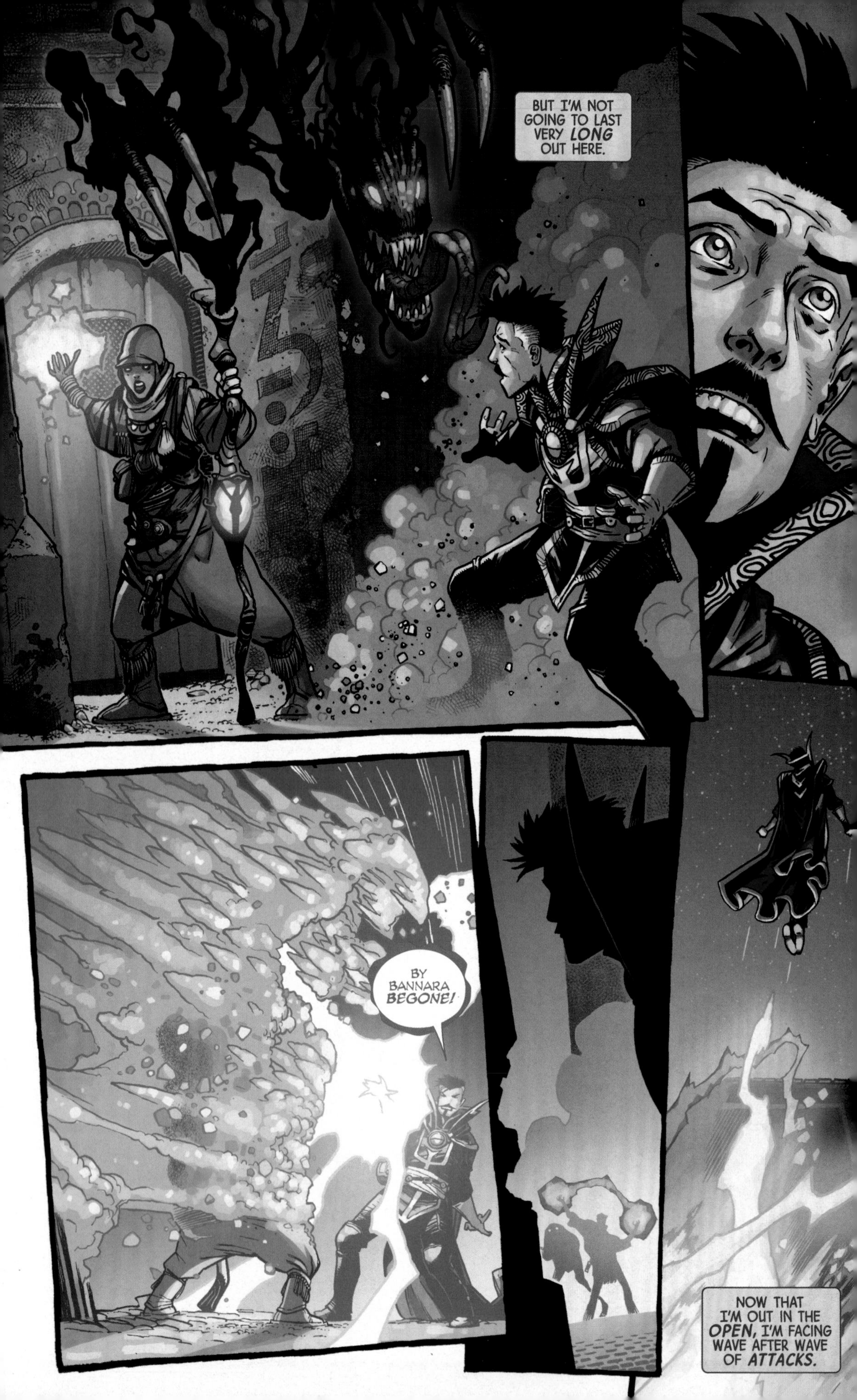
BUT I'M NOT GOING TO LAST VERY LONG OUT HERE.
BY BANNARA BEGONE!
NOW THAT I'M OUT IN THE OPEN, I'M FACING WAVE AFTER WAVE OF ATTACKS.

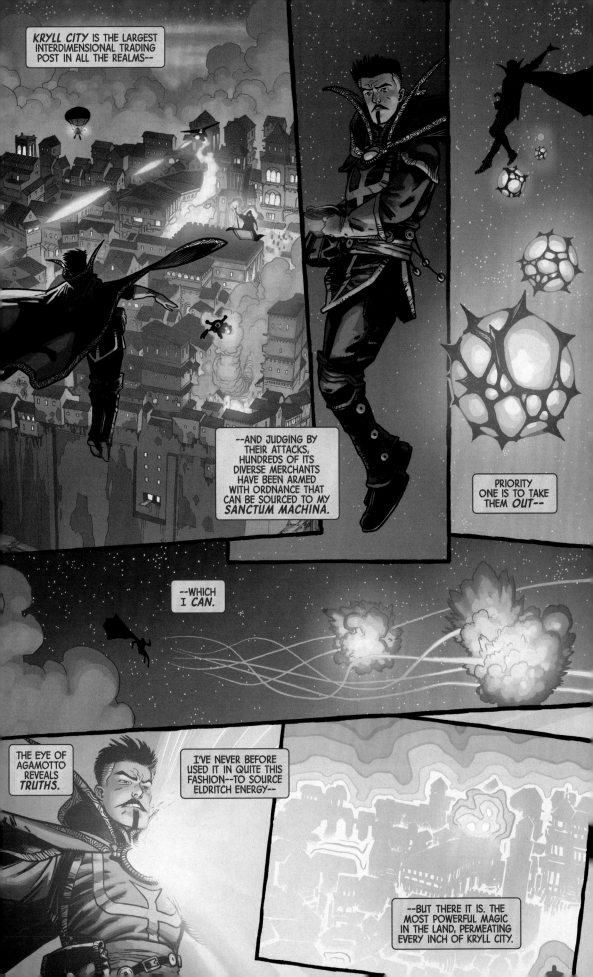

KRYLL CITY IS THE LARGEST INTERDIMENSIONAL TRADING POST IN ALL THE REALMS--

--AND JUDGING BY THEIR ATTACKS, HUNDREDS OF ITS DIVERSE MERCHANTS HAVE BEEN ARMED WITH ORDNANCE THAT CAN BE SOURCED TO MY *SANCTUM MACHINA.*

PRIORITY ONE IS TO TAKE THEM *OUT*--

--WHICH I *CAN.*

THE EYE OF AGAMOTTO REVEALS *TRUTHS.*

I'VE NEVER BEFORE USED IT IN QUITE THIS FASHION--TO SOURCE ELDRITCH ENERGY--

--BUT THERE IT IS. THE MOST POWERFUL MAGIC IN THE LAND, PERMEATING EVERY INCH OF KRYLL CITY.

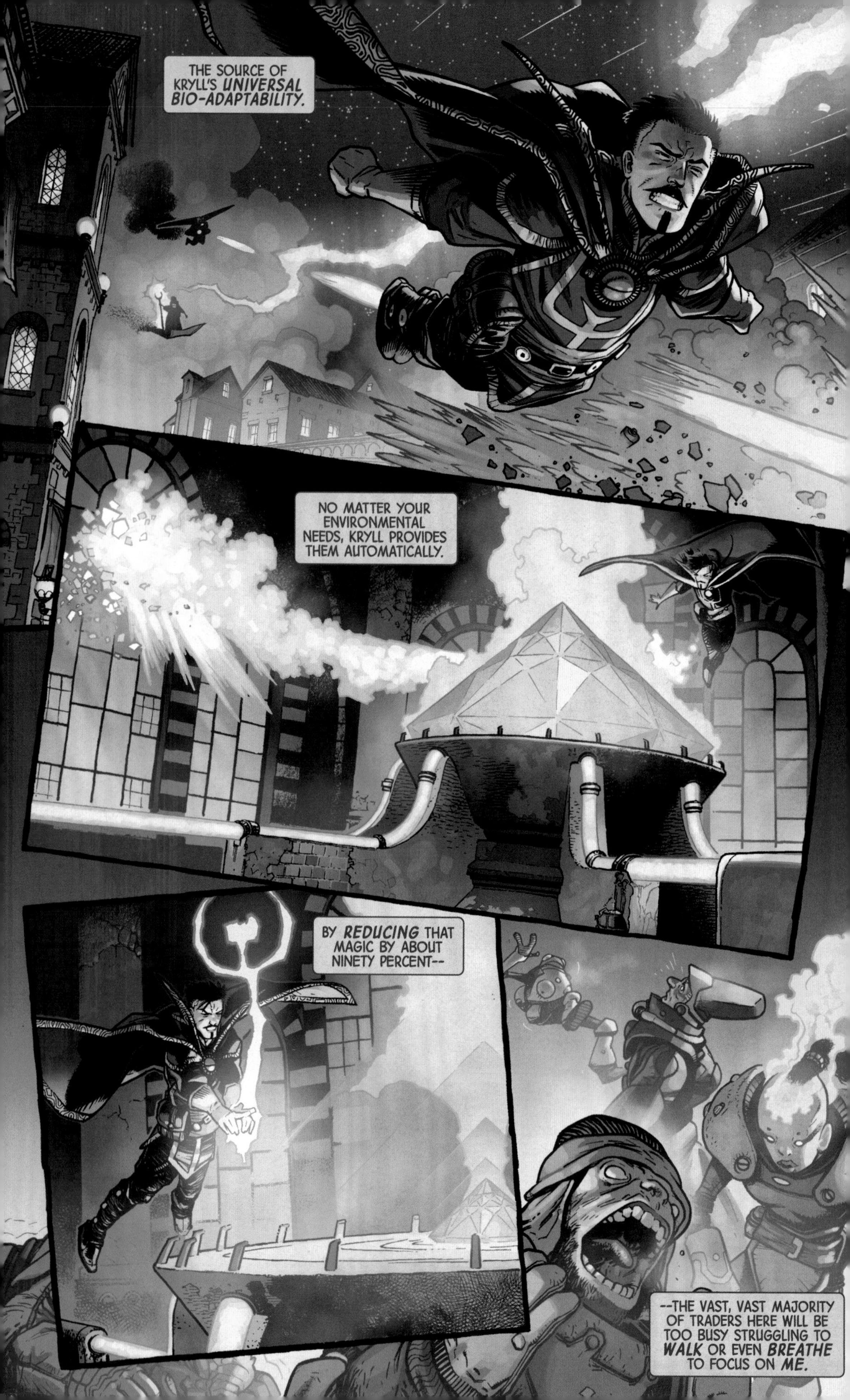
THE SOURCE OF KRYLL'S *UNIVERSAL BIO-ADAPTABILITY.*
NO MATTER YOUR ENVIRONMENTAL NEEDS, KRYLL PROVIDES THEM AUTOMATICALLY.
BY *REDUCING* THAT MAGIC BY ABOUT NINETY PERCENT--
--THE VAST, VAST MAJORITY OF TRADERS HERE WILL BE TOO BUSY STRUGGLING TO *WALK* OR EVEN *BREATHE* TO FOCUS ON *ME.*

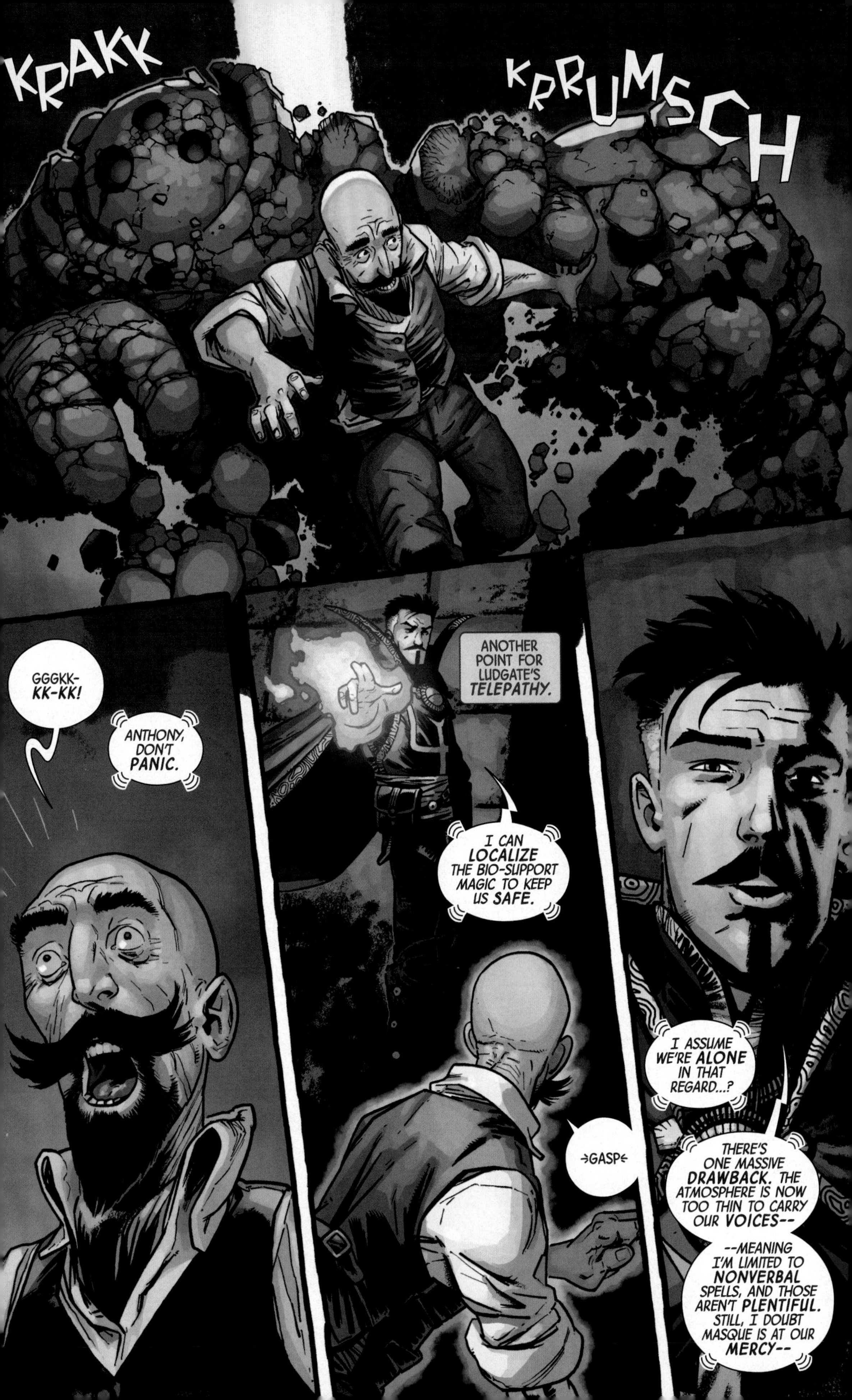
KRAKK
KRRUMSCH
GGGKK-KK-KK!
ANTHONY, DON'T PANIC.
ANOTHER POINT FOR LUDGATE'S TELEPATHY.
I CAN LOCALIZE THE BIO-SUPPORT MAGIC TO KEEP US SAFE.
GASP
I ASSUME WE'RE ALONE IN THAT REGARD...?
THERE'S ONE MASSIVE DRAWBACK. THE ATMOSPHERE IS NOW TOO THIN TO CARRY OUR VOICES--
--MEANING I'M LIMITED TO NONVERBAL SPELLS, AND THOSE AREN'T PLENTIFUL. STILL, I DOUBT MASQUE IS AT OUR MERCY--

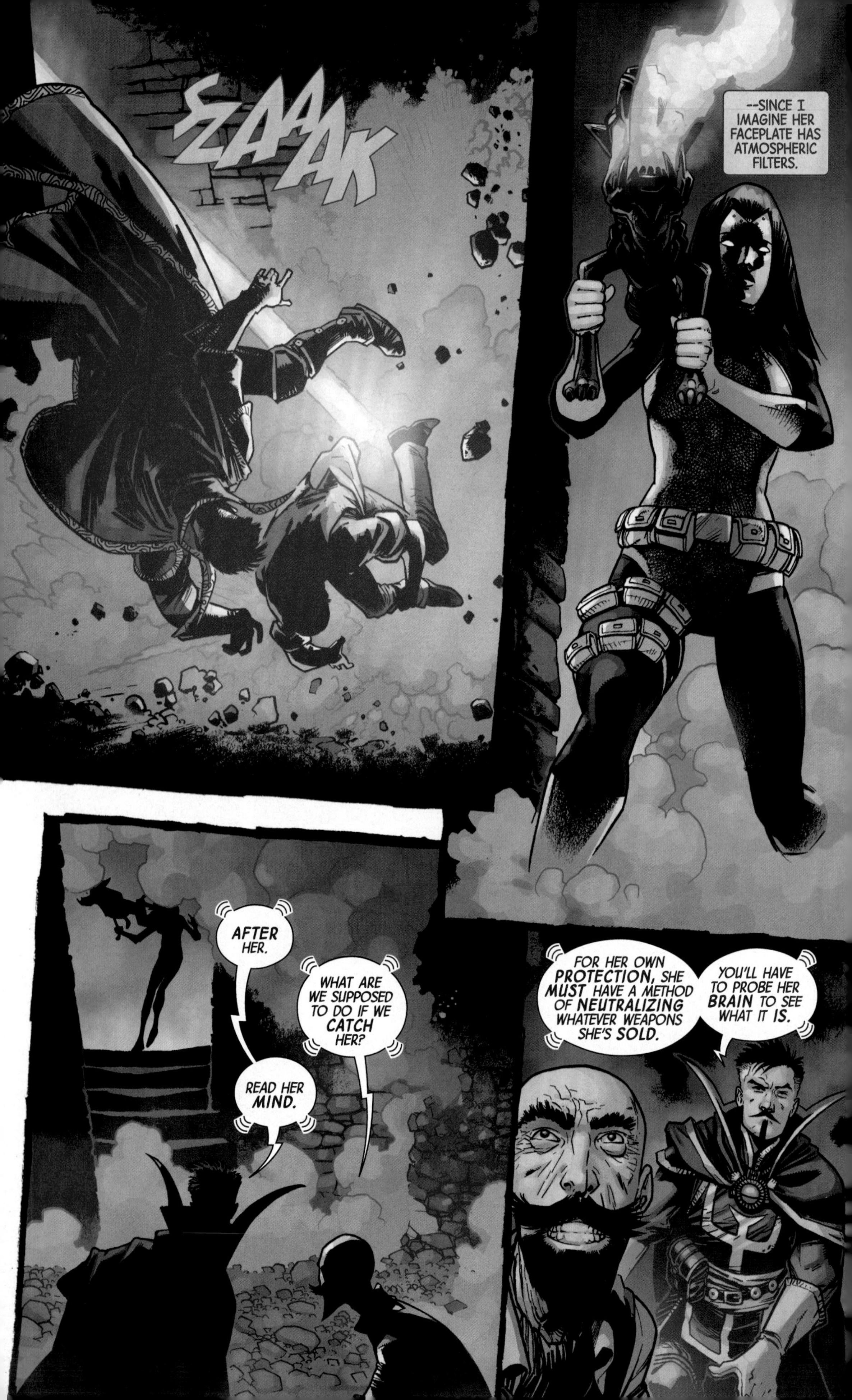
SZAAAK
--SINCE I IMAGINE HER FACEPLATE HAS ATMOSPHERIC FILTERS.
AFTER HER.
WHAT ARE WE SUPPOSED TO DO IF WE CATCH HER?
READ HER MIND.
FOR HER OWN PROTECTION, SHE MUST HAVE A METHOD OF NEUTRALIZING WHATEVER WEAPONS SHE'S SOLD.
YOU'LL HAVE TO PROBE HER BRAIN TO SEE WHAT IT IS.

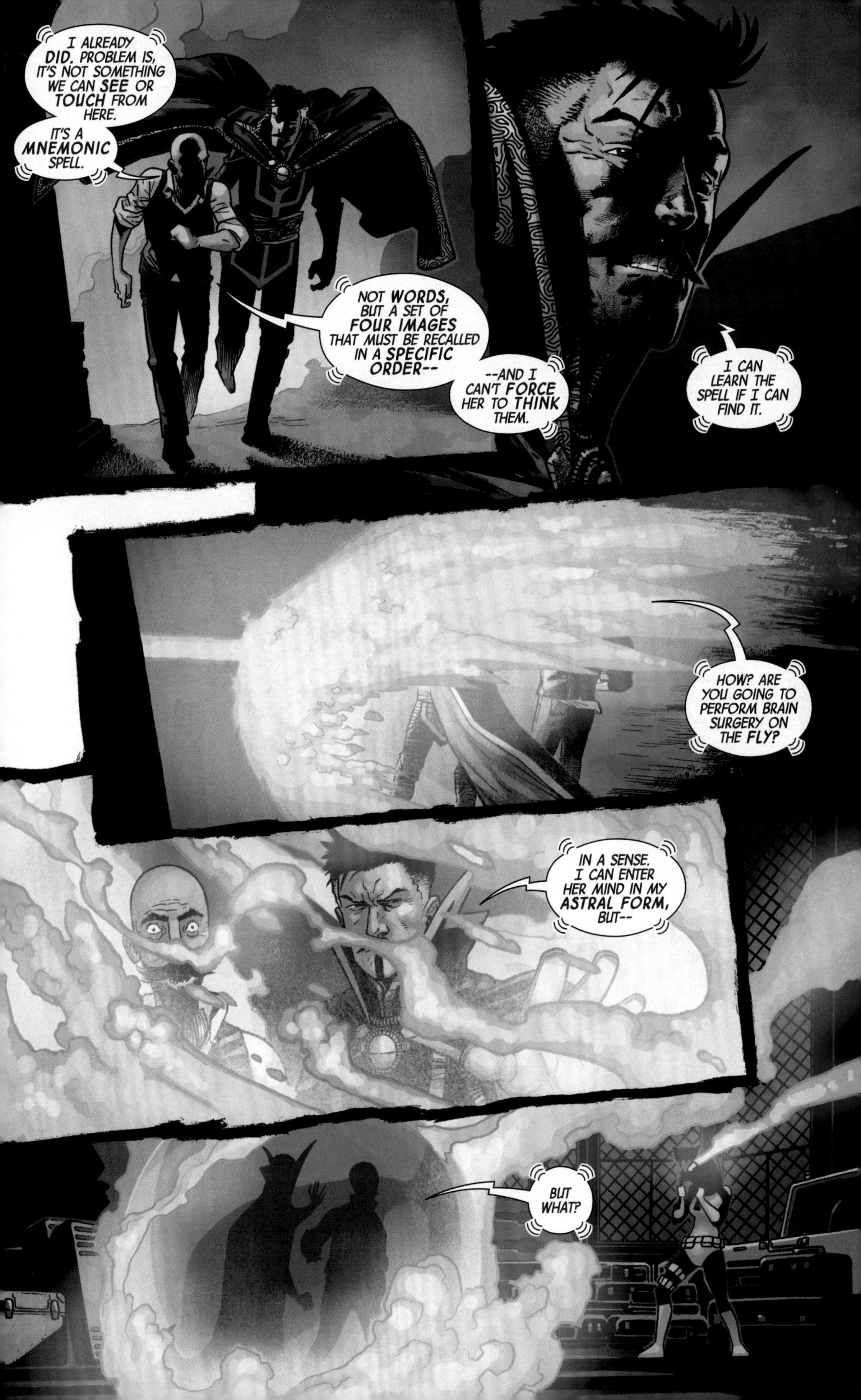
I ALREADY DID. PROBLEM IS, IT'S NOT SOMETHING WE CAN SEE OR TOUCH FROM HERE.
IT'S A MNEMONIC SPELL.
NOT WORDS, BUT A SET OF FOUR IMAGES THAT MUST BE RECALLED IN A SPECIFIC ORDER--
--AND I CAN'T FORCE HER TO THINK THEM.
I CAN LEARN THE SPELL IF I CAN FIND IT.
HOW? ARE YOU GOING TO PERFORM BRAIN SURGERY ON THE FLY?
IN A SENSE. I CAN ENTER HER MIND IN MY ASTRAL FORM, BUT--
BUT WHAT?

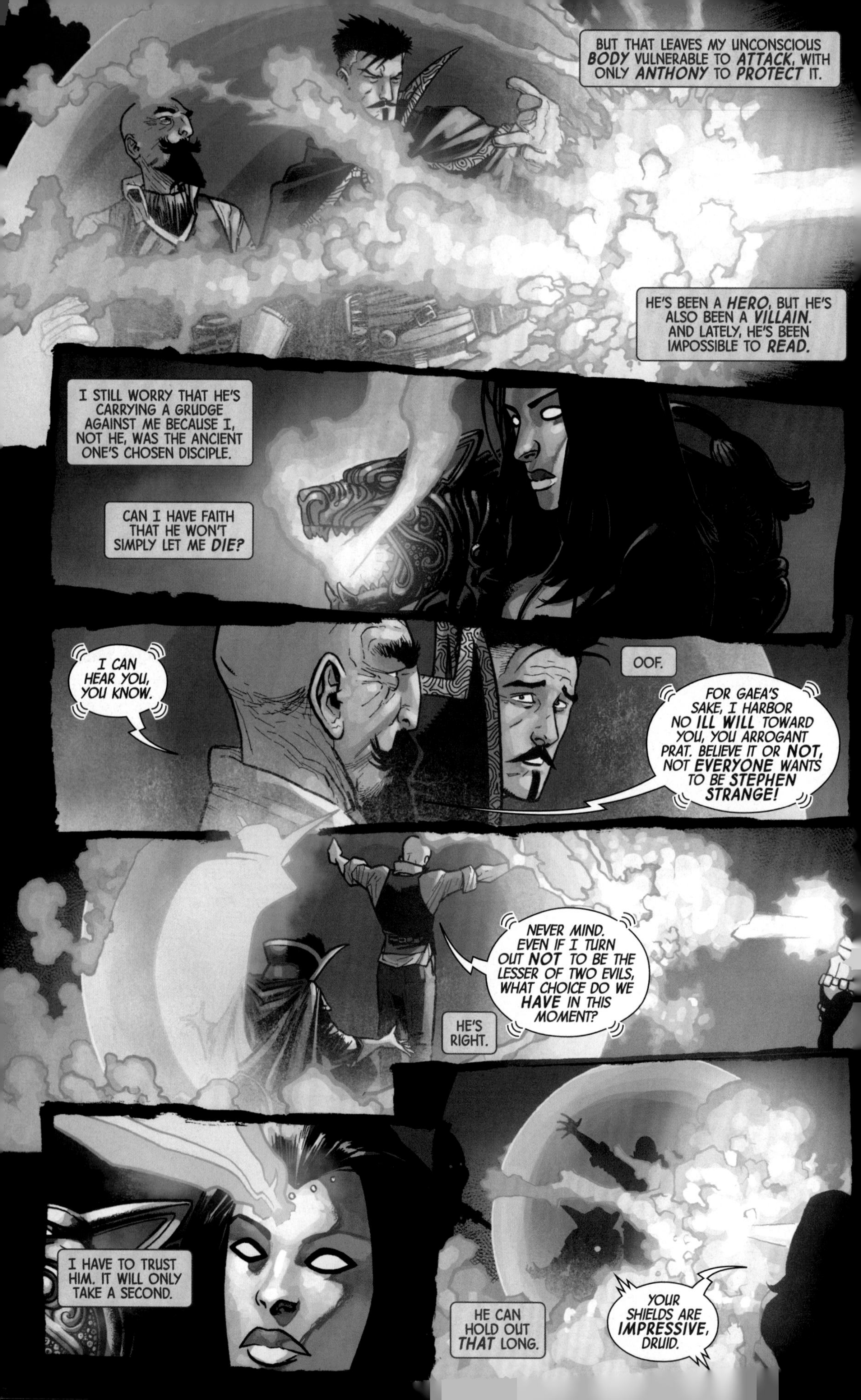

BUT THAT LEAVES MY UNCONSCIOUS BODY VULNERABLE TO ATTACK, WITH ONLY ANTHONY TO PROTECT IT.
HE'S BEEN A HERO, BUT HE'S ALSO BEEN A VILLAIN. AND LATELY, HE'S BEEN IMPOSSIBLE TO READ.
I STILL WORRY THAT HE'S CARRYING A GRUDGE AGAINST ME BECAUSE I, NOT HE, WAS THE ANCIENT ONE'S CHOSEN DISCIPLE.
CAN I HAVE FAITH THAT HE WON'T SIMPLY LET ME DIE?
I CAN HEAR YOU, YOU KNOW.
OOF.
FOR GAEA'S SAKE, I HARBOR NO ILL WILL TOWARD YOU, YOU ARROGANT PRAT. BELIEVE IT OR NOT, NOT EVERYONE WANTS TO BE STEPHEN STRANGE!
NEVER MIND. EVEN IF I TURN OUT NOT TO BE THE LESSER OF TWO EVILS, WHAT CHOICE DO WE HAVE IN THIS MOMENT?
HE'S RIGHT.
I HAVE TO TRUST HIM. IT WILL ONLY TAKE A SECOND.
HE CAN HOLD OUT THAT LONG.
YOUR SHIELDS ARE IMPRESSIVE, DRUID.

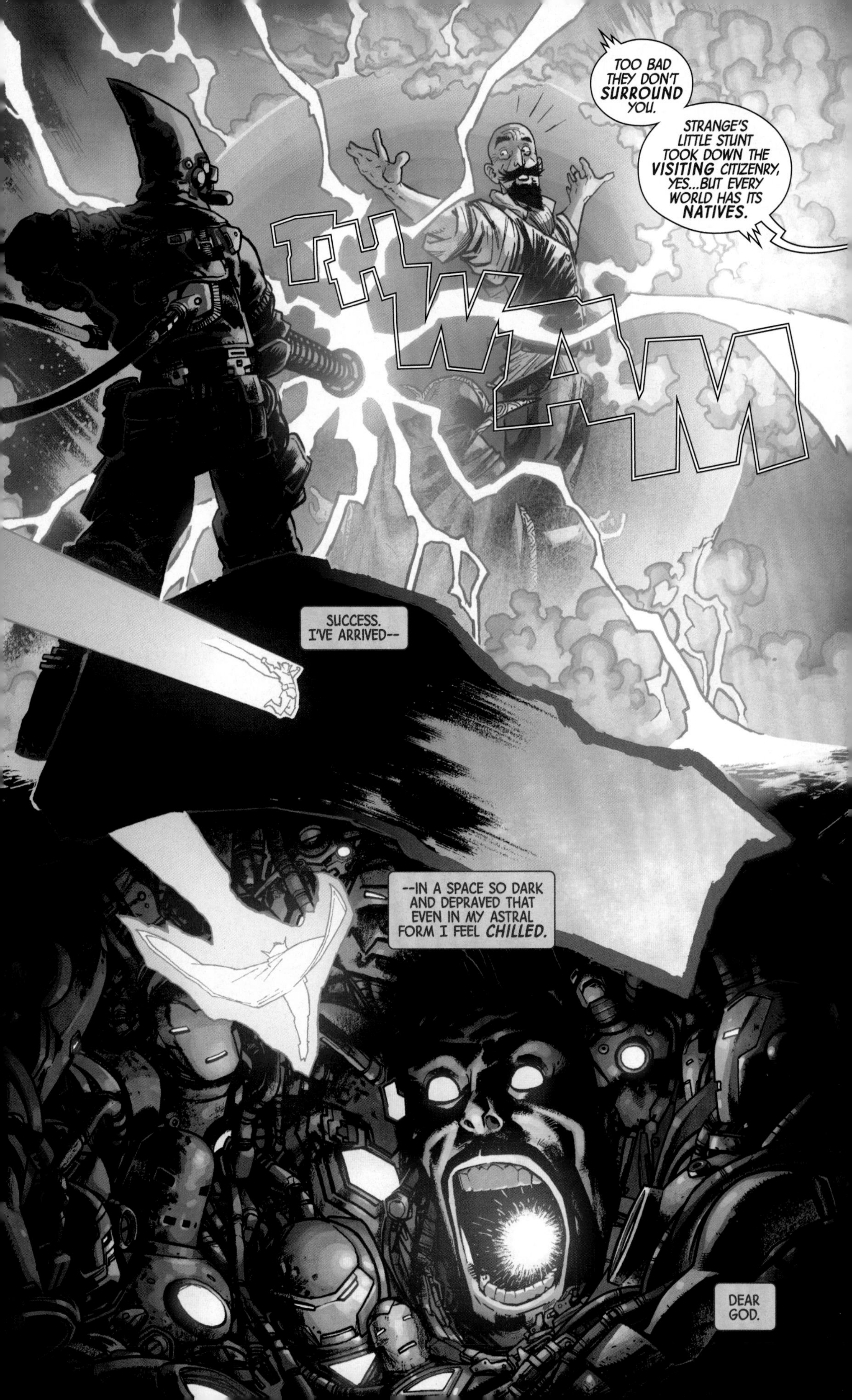

TOO BAD THEY DON'T SURROUND YOU.
STRANGE'S LITTLE STUNT TOOK DOWN THE VISITING CITIZENRY, YES...BUT EVERY WORLD HAS ITS NATIVES.
THWAM
SUCCESS. I'VE ARRIVED--
--IN A SPACE SO DARK AND DEPRAVED THAT EVEN IN MY ASTRAL FORM I FEEL CHILLED.
DEAR GOD.

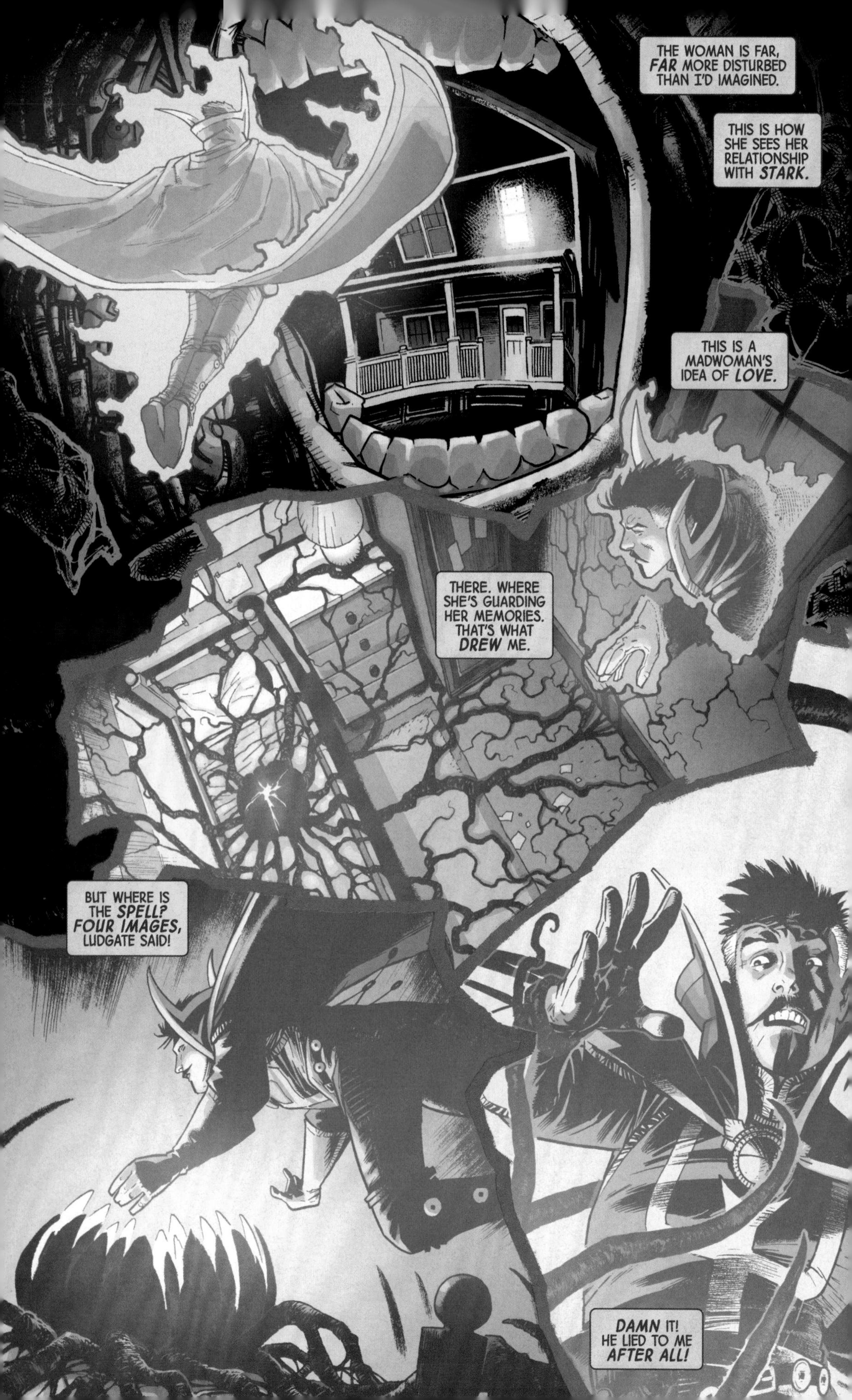

THE WOMAN IS FAR, FAR MORE DISTURBED THAN I'D IMAGINED.
THIS IS HOW SHE SEES HER RELATIONSHIP WITH STARK.
THIS IS A MADWOMAN'S IDEA OF LOVE.
THERE. WHERE SHE'S GUARDING HER MEMORIES. THAT'S WHAT DREW ME.
BUT WHERE IS THE SPELL? FOUR IMAGES, LUDGATE SAID!
DAMN IT! HE LIED TO ME AFTER ALL!

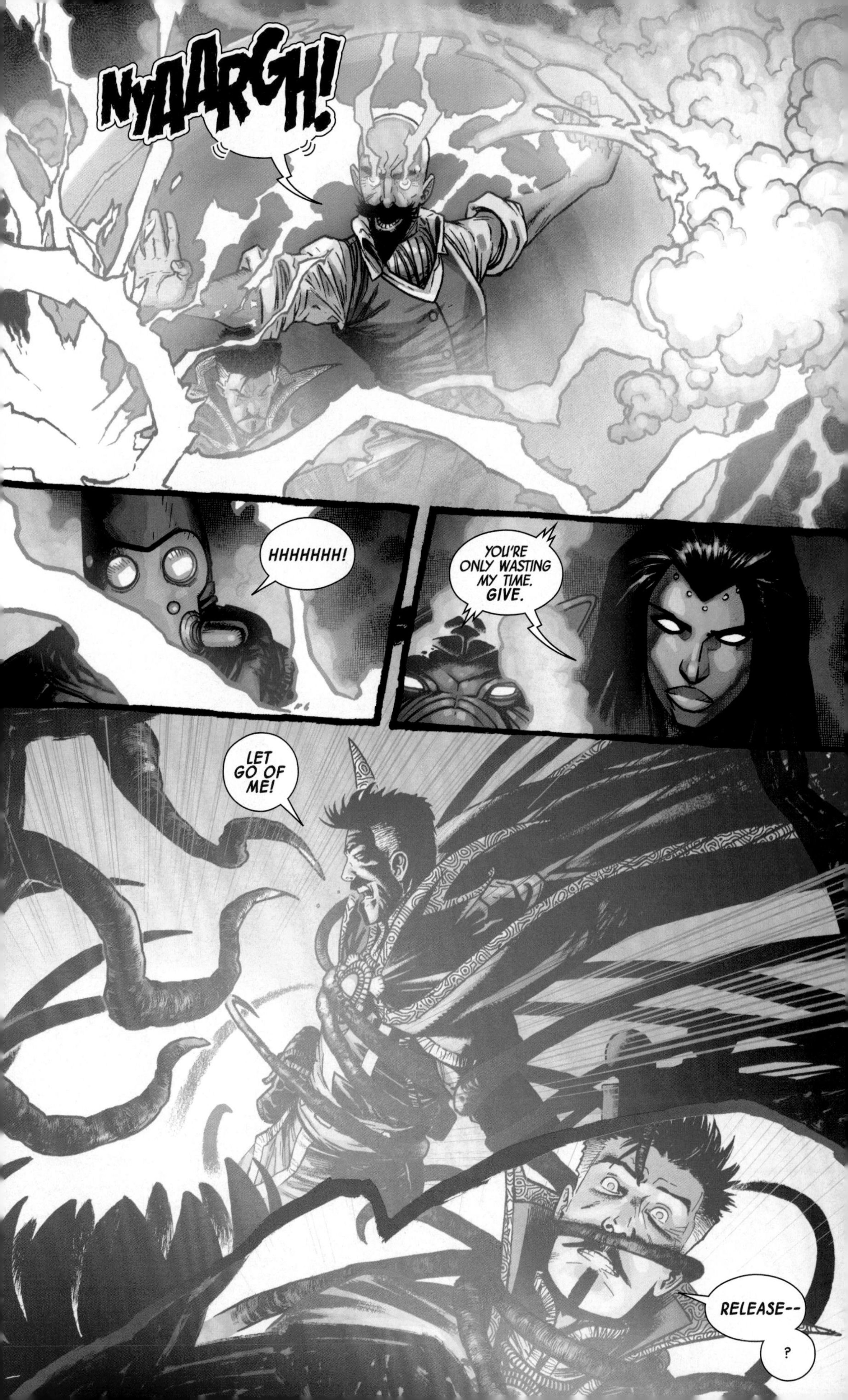
NYAARGH!
HHHHHHH!
YOU'RE ONLY WASTING MY TIME. GIVE.
LET GO OF ME!
RELEASE--
?

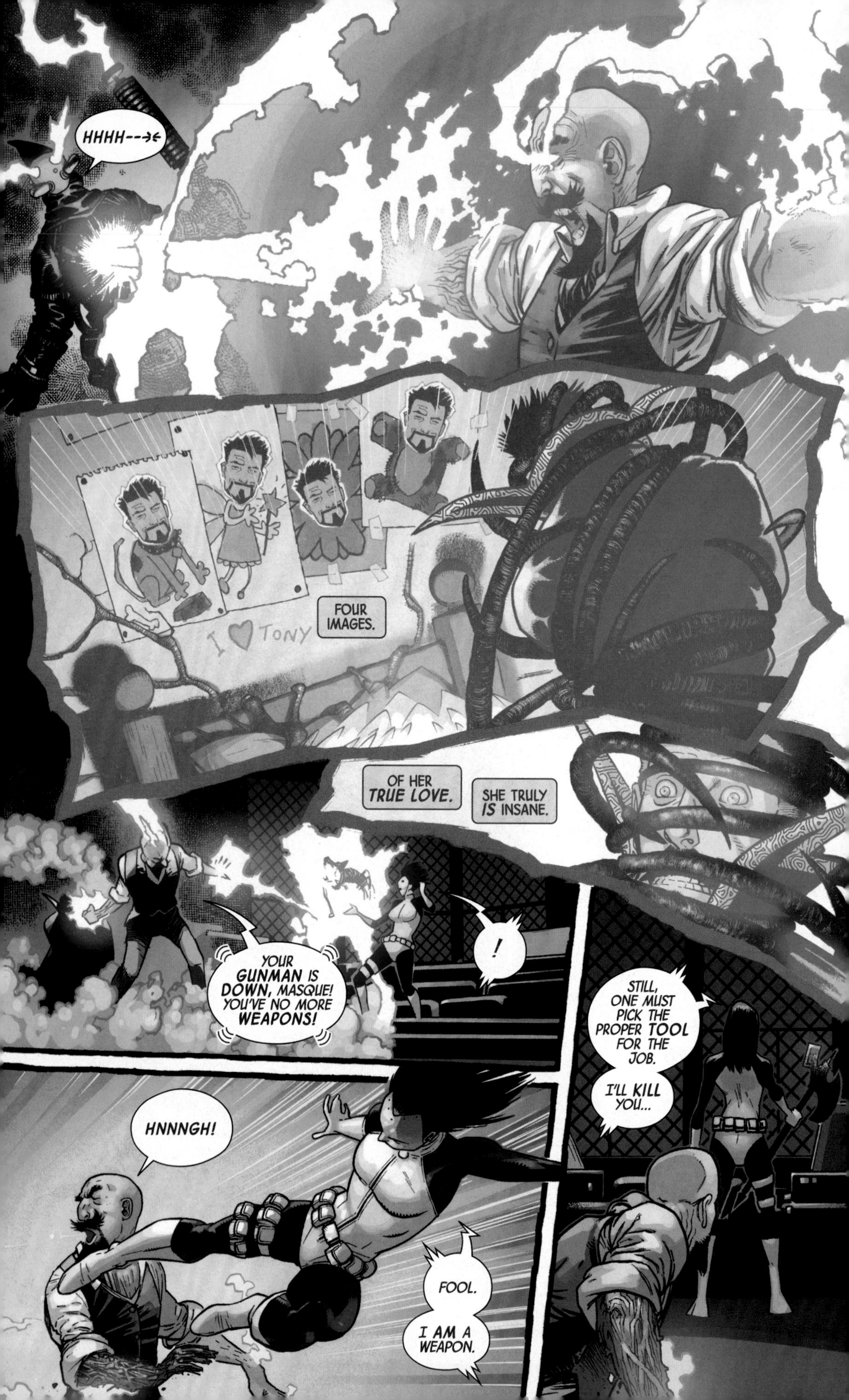
HHHH--→←
FOUR IMAGES.
I ♥ TONY
OF HER TRUE LOVE.
SHE TRULY IS INSANE.
YOUR GUNMAN IS DOWN, MASQUE! YOU'VE NO MORE WEAPONS!
!
STILL, ONE MUST PICK THE PROPER TOOL FOR THE JOB.
I'LL KILL YOU...
HNNNGH!
FOOL.
I AM A WEAPON.

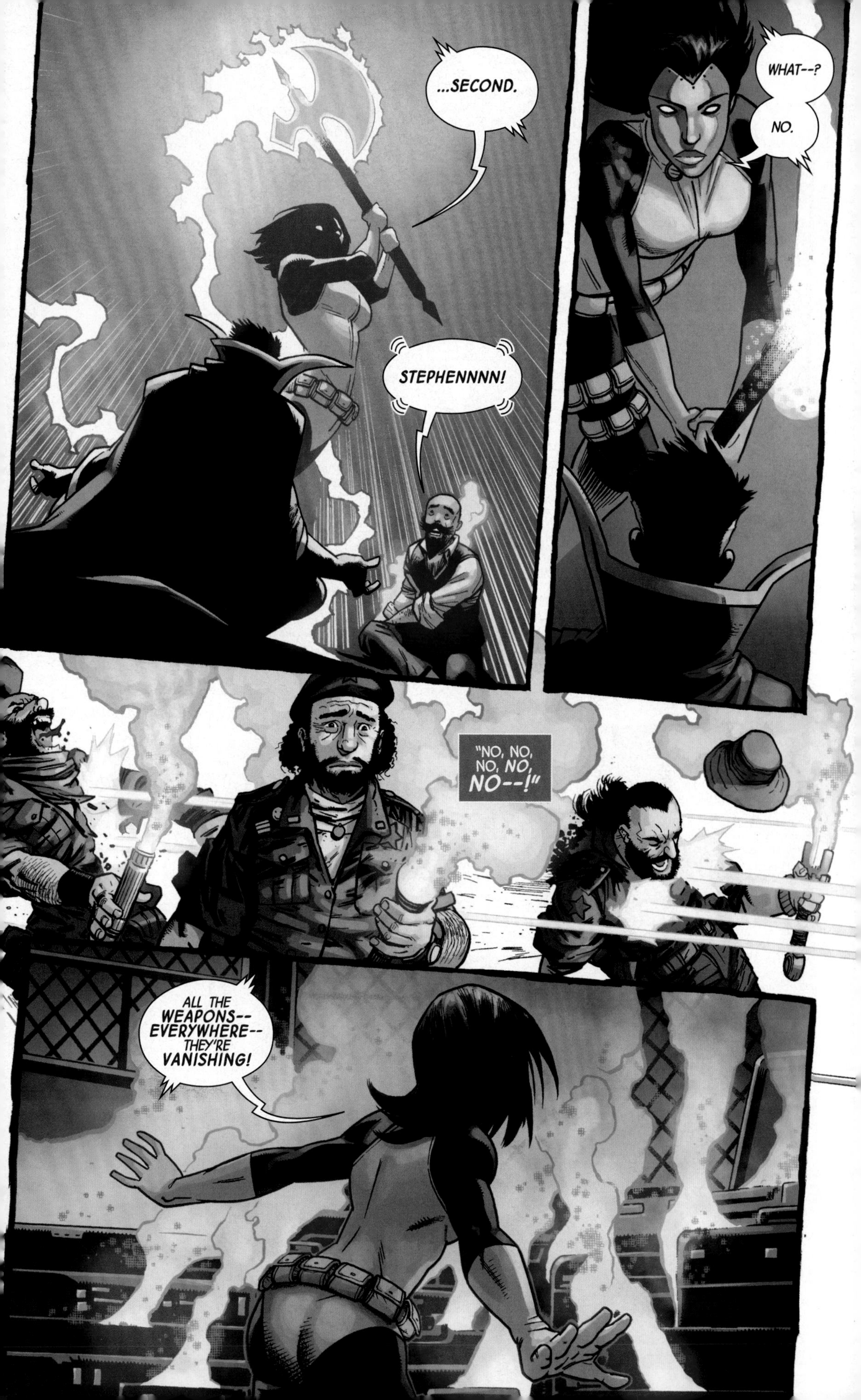
...SECOND.
STEPHENNNN!
WHAT--?
NO.
"NO, NO, NO, NO, NO--!"
ALL THE WEAPONS-- EVERYWHERE-- THEY'RE VANISHING!

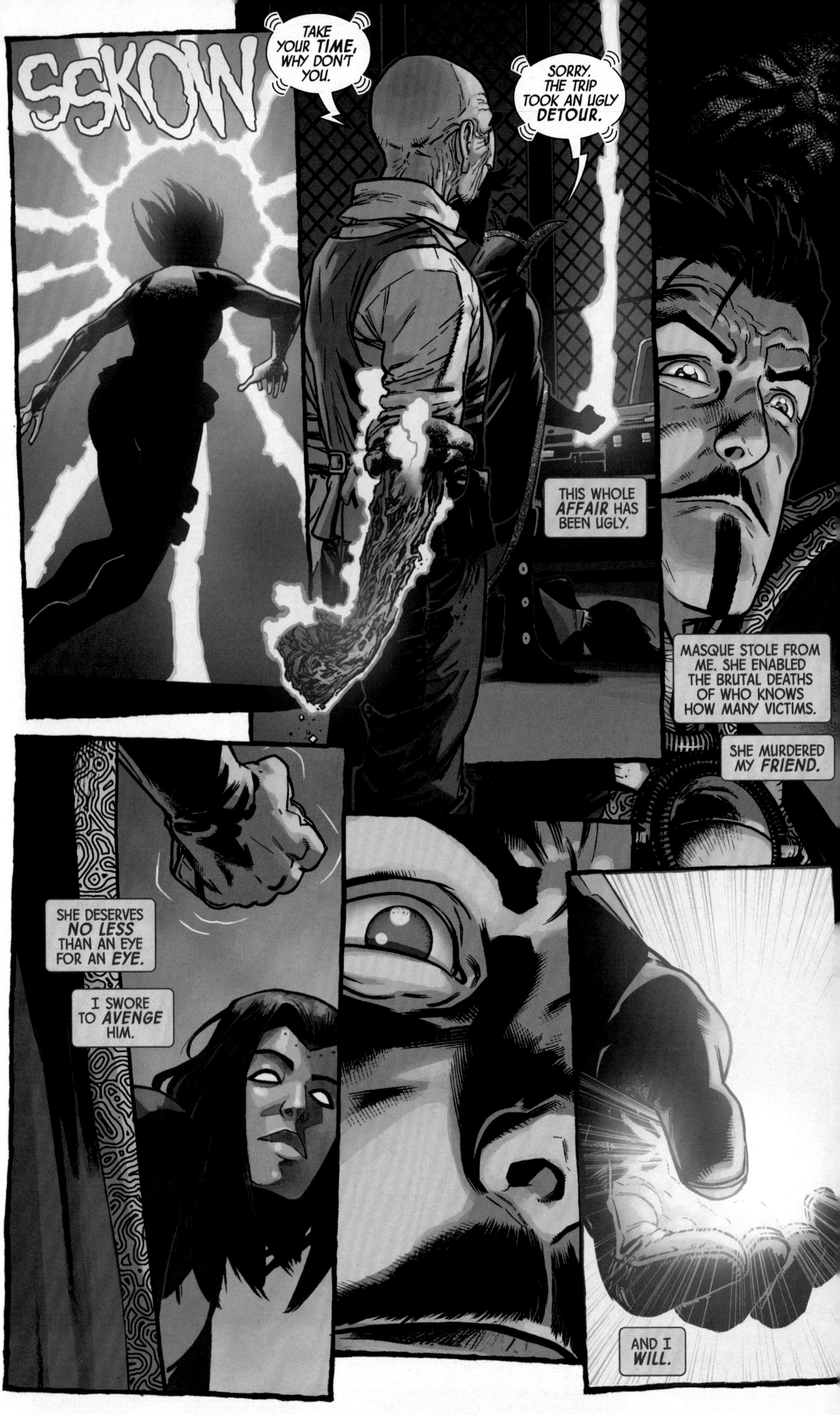
SSKOW
TAKE YOUR TIME, WHY DON'T YOU.
SORRY. THE TRIP TOOK AN UGLY DETOUR.
THIS WHOLE AFFAIR HAS BEEN UGLY.
MASQUE STOLE FROM ME. SHE ENABLED THE BRUTAL DEATHS OF WHO KNOWS HOW MANY VICTIMS.
SHE MURDERED MY FRIEND.
SHE DESERVES NO LESS THAN AN EYE FOR AN EYE.
I SWORE TO AVENGE HIM.
AND I WILL.

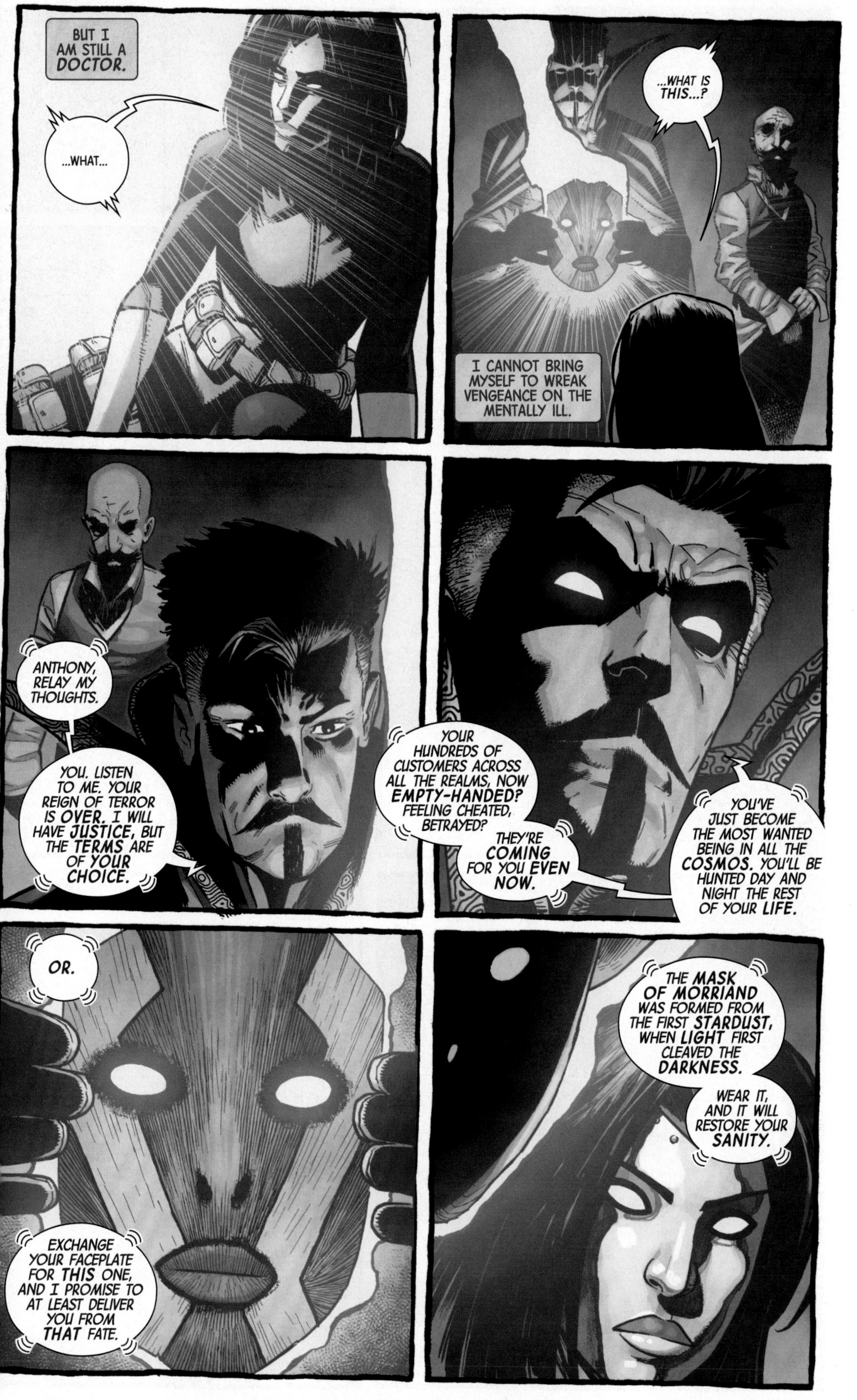

BUT I AM STILL A DOCTOR.
...WHAT...
...WHAT IS THIS...?
I CANNOT BRING MYSELF TO WREAK VENGEANCE ON THE MENTALLY ILL.
ANTHONY, RELAY MY THOUGHTS.
YOU. LISTEN TO ME. YOUR REIGN OF TERROR IS OVER. I WILL HAVE JUSTICE, BUT THE TERMS ARE OF YOUR CHOICE.
YOUR HUNDREDS OF CUSTOMERS ACROSS ALL THE REALMS, NOW EMPTY-HANDED? FEELING CHEATED, BETRAYED?
THEY'RE COMING FOR YOU EVEN NOW.
YOU'VE JUST BECOME THE MOST WANTED BEING IN ALL THE COSMOS. YOU'LL BE HUNTED DAY AND NIGHT THE REST OF YOUR LIFE.
OR.
EXCHANGE YOUR FACEPLATE FOR THIS ONE, AND I PROMISE TO AT LEAST DELIVER YOU FROM THAT FATE.
THE MASK OF MORRIAND WAS FORMED FROM THE FIRST STARDUST, WHEN LIGHT FIRST CLEAVED THE DARKNESS.
WEAR IT, AND IT WILL RESTORE YOUR SANITY.

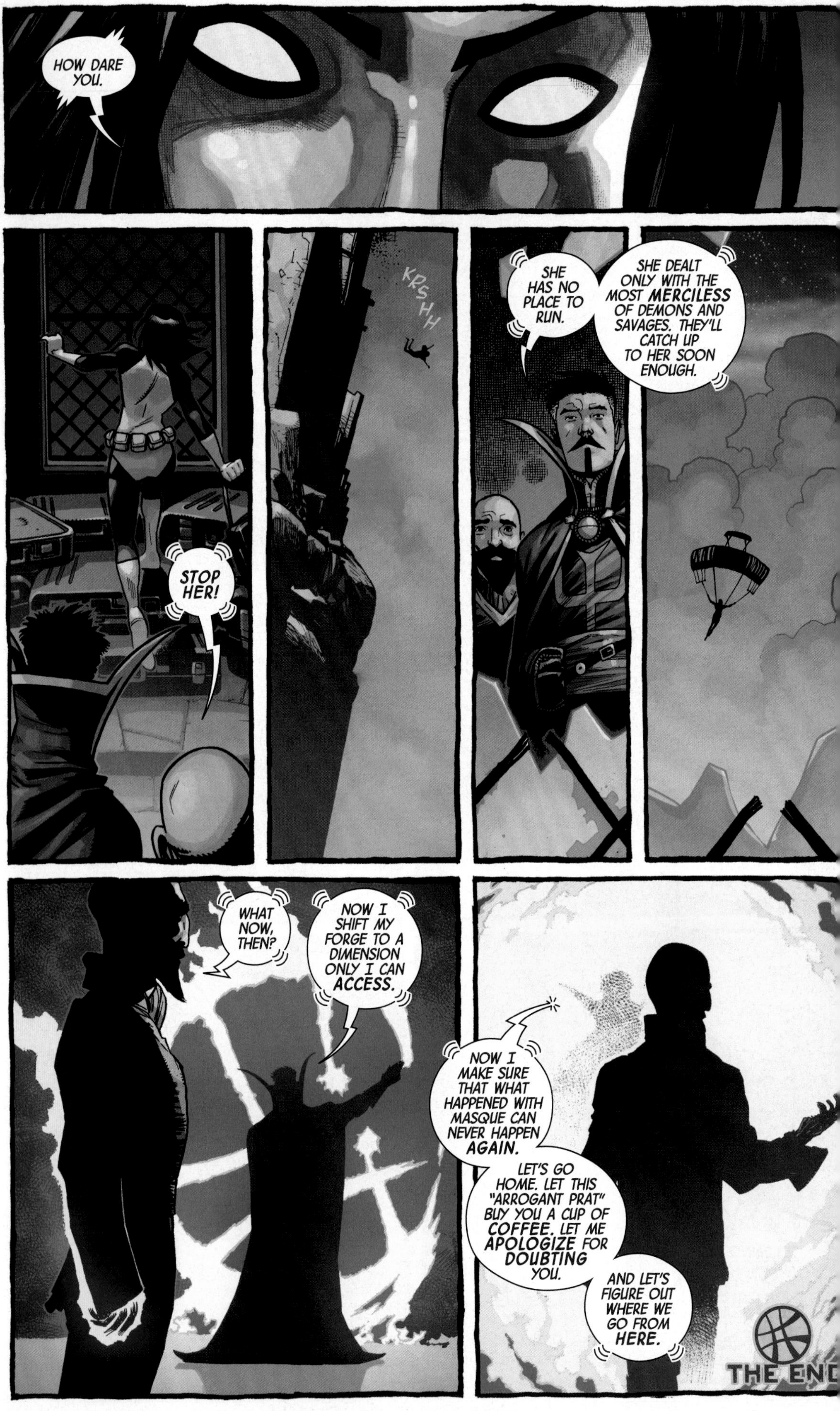
HOW DARE YOU.
STOP HER!
KRSHH
SHE HAS NO PLACE TO RUN.
SHE DEALT ONLY WITH THE MOST MERCILESS OF DEMONS AND SAVAGES. THEY'LL CATCH UP TO HER SOON ENOUGH.
WHAT NOW, THEN?
NOW I SHIFT MY FORGE TO A DIMENSION ONLY I CAN ACCESS.
NOW I MAKE SURE THAT WHAT HAPPENED WITH MASQUE CAN NEVER HAPPEN AGAIN.
LET'S GO HOME. LET THIS "ARROGANT PRAT" BUY YOU A CUP OF COFFEE. LET ME APOLOGIZE FOR DOUBTING YOU.
AND LET'S FIGURE OUT WHERE WE GO FROM HERE.
THE END

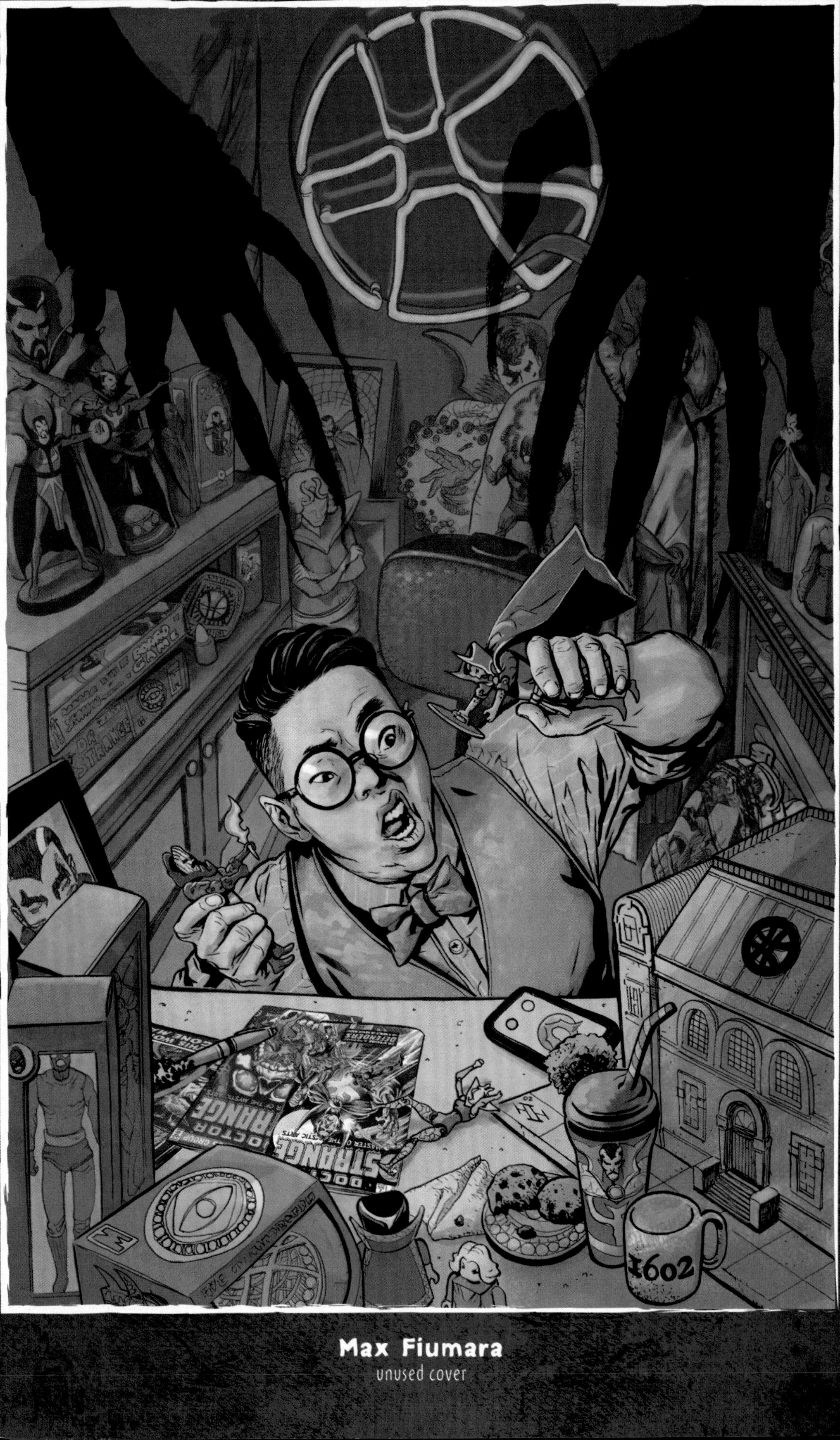
BOARD GAME
DR STRANGE
DEFENDERS
1602

Max Fiumara
unused cover

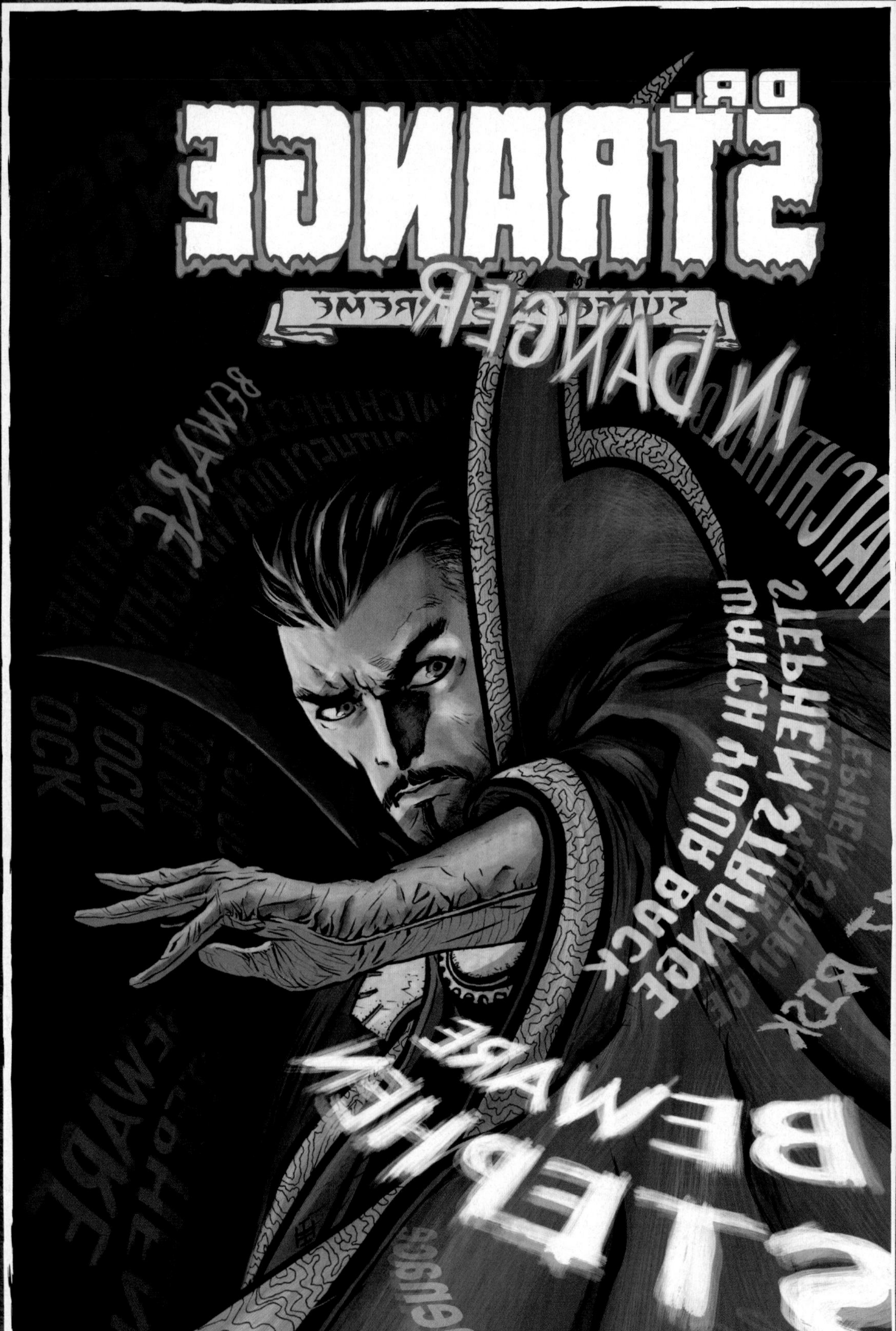
DR. STRANGE
IN DANGER
STEPHEN STRANGE
WATCH YOUR BACK
BEWARE
BEWARE STEPHEN

Max Fiumara
unused cover

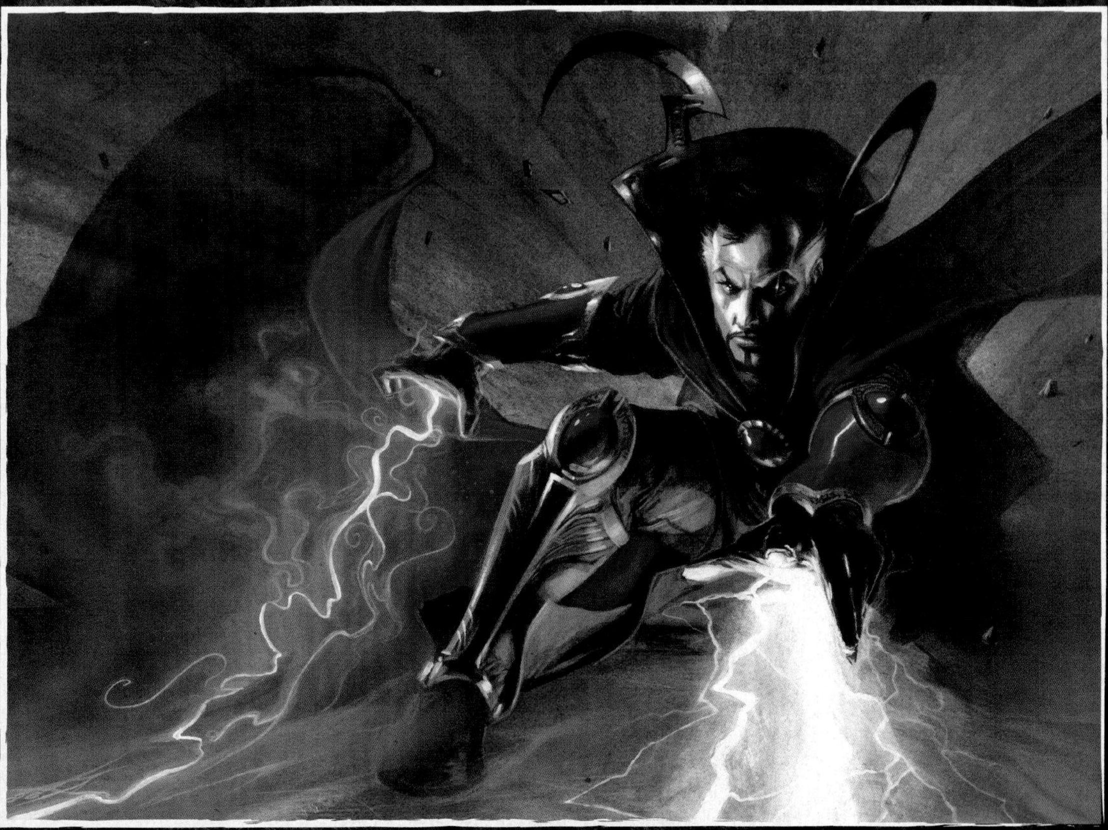

Gabriele Dell'Otto
#1 variant

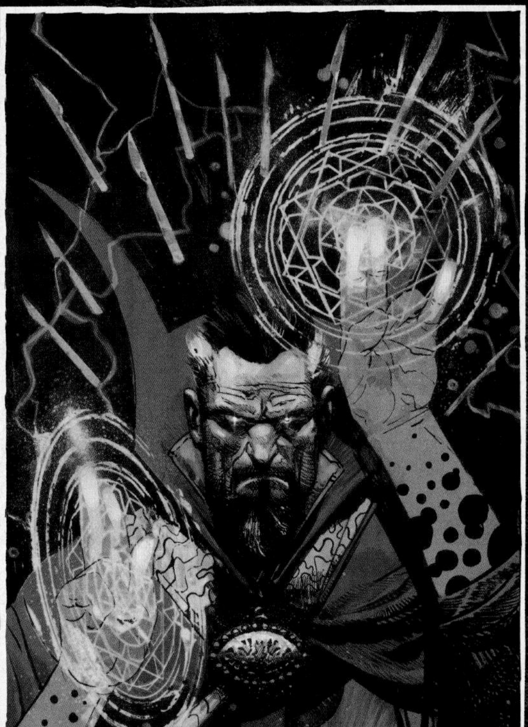

Gerardo Zaffino
#1 variant

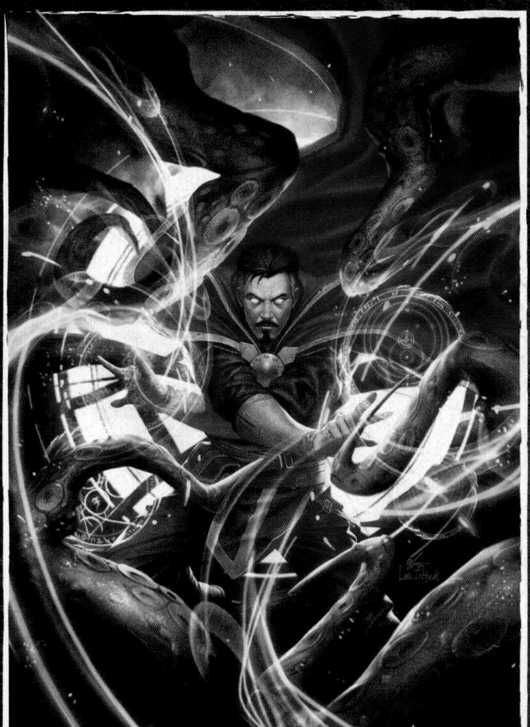

InHyuk Lee
#1 variant

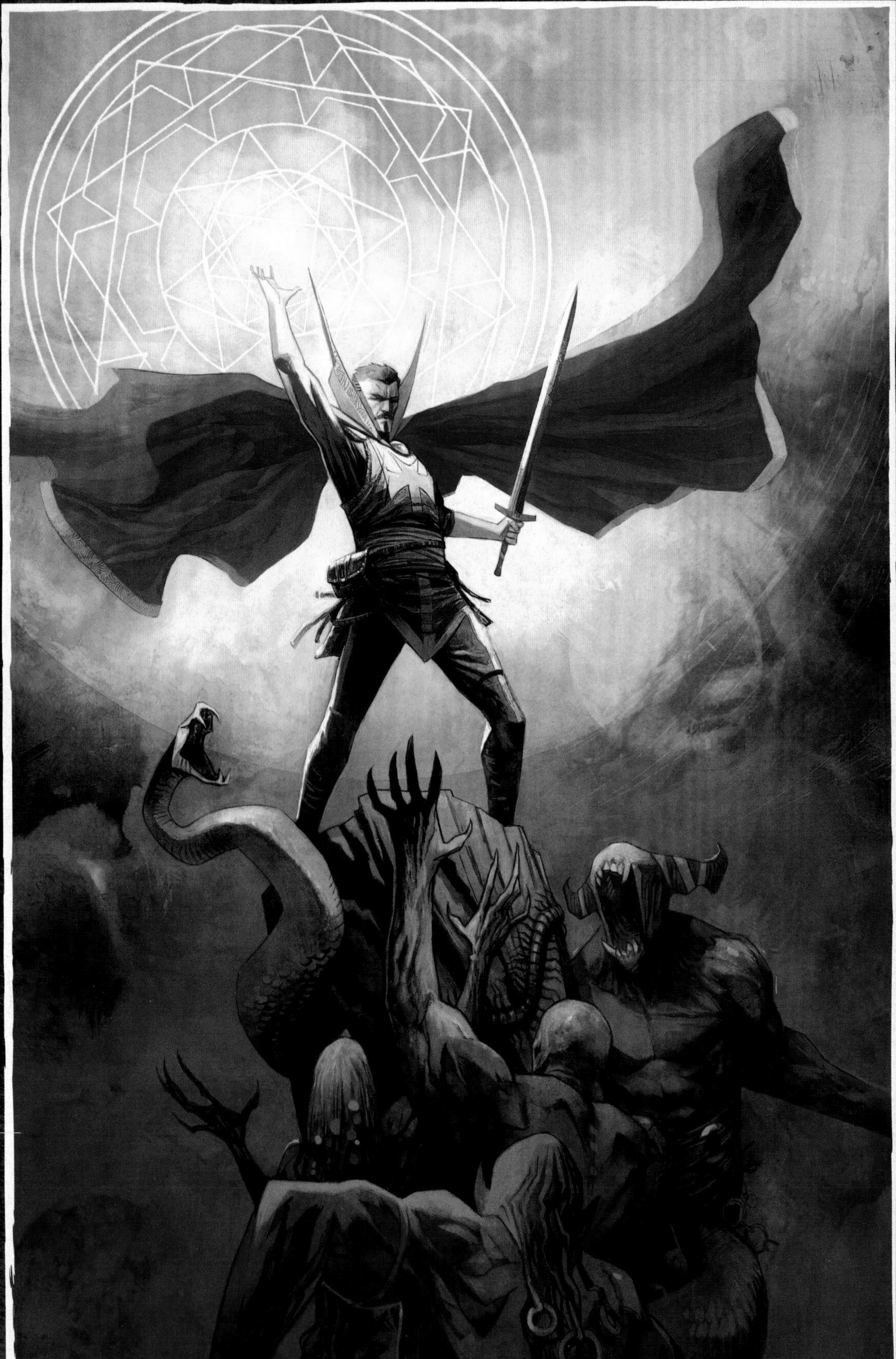

Mike Huddleston
#2 variant

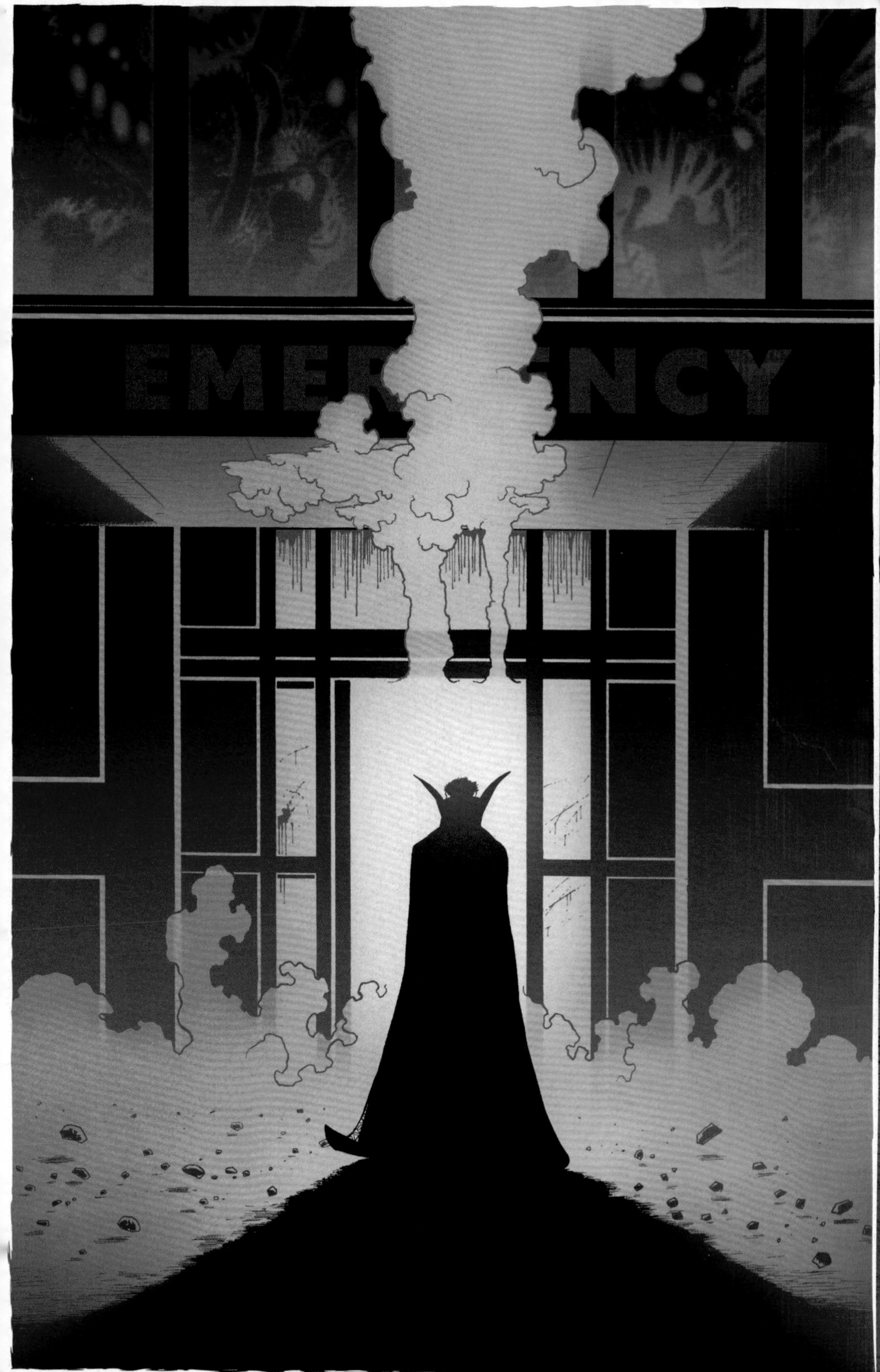
EMERGENCY

Kev Walker
#3 variant

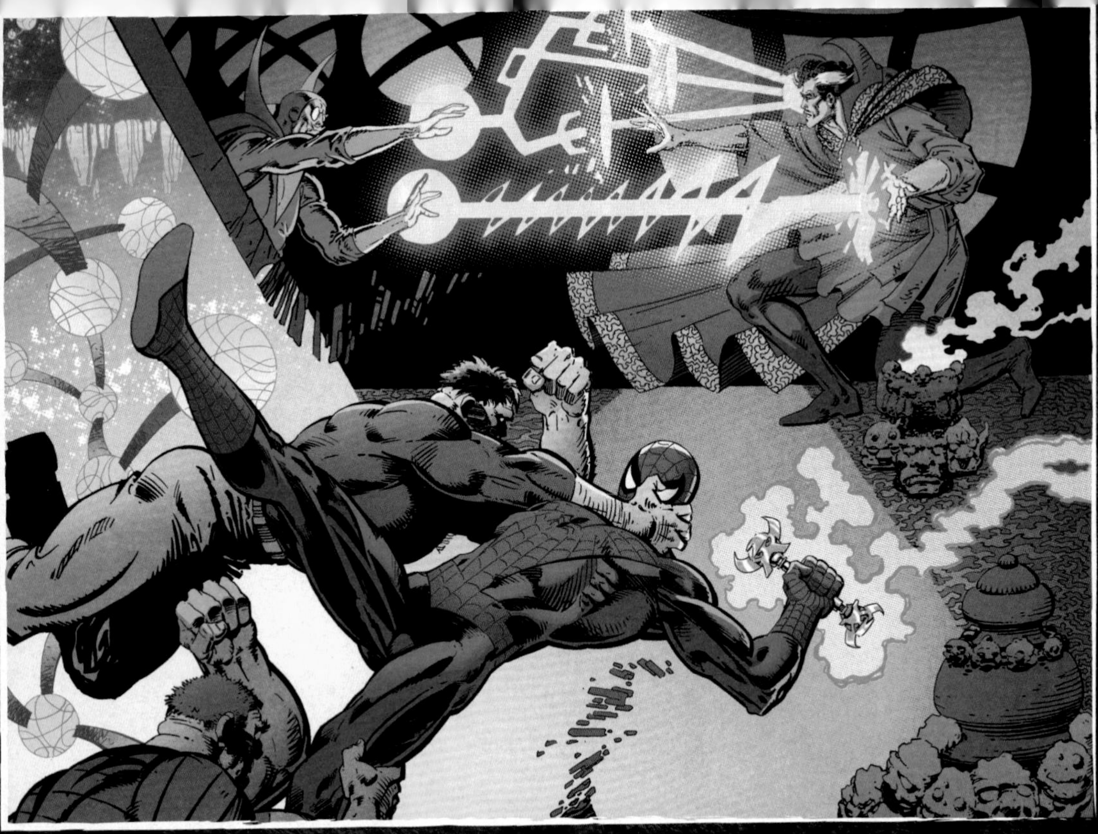

Frank Miller & Matthew Wilson
#1 Hidden Gems variant

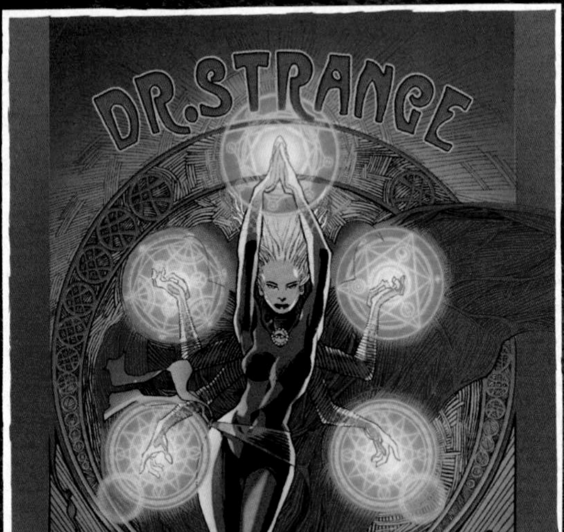
DR.STRANGE

Olivier Vatine
#2 Marvels X variant

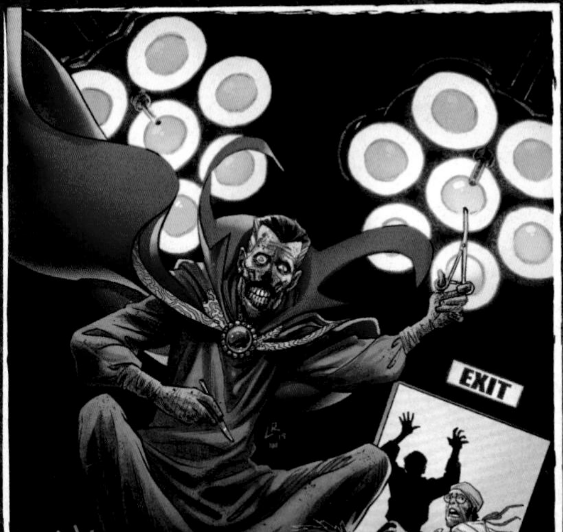
EXIT

Luke Ross
#1 Marvel Zombies variant